Giving the
Body Its Due

SUNY Series, the Body in
Culture, History, and Religion
Howard Eilberg-Schwartz, Editor

Giving the Body Its Due

Maxine Sheets-Johnstone,
Editor

STATE UNIVERSITY OF NEW YORK PRESS

Published by
State University of New York Press, Albany

For information, address State University of New York
Press, State University Plaza, Albany, N.Y., 12246

Production by E. Moore
Marketing by Bernadette LaManna

Library of Congress Cataloging in Publication Data

Giving the body its due / [edited by] Maxine Sheets-Johnstone.
        p.   cm. — (SUNY series, the body in culture, history, and
    religion)
      Essays from an interdisciplinary conference held November 4–5,
    1989 in Eugene, Or.
      Includes bibliographical references.
      ISBN 0-7914-0997-X (alk. paper). — ISBN 0-7914-0998-8 (pbk. :
    alk. paper)
      1. Body, Human (Philosophy)   I. Sheets-Johnstone, Maxine.
    II. Series.
    B105.B64G58   1992
    128—dc20
                                                    91-17594
                                                       CIP

10 9 8 7 6 5 4 3 2 1

What do we owe?
A debt of gratitude.

   Karen Nelson
   Joint Forces
   Contact Improvisation Dance Company

Contents

Preface

In keeping with its interdisciplinary character, this book is addressed to an interdisciplinary audience, and in more than one sense. The people who have contributed to this volume of essays come from the fields of philosophy, anthropology, linguistics, and psychology. The fact that individuals from such disparate callings can contribute to the same volume means not only that their own backgrounds and vistas are broad but that the very topic itself—*Giving the Body Its Due*—is broad. Indeed, the need to challenge Cartesian dualism—the thinking that separates mind from body and in the process devalues the body as mere physical substance—is not at all the province of any one academic domain; the need is symptomatic of a pervasive need within our very culture. It is perhaps most visibly evident in the surge of 'body scholars'/'body practitioners' who today have come to occupy solid if still marginal corners of our culture. These scholars/practitioners would all seem to share the thought that something is "out of joint" in the ways we Americans think of and treat our bodies. For these twentieth-century pioneers of the body, the present volume of essays should be of singular import. For health professionals, psychologists, nurses, physicians—all whose daily work sustains, and is sustained by, the thought that "people are their bodies"—these diverse essays from the sciences and the humanities offer support and insight.

The book is addressed equally to people who are body pioneers in a different sense, people who, whatever their actual work, whatever their everyday lives, take being a body seriously. These are people who listen. These are people who enjoy. They are not necessarily professional "thises" or "thats." They are not die-hard compulsives about exercise. Neither are they mindless drudges cultivating fitness. They are simply quite ordinary people who are attuned to being a body and to cultivating themselves as bodies—which is why they listen and enjoy. This volume of essays is for them also. It offers to them the possibility of opening new terrains of self-understanding and deepening the grounds of older truths.

These interdisciplinary essays are furthermore addressed to academic pioneers of the body. By the richness of their interdisciplinary roots, these essays clearly demonstrate that Cartesian dualism does not exist solely in nooks and crannies of philosophy departments across the country. It exists across academia; distinguishing ourselves as minds and bodies, and giving top billing to our minds are, as indicated above, practices endemic to our culture. Awakening to this fact means awakening to the possibility of challenging it from multiple perspectives—regardless of one's home academic discipline. As these essays so deftly show, one does not have to be a philosopher to understand or to challenge Cartesian dualism. By the same token one does not have to be an anthropologist, linguist, or psychologist to understand the problems with Cartesian dualism from the perspective of anthropology, linguistics, or psychology. Precisely because of the multiple viewpoints they bring and the enriched understandings they contribute, the gathered essays can readily serve as a lively, issue-rich collateral text for courses not only in metaphysics, but also in medical anthropology, in clinical and counseling psychology, in cultural history programs, in medical school curricula, and in human service and health professional training programs.

Acknowledgments

This gathering of essays is the outgrowth of an earlier gathering: *Giving the Body Its Due: An Interdisciplinary Conference*—a Conference I conceived, organized, and directed. The Conference took place on 4–5 November 1989 in Eugene, Oregon and was sponsored by both the Oregon Humanities Center and the Continuation Center of the University of Oregon, by the Oregon Committee for the Humanities—the state equivalent of the National Endowment for the Humanities—and by Lane Regional Arts Council. A diversity of humanities and human science scholars and a diversity of artists came together for the purpose of examining and sharing ways of giving the body its due. The breadth of the interdisciplinary undertaking made the enterprise particularly challenging and rewarding. It was personally satisfying to weave together the research of the many people who participated in the Conference. It has been personally satisfying for the same reason to weave together this volume of writings, which grew out of the Conference. The Continuation Center at the University of Oregon, and particularly Paul Katz, its Associate Director, have been as consistently supportive of this latter enterprise as they were of the Conference itself. I am grateful to them for providing resources and services in the preparation of this book.

MAXINE SHEETS-JOHNSTONE

1

Charting the Interdisciplinary Course

We are all bodies—sensing, moving creatures, wonderfully simple, wonderfully complex. We draw, we write, we walk, we dance. We are sound-makers and song-makers. We are creatures of habit, but also creatures of change, creativity, and curiosity. We are all these dimensions and more, potentially and actually. In the flesh, down to and into our bones, we are all bodies.

This gathering of essays brings together an interdisciplinary array of understandings of what it is to be the bodies we are. It is an opening movement aimed at redressing the imbalance created by Cartesian dualism. In its own way, each essay calls into question certain culturally embedded ways of valuing the body that deride or ignore its role in making us human. In its own way, each essay thus helps restore what is properly due the body since seventeenth-century philosopher René Descartes convinced us that mind and body are separate, and that mind is the primary value. Moreover in its own way, each essay helps elucidate what is properly due the body since the more recent Western twentieth-century emphasis

1

upon vision effectively reduced the richness of the affective and tactile-kinesthetic body—the body of felt experience—to a simple sum of sensations.

The time is ripe for a thoroughgoing reappraisal of the body. The legacy of Descartes's metaphysics has been not only to divide the fundamental integrity of creaturely life, but also to depreciate the role of the living body in knowing and making sense of the world, in learning, in the creative arts, and in self- and interpersonal understandings. The Cartesian legacy has in essence reduced the body by turns to a static assemblage of parts and to a dumb show of movement. The living sense of the body, and its propensity for sense-making, have been blotted out by top-heavy concerns with brains, minds, consciousness, and language, these latter being construed by many people as virtually self-sufficient "mental" systems, all the rest being just so much in the way of mechanical peripheral support.

It is this conception of the body as mere handmaiden to the privileged that is in process of revision. The revision, be it noted, is no mere cosmetic surgery. The traditional Cartesian view of the body as drone to an all-powerful, rational mind has complex as well as deep roots. Their complexity and depth are apparent in the everyday attitudes, interests, values, and behaviors that in general define twentieth-century American society and that are daily reinforced and reflected back in one way and another by Western media. For example, the body is not only something to be ministered to when sick, fed when hungry, exercised regularly, and put to bed when tired. It is more finely conceived as something to protect and care for like a possession—a car, for example; as something to read about regularly—up-to-date scientific information is essential; as something to assess sexually at various levels and according to various standards of beauty; and more. We are advised, for instance, to have the body appraised physically once a year, to air it daily, but also to shelter it from damaging sun rays. We are advised to give it pills to safeguard its heart, and certain vegetables to insure the proper functioning of its bowels. We are advised to flatten its "stomach," and to clothe it in alluring and enticing ways. We are advised to keep its desires in check, to "manage" its stress, and to obliterate its wrinkles, odors, and unwanted hairs. Clearly, a complex of attitudes and values feeds into the traditional view, all of them buttressing a conception of our bodies as a kind of personal dumbwaiter each of us has at our disposal. To assure a smooth and continuous performance, we must on the one hand keep abreast of the latest in dumbwaiter science and technology, and aesthetic maintenance, and on the other hand know how to trouble-shoot in case of breakdowns and accidents.

The picture is perhaps exaggerated. Yet when attention is turned to the dominant ways in which the body is viewed in our society—one need only glance at popular magazines and tabloids, peruse the daily newspaper, glimpse summaries of television programs about the body, or notice movie advertisements—the picture of the body as "an extended substance"—a purely physical object—seems unmitigated. It is against this background of what might be called "popular body noise" that the need to promote humanistic understandings of the body becomes clearly and readily apparent. When the body is treated as a purely material possession, our humanness is diminished. Popular body noise drowns out the felt sense of our bodies and a felt sense of our individual aliveness. In place of these felt senses is a preeminently visual object groomed in the ways of quite specific, all–pervasive, culturally–engrained attitudes and values. What is diagnosed as needing thinner thighs, increased fiber, stress–reduction, or an at–home aerobic device, is precisely a culturally–seduced visual object. We no longer listen to our bodies directly, but only to what modern science tells us about our bodies, and not just at the level of food, sex, and stress, but at the level of neuroanatomical/physiological *facts:* how our brains work, how our eyes see, how our hearts react to trauma, and so on. The *living* sense of ourselves vanishes in the din of popular body noise.

The view of the body as something that in time will wear down—and out—as something whose parts can be replaced by parts from other individuals, as something whose material insides are as accessible as its material outsides, and so on, is part of the same view of the body as an object. As suggested above, the view is strongly undergirded by scientific perspectives which not only reduce the body to a thing, treating it as a finely functioning machine, but which also are concerned with it as an essentially visual object, an amalgam of structures, tissues, cells, genes, and so on. From the grossest to the finest level, the body is analyzed in terms of things seen—object(ive) realities. Given this purview, it is not surprising that the somatically felt body—the body that feels joy, sadness, and anger, the body that feels nostalgia and despair—and the tactile-kinesthetic body—the body that feels itself in the act of moving and touching—are all but repudiated. What is not objectified by sight does not invite twentieth-century Western scientific study.

It is one thing to acknowledge the limitations of a particular approach and quite another to presume that there are *no* limitations, that is, that a given approach is exhaustive. The latter presumption threatens integrity. Blind allegiance to the tenets of twentieth-century Western science culminates in hypervisualism, a theoretical stance in which vital, living aspects of persons, particularly those having to do with bodily feelings of emotion and bodily feelings of movement and touch, are not given their due.

What is needed merely to *balance* the equation are values that substantiate the human aspects of being a body. The need is for understandings which do justice to the multiple ways in which the body has been, and is, part of our living human heritage—from the beginnings of human language, for example, to body-mind transformations achieved through 'just sitting' Eastern methods of meditation. In short, the promotion of humanistic understandings of the body is a much needed counter to the more familiar, and certainly more widely publicized, scientific understandings of the body everywhere apparent in present-day American society from choice of fish oils to the most effective aerobics. The essays which follow delineate just such fundamental bodily aspects of our humanness.

There is a further dimension in which humanistic understandings of the body can be realized. Ways in which the body is treated, and attitudes toward it, are quintessentially informative of a civilization's basic tenets and values. We are only just beginning to appreciate this fact both through socio-historical studies of the body and through ever-increasing awarenesses of the connection between "our bodies ourselves" and the body which is earth. Such beginning appreciations can lead to the broad and deep socio-political realization that understandings of what it is to be human necessarily include, if not begin with, understandings of something common to all peoples and to all civilizations, something not outside of, but fundamental to, each and every personal existence: the living body. Precisely this kind of awareness was promoted by the earthquake in Armenia in 1987. As one newspaper article quoted a Soviet embassy official in Washington, "Suddenly [Americans] realize that we are the same human beings, [that] we can feel the pain as well." That we seem to need devastating natural disasters to remind us of our common humanity says something about our highly touted "humanness," and our elevated sense of ourselves as distinct from "the beasts." Clearly, we have much to learn about ourselves and the world. Our bodies provide us the most fundamental starting point. Precisely because they provide us a common denominator, *bodily* understandings have the possibility of ransoming us, as much from insulated arrogance as from indifferent violence.

The aim of the essays which follow is to awaken basic dimensions of ourselves as living bodies, in German poet Rainier Rilke's memorable words, to awaken the "unlived lines of our bodies." The achievement of this aim should eventuate at the same time in an awakening of a sense of our human condition, a heightened awareness not merely of our immediate culture, but a heightened awareness of our cultural and evolutionary heritage, and in consequence of the *commonalities* undergirding human experience. The pursuit of self-understandings ultimately demands such an evolutionary perspective and pan-cultural attentiveness. The interdisciplinary scope of the essays is of singular value in this respect since it attests to a variety of commonalities in human experience, thus to the importance of recognizing the foundational relationship between human bodies and human cultural and evolutionary histories.

Albert A. Johnstone's essay offers the first challenge. His essay shows why Descartes should have listened more carefully to the several objections formulated by his favorite disciple, Princess Elizabeth of Bohemia. In particular, it examines the keystone of Descartes's view, namely, his claim that a thinking being (which for him is a being which doubts, denies, wants, feels, perceives) is conceivable independently of extended or bodily being. Descartes's claim is tested with regard to three aspects of thinking: (a) feeling, (b) willing, and (c) thinking proper. Johnstone shows how the introspective approach advocated by Elizabeth, and adopted by Descartes himself on related issues, finds Elizabeth to have made the more perceptive observations. In each case, the tactile-kinesthetic body is found to be an inalienable constituent of the thinking subject. Johnstone shows incidentally how the Cartesian formula is affected by this finding. "I think, therefore I am," becomes "I, possibly a hoax, think; therefore I, possibly a hoax, am"—surely a devastating blow to the self-image of Cartesian thinking substances.

In his essay on contemporary Japanese philosopher Yasuo Yuasa, Shigenori Nagatomo invites us to consider a conception of minds and bodies quite different from Descartes's. Yuasa's 'body-scheme' is an attempt to bring together four different 'circuits' of the body: the neurophysiological, the kinesthetic and somesthetic, the emotional-instinctual, and the psychological. In contrast to Western scientific construals, these circuits or planes of body functioning are not separate self-sufficient systems to be ministered to in piecemeal fashion by specialists. They are thoroughly integrated, entwined facets of bodily life. As Nagatomo demonstrates, only through the recognition of such a comprehensive body-scheme do phenomena such as ki-energy, systems of medicine such as acupuncture, and meditational practices eventuating in altered states of consciousness become explainable. Most importantly, as Nagatomo shows, self-cultivation as an epistemological undertaking is somatic in character: knowledge is gained *through the body*. At one level, self-cultivation as an Eastern concept is the epistemological equivalent of Socrates's "Know thyself." But it is at the same time a radically different precept on three counts: it originates in a disciplined practice of the body rather than a disciplined practice of the intellect; it culminates in a different kind of knowledge of the self; and it underscores the continuity and unity of self and world.

Daniel Moerman is an anthropologist who has long been concerned with the metaphysical implications of Western medicine. His studies of native American herbal medicines not only offer the most complete inventory and account of how plants were and are used by American Indians to cure human ailments; they pose questions concerning why such a therapeutic relationship should exist between humans and plants in the first place, and how the curative—and poisonous—effects of certain plants are mediated and how those effects might have been discovered. In his essay, "Minding the Body: The Placebo Effect Unmasked," Moerman is concerned with the same basic metaphysical question: Why and how are certain medical treatments effective? The only difference here is that his concern is not with the efficacy of culturally recognized drugs but on the contrary, with the inexplicable power of culturally "disenfranchised" placebos. Moerman presents an array of research findings substantiating the fact that pills containing virtually nothing but sugar have healing powers, and that to the publically unacknowledged consternation of the medical community, the color of a pill, for example, as well as patients' estimations of their physicians, influence whether and to what degree a prescribed pill has a positive effect. His review of the research on placebos shows beyond doubt that starch tablets or injections of saline solution can cure any condition which can be cured, and further, that sometimes such cures are better and longer lasting than those produced by standard pharmaceutical drugs. As Moerman points out, the realities of the placebo effect indicate that simplistic explanations—such as "mind over matter"—or easy scientific labelings—such as "psychosomatic medicine"—cannot adequately account for the complexities of the situation. His suggestion, of course, is that physiognomic aspects of treatment must first of all be recognized as existing by the medical community, whether a matter of pill color, tacit beliefs about size vis à vis the efficacy of a pill, or the interpersonal dynamics—the unspoken "dance," as Moerman calls it—that regularly takes place between patient and doctor. If Descartes was troubled by phantom limbs as evidence of how our senses can deceive us, he would have been that much more troubled by placebos as indicators of how our senses, our sense of a situation, our sense of the pills we take, and our sense of our physician, can cure us. Clearly there is more to relieving the pains of a suffering material body than controlled (or uncontrolled) substances would have us believe. To account in forthright fashion for such aspects of medicine would not simply show Cartesian dualism to be a thoroughly spurious doctrine. It would be to forge the beginnings of new, evidentially based understandings of how 'minds' and 'bodies' are all of a piece.

Peter Levine's challenge to Cartesian dualism is through an examination of trauma and of the natural resources of the body, specifically, the natural capacity of the body to defend itself and cure itself. When allowed to complete its particular course of action—when left to its own self-protective devices, in other words—the body's inherent wisdom sees it through. Levine explains how, when we thwart the completion of a self-saving action, "tonic immobility" results: the body freezes up. We are left in a state of heightened inner activity (anxiety) while outwardly little if any sign of motion is evident. He compares situations in which humans experience anxiety to situations in which nonhuman animals react to inescapable threat. As Levine tells us, it was in fact through his insights into the behavior of nonhuman animals that he began reassessing body therapy theories and methodologies. In his clinical work, he found that a fundamental way of addressing anxiety was to "renegotiate" maladaptive stress responses, that is, to relive threatening or frightening situations in such a way that thwarted bodily acts are consummated. Through renegotiation we acknowledge our need to complete patterns of thoughtful action. In acceding to the body's wisdom, we bridge the debilitating chasm opened by trauma.

When one considers the proliferation of stress management and wellness programs, one might conclude that finally the needs of the body are no longer being subordinated to the demands of production and consumption: at long last, one might think, "we have overcome Cartesian dualism and have gotten in touch with our bodies." To this optimistic spirit, Robert Kugelmann responds with strikingly original and cautionary notes. In his essay, he calls into question common present-day cultural practices and attitudes with respect to "engineering stress." In the most general terms, Kugelmann's response is to challenge stress management programs as being simply means of disciplining the body. The goal of such programs is to enable adjustment to workplaces and to social relations that are transitory—chiefly from the driving pressures of technological innovation—and to a temporality characterized by speed. Kugelmann aptly shows how these programs motivate people to work with diligence in settings that are acknowledged to be intrinsically meaningless. People "get in touch with their bodies" in the sense of imagining them to be strong and flexible in demanding situations, and relaxed in threatening ones. Managing the body in the prescribed ways, Kugelmann believes, actually precludes us from listening to the meaning of stress as it is lived, namely, as a continually aborted grief in face of a world become a Heraclitean flux. To reckon honestly with our stressful world, Kugelmann urges, what we need are rituals to remember our losses, not techniques to make us more flexible and resilient in the face of change.

There are two major theses that anchor my essay, "The Materialization of the Body." The first is that materialization is the metaphysical corollary of animism (understood simply as "imbued with life"); the second, that radical materialization of the body has both de-humanizing and ethically noxious effects: it culminates in an eroded sense of self and an eroded sense of personal responsibility. The theses undergird my abbreviated chronicling of the history of Western medicine as a metaphysical history of the body. Since cultural medical practices of whatever time and place bespeak a certain conception of the body, it is not surprising that any particular history of medicine can be written as a metaphysical history of the body. Accordingly, an analysis of changing understandings of sickness and of changing medical practices in the history of Western culture offers a ready-made and unique approach to a critique of Cartesian metaphysical claims. In chronicling the materialization of the Western body—its progressive "fossilization," first at the hands of the developing medical sciences of anatomy and physiology in the sixteenth century, and then at the later hands of developing medical aspects of molecular biology in the twentieth century—the essay focuses on the progressive fragmentation of the body as a purely physical object. It shows how the adage, "a place for everything, and everything in its place" is an exemplar of the unifying principle undergirding material systematization. It furthermore shows how the metaphysics of sickness, bodies, and people that has evolved in conjunction with Western medicine contrasts starkly not only with Eastern concepts of sickness, bodies, and people, but also with earlier Western notions as well. The contrasts are demonstrated by juxtaposing Western and Eastern conceptions of sickness, and ancient Greek and present-day Western conceptions of certain bodily realities, among which the breath.

Robert Romanyshyn, a clinical and cultural psychologist, has written a powerful narrative of a body transmogrified by sight, not a sight which through reflection allows a reciprocal relationship between seer and seen but a sight that categorically fixes the body on a geometrically-absolute grid of lines far removed from the lived lines of the living body. Romanyshyn shows how the history of this body has culminated in our own time in the body of the astronaut, a body suited up for a contrived, unearthly life in outer space, a body whose gift and legacy of immediate contact with the world of things has been withdrawn, remanded by the mechanics and physics of inhuman space. Romanyshyn's point is far from being a negative value judgment on space exploration; it is an observation on how cultural practices can and do reinforce already dominant themes within a culture. Linear perspective vision was discovered in the fifteenth century, and became a psychological convention, a cultural habit of mind. But as Romanyshyn shows, the vectoral demands of linear perspective vision result in a line which human vision cannot follow, a vanishing point. What he goes on to show is how perspectival vision establishes an hegemony of the eye, which transforms the self into a spectator, the body into a specimen, and the world into a spectacle. In his history of the abandoned body and its shadow, Romanyshyn draws on the history of art, on literature, and on science. He ends by considering how the astronaut is a living symbol of the vanishing point of linear perspective vision. At the same time, he considers how the astronaut as a living reality leaves behind a shadow. By a shadow Romanyshyn means all those marginal figurations of the body that have haunted European linear consciousness since the fifteenth century—the witch, the madman, the monster, and in our own time, the anorexic. The shadow body left behind by the astronaut is indeed an anorexic body, a body barely capable of living by itself. This shadow body measures out its livelihood, rationing living to bare bones. As Romanyshyn aptly shows, this body too is an apt symbol of our times: it is a reflection of our concern with "light matters"—matters having to do with the visual appearance of things.

The visual appearance of things might be said to be the focus of Mical Goldfarb's essay, but in a quite different sense. Goldfarb, a psychotherapist and artist, is concerned to show how in artistic creation the body is something other than a convenient tool for making art objects. The body is part of the very process of creating, part of the very thinking that goes into the making of a painting. By listening to "inner experience," artists succeed in capturing the felt quality of things. Attention to inner experience can furthermore facilitate the process of creation at times when impasses seem suddenly to constrict all creative activity. Using her own artistic experience and the experience of other artists as examples, Goldfarb shows how artist's block—that seemingly impassible solidity that obtrudes itself sometimes with obdurate firmness—can actually open the way to a clarity of vision. Rather than fighting the block, attempting to ignore it, or otherwise deal with it as an altogether negative experience, Goldfarb shows how attending to the block in a bodily sense frees one's energies. Indeed, rather than playing deaf to the impasse, the artist listens to it in depth; she/he not only makes room for it but hears it out.

Eugene Gendlin, well-known founder of the psychotherapeutic technique of focusing, examines ways in which a bodily felt sense operates in everyday life situations as well as in deeper self-understandings. In his essay, "The Wider Role of the Body in Thought and Language," he shows us in new and distinctive ways how a bodily felt sense is fundamental to our acts of thinking and speaking. In particular, he invites us to consider how the body *implies*, and how, by listening to its 'implyings' we come to fresh awarenesses and create new meanings. Drawing both on the most common of daily human experiences and on his own clinical experience, Gendlin shows us that there is an intricacy to our bodily life that not only far exceeds the possibilities of any merely material substance or mere robot utterly wed to culturally-derivative fads and forms of experience, but that far exceeds the categories and distinctions we take to order our lives. He sees this bodily "excess" as itself an order, an order of meanings—bodily implyings. He furthermore sees this order of meanings as literally *coming* from the body in the same way that sleep, appetite, orgasm, and emotions *come* from the body. In a broader sense, his research demonstrates that there is indeed such a thing as human nature, and that what is necessary to its appreciation is an opening to the ways in which the body speaks to us, ways that are not part of the established cultural order but that break through to a different order.

An equally new perspective on the body and language is presented by Mary LeCron Foster, an anthropological linguist. Recent investigations into the origin and evolution of human language point toward the centrality of the body and of bodily awarenesses in the very genesis of language. The relationship of the body to the beginnings of language might at first seem complex and remote in comparison to the relationship of the body to, say, illness, or the emotions, and this because in sickness and in our everyday emotional lives we are immediately aware of experiences of the body and can thus readily recognize and recall such experiences. In contrast, not only does a discussion of the origin of language take us far back in evolutionary time, but an awareness of our articulatory gestures in the course of our everyday speech is virtually absent: we are attentive not to the means whereby we are making speech sounds, but to speech itself. Yet the awareness of both movement and touch, as when the tongue touches the palate in sounding a *t*, or when top and bottom lips touch in sounding an *m*, was once the origin and anchor of linguistic meanings. In her essay, Foster shows how language arose as an extension of a mammalian mimetic use of the body or of body parts, or in broader terms, how analogical thinking is at the very core of human thinking. She demonstrates how spatial relationships and movements observed in nature were imitated and communicated by shaping and manipulating the tongue and the lips—how, in other words, articulatory gestures and their referents were analogically related. The articulatory gesture *m*, for example, is analogically related to such meanings as "bringing together," and "pressing against." Though vastly changed, our language today still preserves in an attenuated form vestiges of these analogical beginnings. As Foster shows, we can still sense in our articulatory gestures the tactile-kinetic relationships obtaining between gesture and meaning. A true appreciation by the reader of these relationships necessitates a "mouths-on" approach, something akin to an appreciation of what we must have experienced when we first learned a language, specifically when we first learned the intricacies of our own mother tongue, and not those of some other tongue. Foster's theory of monogenesis—a single origin of language—is based upon her extensive knowledge of languages, and on her systematic reconstruction of early language through the postulation of regular sound change. Her essay brings to light the essential role of the body in the origin and evolution of language, and in particular underscores the significance of the tactile-kinesthetic body to consistent and systematic linguistic patterning. In her analysis, the articulate tactile-kinesthetic body is clearly recognized not as the simple means by which human language is uttered, as if language were in the head, and the body were simply a convenient tool for chattering out its messages. It is recognized as the very source both of the conception of language and of original linguistic meanings.

An internal connectedness is readily apparent in the progression of essays, each one opening in a further way a particular dimension of the one preceding. Common themes are equally readily apparent in the original inquiries and findings summarized above. Some of these themes may seem startlingly new, yet like newly discovered stars or galaxies, they have been there all along, hidden behind either cultural or theoretical blinders. That thinking is not something a mind does in a metaphysical vacuum is a notion that permeates Johnstone's, Gendlin's, Foster's, Goldfarb's, and Moerman's essays. That cultural histories inform our lives is a theme permeating both Romanyshyn's essay and my own. At the same time, as Foster's essay shows explicitly, as Levine's work demonstrates, and as Johnstone's, Gendlin's, and Nagatomo's analyses each strongly suggests, something far deeper than culture also informs our lives. Something called "human nature" transcends the bounds imposed by any cultural standards, or perhaps better, *subtends* cultural norms—the experience of seated meditation, for example, as Nagatomo shows us; or the experience of a bodily felt sense, as Gendlin show us; or the experience of working through artist's block, as Goldfarb shows us; or the experience of feelings of love or anger, as Johnstone shows us. All such experiences are pan-cultural possibilities; they are not the treasure of a particular culture. Whether identified specifically as evolutionary dimensions of humanness or not, fundamental human capacities and possibilities— pan-cultural invariants—clearly inform our lives no less than particular cultural capacities and possibilities.

It is pertinent in this context to underscore the common body that not only subtends cultural differences but also subtends gender differences. None of the essays addresses current gender issues. This is not because gender issues are thought unimportant but because more fundamental issues are of concern here. The body that is conceived as an assemblage of parts or as a dumb show of movement is a gender-neutral human body. In more immediate terms, the body that responds to placebos, that experiences trauma and anxiety, that sounds the letter m, that becomes ill with a cold, that is illuminated by a felt sense, that creates art, that 'just sits' meditating and in 'just sitting' is transformed from the everyday—this body is foundationally a *human* body. It is specific to neither a male nor a female body exclusively. Indeed, an array of fundamental human phenomena point to the body not only as cultural universal but also as gender-neutral. All humans feel pain, for example. In recognizing and acknowledging this basic human phenomenon, we could say, paraphrasing the earlier cited remark of a Soviet official, that "Suddenly men and women realize that they are both human beings, that men as well as women, women as well as men, can feel pain." Similarly with the foundational human phenomenon (or phenomena) addressed in each essay. Gender differences, where they arise in the context of the discussion or analysis, do so on the ground of the fundamental human phenomenon in each case. Thus Moerman, for example, reviewing studies of the placebo effect, cites gender differences in color choice; Romanyshyn, describing the bodily legacy of a culture-induced linear perspective vision, speaks of the (male) astronaut and the (female) anorexic, though neither astronaut nor anorexic are always male and female bodies respectively; Goldfarb describes both male and female artists' ways of working, but the ways are peculiar to neither male nor female. In each case gender difference is subtended by something more basic. The current concern and predilection for uncovering and analyzing gender differences should not blind us to the corporeal ties that bind us in a common humanity—nor to the importance of devoting ourselves equally to the understanding of those ties. That there are such corporeal ties and that they are of foundational significance in our everyday lives are powerful if tacit themes uniting the gathered essays.

That our present-day Western culture is mesmerized by vision and that we have all but forgotten the felt body, the body of both tactile-kinesthetic and affective experience, is a theme that permeates Romanyshyn's essay, and one that is also very much present in Nagatomo's and Johnstone's essays. In fact another recurrent theme explicitly addressed in detail in Johnstone's and Nagatomo's essays is that emotions—somatic/tactile-kinesthetic feelings—are bodily realities and belong to the whole body, not just selected parts of it. This same theme surfaces in other essays—in Kugelmann's, Levine's, Moerman's, and my own essay—precisely because of the concern of these essays with sickness and health. Indeed, given the fact that many if not all of the above specified themes are in various ways integrally related to sickness and health, it is not surprising that sickness and health themselves emerge as themes in challenges to a Cartesian metaphysics.

Another common theme of great import is that of wholeness,

and wholeness in two senses: the body is neither an amalgum of separate systems nor is it an entity separate from a mind. All of these essays in one way and another offer evidence of that wholeness; each thereby substantively challenges conceptions of bodies and persons that denigrate or ignore their integrity. In this respect it should be emphasized that the mind-body issues addressed in this book are not those arising within what is commonly called the "representational theory of perception." As Johnstone deftly points out in the opening essay, there are at least two mind/body problems: the thought/body problem and the mind/brain problem. Problems of the latter sort are met with in the context of the representational theory of perception. What that theory attempts to explain are phenomena such as bent pencils in glasses, red suns at sunset, and the physical indistinguishability of nerve impulses in spite of their distinctive sensory origins. It explains such phenomena by affirming the brain to be the fabricator of representations of the external world. The interdisciplinary challenges gathered together here are in effect not addressed to the issues arising within what is basically a scientific explanation of how we perceive what we do; they are addressed to the thought/body problem—to the conceptual dichotomy introduced by Descartes with his thinking and extended substances. Each essay shows in its own way how in our everyday thoughts, feelings, and actions, in our illnesses, in our recoveries, in our paths of self-cultivations, and so on, we are not two substances, one definitively reigning supreme, one definitively diminished. We are all of a piece. By giving the body its due, each essay brings to the fore the possibility of ultimately restoring to wholeness precisely what was conceptually sundered by Descartes and what in turn became the dominant problem in Western metaphysics.

Another recurrent theme is in fact the body's capacity to cure itself. The theme is readily apparent in Levine's, Moerman's, and my own essay, and it is evidentially supported by each of us in different ways. In his essay, too, Kugelmann implicitly recognizes the body's capacity to cure itself and in this respect, his analysis closely compliments Levine's. Where Levine speaks explicitly of the body curing itself by "renegotiating" trauma, Kugelmann speaks of the need of rituals by which the body might acknowledge its "continually aborted grief." By whatever name, and whatever its particular dynamic form, stress is loss, and loss is recovered only by recovering the body that was once integrally present but now remains unattended or left behind. Nagatomo, Gendlin, and Goldfarb also implicitly emphasize the body's capacity to cure itself.

Their essays affirm that the quite ordinary body of quite ordinary human experience holds the key to lightening its own miseries, provided one stops to listen to it and gives it its due. Indeed, the lore and wisdom of "the ordinary body" is thematic throughout the whole.

Wholeness, self-healing, cultural histories, pan-cultural invariants, thinking, emotions, the tactile-kinesthetic body, the body's wisdom—what are these themes telling us? Surely they are awakening us to the richness of our bodily lives, and asking us to listen to that richness and to question received notions that devalue our sense of our bodies. Just as surely they are telling us that cultural influences can be pernicious, as pernicious as biological "influences" in the form of certain viruses, bacteria, and chemicals. Not only are stress, hypervisualism, popular body noise, a wholly material view of bodies, and the like, *cultural diseases*, Cartesianism itself is a cultural disease. Cartesianism tells us that we are schizoid creatures, one-half of which is little more than a mechanical rig for getting us about in the world. When we unquestioningly accept this diagnosis of our nature, we give up living in our bodies and enter a cultural *in*sanitarium. Our only way out is through corporeal reflection. Through a recognition and contemplation of the 'deep structures' of our bodily selves, we have the possibility of rediscovering and reaffirming wholeness, self-healing, emotions, tactile-kinesthetic experience—all those dimensions of our bodily lives which we deposited at the doorstep when we entered.

Given the depth, breadth, and implications of these new and original essays, the recovery and revaluation of the body augurs well. There is too much awaiting discovery and understanding—even too much now at stake—for bodies to be catapulted to prominence merely for fifteen minutes of twentieth-century fame or for them to become merely an arcane delight at specialist gatherings or the *dernier cri* in purely academic discussions. Through ever-widening and deepening experiences and through researches which take account of the body in language, philosophy, medicine, ethics, society, culture, and more, including an ecological sense of a world in which bodies find their proper place, a profound and lasting appreciation of the body is possible. In this extended sense, the body is already being given its due. An attentive turning toward the body, "the corporeal turn," is already under way. In this extended sense, burgeoning new inquiries and findings, as they mature and coalesce, will surely come to prevail as a metaphysics that upholds the truths of experience.

ALBERT A. JOHNSTONE

2

The Bodily Nature of the Self or What Descartes Should Have Conceded Princess Elizabeth of Bohemia

THE CARTESIAN CONCEPT OF SELF

One of the declared goals of Descartes's *Meditations on First Philosophy* is to establish the proposition that the soul, or the self, is a pure thinking being, a being devoid of spatial characteristics, and hence one that could conceivably exist independently of a body. The proposed view of the self is the source of the Cartesian dualistic doctrine of the existence of two distinct substances, one thinking, one extended. It is consequently one of the central supports of the mind/body dichotomy which haunts everyday Western thinking and its more sophisticated philosophical counterpart.

The Cartesian view of the self is very much mistaken. To claim as much is not to add one further voice to the chorus of linguistic, hermeneutic, coherentist, or reductionist criticisms, which in phil-

osophical circles habitually relegate Cartesianism to the role of ideational scratching post. Contrary to currently fashionable opinion,
Descartes is quite right in his general approach to philosophical
issues—in his rigorous rationalism, in his high regard for introspection, in his skeptical scrutiny of received opinion, and in his incip-
ient epistemic foundationalism—although lack of space precludes a
serious defense of Cartesian epistemic values.[1] Where Descartes
may be properly criticized is in his failure to be faithful to his own
approach, a failure pointed out in his own time by his favorite disciple, Princess Elizabeth of Bohemia.[2] The aim of the present paper is
to show that if Descartes had indeed paid greater heed to Princess
Elizabeth's objections to his account of the self, he would have been
led through the application of his own principles to a more coherent
and experientially faithful view of the corporeal nature of the thinking self.

Thinking as envisioned by Descartes encompasses a very broad
range of activities. When in the *Meditations* Descartes concludes
that he is "a thing that thinks," he glosses this characterization as
"a thing that doubts, understands, affirms, denies, is willing, is unwilling, and also imagines and has sensory perceptions."[3] The
thinking, which according to Descartes is constitutive of each of
these activities, is something nonsensuous—noncorporeal or nonspatial. The point is sometimes misunderstood, although it follows
readily enough from Descartes's talk of two distinct substances of
which one is characterized as extended substance; by implication,
the second substance must be nonextended or nonspatial. In addition, any number of Descartes's remarks make little or no sense
unless thinking substance is understood to be literally nonspatial.
In a letter to Father Marin Mersenne (July 1641), Descartes explicitly
states that by the term 'idea' he means a concept and not an image
conjured up in imagination.[4] In *Meditation VI* he takes pains to
distinguish pure understanding from imagination, and speaks of
the mind as turning toward itself and its own ideas in understanding, and as turning toward body in imagining.[5] He makes a similar
point in his "Author's Replies to Second Set of Objections" when,
as an illustration of a thought, he says that "whenever I express
something in words, and understand what I am saying, this very
fact makes it certain that there is within me an idea of what is
signified by the words in question."[6] Thought, in this case, is identical with the meaning that words have for oneself in the process of
speaking them, and as such is not something sensuously present in
experience.

Descartes's characterization of thinking and of thoughts as nonspatial is much more warranted than one might at first be inclined to think. Consider a few examples. Let us suppose that I go out into the hall to get a drink of water. I am aware of my intention, of where I am going and what I want, and yet that intention is not sensuously present in my experience. To borrow a well-borrowed image from philosopher Ludwig Wittgenstein, if God were to look into my mind, he (or she) could not tell from anything *sensuously* present what that intention was. Certainly there are many sensuous clues to be found in my experience—the dryness in my throat and mouth, the direction of my determined gait, perhaps a fleeting image of water or of a water fountain—and anyone combing through my experience might well guess from these sensuous clues what my intention is. Yet the intention itself is not sensuously present. It is nevertheless an essential ingredient in the experience, since it commands and constitutes the purpose of the activity underway. Furthermore, I, the one having the experience, am quite certain what my intention is (unless of course I get distracted and forget what I am doing), and I could immediately inform anyone who asked what I intend to do. Any adequate description of the experience would have to include the intention, despite its apparent absence from an inventory of the sensuous constituents of the experience.

Similarly, when I look out of a window and see hats and coats moving about in the street below, I know that the coats cover people, and not machines. That knowing would seem to be an essential part of the experience, since without it the experience would be a quite different one from the one it is. Yet the knowing or what is known is not something actually present sensuously in the experience. Anyone looking into my mind and rummaging through the sensuous constituents of the experience would fail to find it.

The apparently incorporeal nature of thought and thinking leads Descartes to make the not implausible claim that the thinking self, the being that knows, intends, understands, and means, is of the same immaterial and non-sensuous nature as the thoughts entertained. Descartes spells out the claim in his above-mentioned letter to Father Mersenne in which he states that the thinking being cannot be imagined or represented by an image; it has neither color nor odor nor taste, nor anything corporeal—and yet it is quite conceivable and is indeed that through which anything is conceived.[7] The notion that the thinking self is an invisible, intangible, incorporeal being present in all experience, is often considered difficult to accept. The eighteenth-century Scottish philosopher David Hume implicitly assumes the notion to be absurd, when, from his failure to find a sensuous self among the materials of experience, he draws the conclusion that there is no self.[8] Hume's assumption would be widely endorsed among present-day thinkers. Yet in fairness to Descartes, it should be pointed out that parity of reasoning leads to the conclusion that there is no knowing, no intending, no understanding, no meaning, insofar as these are taken to be nonsensuous constituents of experiences. Conversely, if nonsensuous knowing, intending, and meaning are admitted to be constituents of experience, then surely the notion that a nonsensuous being is the author of such activities is not only not absurd but also initially plausible, and at the very least deserves serious consideration.

Within his own reflections on the matter, the chief support Descartes offers for the conception of an incorporeal self is the conclusion he reaches in his epistemological enterprise of methodical doubt. Descartes sets himself the task of doubting everything that can be doubted in order to discover whether there is anything indubitable. He finds that he may doubt the existence of anything that is spatial or extended in space since any such item could well be a bit player in a dream he is having, or the fabrication of some deceitful demon attempting to delude him. He reasons that nevertheless he cannot doubt his own existence: in order to doubt, he must exist. Descartes goes on to argue that since he must exist despite the supposition that everything corporeal or spatial is but a dream or a demonic hoax, he cannot himself be anything spatial or corporeal. In his dialogue *The Search for Truth*, he has his spokesman, Polyander, put the matter as follows: "On the contrary, these suppositions simply strengthen the certainty of my conviction that I exist and am not a body. Otherwise, if I had doubts about my body, I would also have doubts about myself, and I cannot have doubts about that. I am absolutely convinced that I exist, so convinced that it is totally impossible for me to doubt it."[9]

Now, the obvious objection to this line of reasoning is that the conception of the self involved is perhaps inadequate; from the fact that one has no awareness of being a body, it does not follow that one is not a body. Descartes was sufficiently impressed with this objection to add in *The Meditations* the further consideration absent from his earlier *Discourse on Method*, that his conception of himself is an adequate one: he has a "clear and distinct idea" both of himself as a "thinking, non-extended thing," and of body as something extended and non-thinking.[10] The addition yields a very powerful argument. If Descartes is right and his conception of the self is an adequate one, then his conclusion that he conceivably could exist without a body would seem to follow unassailably. Of course, if he conceivably could exist without a body, then his body is not essential to the being he is; he is essentially a pure nonsensuous being which simply happens to be conjoined to a body.

The mind/body dichotomy thus traced out by Descartes should not be confused with the one that figures most often in more recent discussions of the body/mind problem. There are in fact two (at least two) distinct body/mind dichotomies. The one with which we are concerned here is a thinking-being/extended-being dichotomy, or a thought/body dichotomy. The other (with which we shall not be concerned) is tied to the representational theory of perception, the account of perception generally accepted in present-day science and, it might be added, also warmly advocated by Descartes. According to the representational theory, the entities present in perceptual experience are not external objects in person but rather mere representations, images or copies of those objects in the external world. These representations, which are in one's mind, are the end product of a long chain of events that includes the emission of light or sound waves, the stimulation of sense organs and the transmission of messages to the brain. The mind/body problem that arises in this context concerns basically the relation of events in the mind to events in the brain. The corresponding mind/body dichotomy is more appropriately termed a mind/brain dichotomy. It is clearly quite different from the thought/body dichotomy with which we are at present concerned. Indeed, the two dichotomies are encountered in different accounts of perception, one in the representational account in which brain events play an essential role, the other in a first person account of what perception is like for the perceiver. It would be a serious mistake to misconstrue Descartes's thought/body distinction as the mind/brain one.

THE IGNORED FELT BODY

The strength of Descartes's argument in favor of a pure thinking self is rarely appreciated, in particular by modern English-speaking commentators. Over the centuries an impressive volume and variety of criticism have been directed against Descartes's account of the thinking subject and the dualism to which it gives rise. Much of it concerns the metaphysical implications of the view and the very possibility of a thinking substance, and often begs the question by assuming criteria of substancehood unfavorable to Descartes's view. Even if successful, such an approach is less than adequate, for it ignores the opposing evidence, the reasoning which leads Descartes to his view in the first place. Among the rare criticisms to attempt to meet Descartes on home terrain are those formulated by Princess Elizabeth in a series of three letters in the spring of 1643.[11] Let us take a brief look at them.

Elizabeth begins what is to blossom into a long and intimate correspondence with Descartes with a query: How is it possible for the soul, a thinking substance, to act on the body so as to produce voluntary movement? She points out that a soul so defined has none of the properties by which one body moves another, and requests a more probing definition. In his answer, Descartes does little more than to liken the action of the soul on the body to the action of gravitation, a phenomenon with which we are all familiar. However, since Descartes has already dismissed gravitation from his physics on the grounds that such a force is impossible, Elizabeth is understandably dissatisfied with this reply. She reiterates her puzzlement, and at two separate points in her second letter speaks of the pernicious effect of troubles, worries, and emotional turmoil on clear philosophical reflection. Such an effect is very difficult to accommodate in Descartes's account of the self, Elizabeth points out, for a pure thinking being which may conceivably exist without a body should not be at the mercy of "a few vapors." The root of Elizabeth's objection thus appears to be the failure of Descartes's account to square very well with her own felt experience. Descartes remains quite oblivious of the fact, and advances the somewhat dubious claim that three distinct modes of knowing—conception, imagination, and sense awareness—are each respectively appropriate to one of three types of being—soul, body, and the union of the two. At this point the discussion between the two strongly resembles the typical misunderstandings which keep marriage counselors busy: for the husband a particular problem is a technical difficulty to be resolved, while for the wife it is a matter of accommodating feelings. Since Descartes is firmly convinced of the validity of the thought/extension dichotomy doctrine, he apparently considers it sufficient to meet Elizabeth's objections with technical fine-tuning rather than serious revision. He appends a recommendation not to spend more than a few days a year on metaphysical matters, which advice, while perhaps not patronizing in spirit, is nowhere extended to Descartes's male correspondents. Undaunted, Elizabeth replies with the suggestion that the root of the problem could well be a faulty conception of the soul as a pure thinking being. She suggests that Descartes is perhaps being unfaithful to his own precept to form judgments only about what is perceived clearly and distinctly, and that it could well be that the bodily nature of the self follows from some other essential function of the soul. Descartes's response to the suggestion, if there ever was one, is now lost. The issue is not discussed in subsequent correspondence.

Since it is unlikely that someone as intellectually acute as Elizabeth would esteem her scruples to be answered satisfactorily, we are left with the somewhat puzzling question as to why the issue was never taken up again. Descartes subsequently devoted considerable attention to related matters of considerable interest to Elizabeth. In later correspondence he was very solicitous of Elizabeth's ill health and bouts of depression, and the extensive advice he offered on living one's life constitutes the quasi-totality of his writings on moral philosophy. He dedicated his *Principles of Philosophy* to her, and seems to have written his treatise, *The Passions of the Soul*, largely in response to her interest in the subject. Yet in none of this is Elizabeth's original query addressed. It may be that Elizabeth simply decided that the philosopher must know better than she on the issue. It may be that she found it would be ungracious of her to push Descartes to the wall with a point the deeper implications of which he was obviously unwilling to envisage. It may be too that she simply lost interest in the question. Whatever the reason, it remains true that in her early correspondence Elizabeth puts her finger on a crucial issue, that of whether the Cartesian notion of a pure thinking being is an experientially adequate concept of the self—adequate to account for the initiation of movement, and adequate to account for the influence of feeling on reflection.

Elizabeth's criticisms point toward the necessity of introducing feeling, and hence the body into the concept of the self. The body involved in feeling is essentially the felt body, or the body as it is felt to be, as distinct from the seen body, or the body as it is seen to be. The body as felt is an aspect of the body given little serious consideration by Descartes. In Descartes's notion of the body, preferential if not quasi-exclusive status is accorded the body as it is seen, the visual body. When Descartes speculates that his body may be part of a dream or a demon conjuration, the body he considers is clearly the visual body. He declares, for instance, "I shall consider myself as not having hands or eyes, or flesh, or blood or senses, but as falsely believing I have all these things."[12] Flesh and blood are properties of the body as seen, not of the body as felt. To convince oneself of the fact, one need only close one's eyes and become attentive to what one actually feels of the body, what its salient, sensed features are, and how they might be most appropriately characterized. Clearly, what is felt is a weighty, three-dimensional mass that includes, among other things, elongated appendages that are sensitive and mobile in odd ways. Flesh and blood are simply not part of what is felt. Similarly, when Descartes concludes that his own existence is certain, and he asks what sort of being he used to think he was, he remarks quite significantly, "Well, the first thought to come to mind was that I had a face, hands, arms and the whole mechanical structure of limbs which can be seen in a corpse, and which I called the body."[13] Once again, the body to come to mind for Descartes is the visual, not the felt body. The face as such is quite certainly not a predominant feature of the felt body; it is simply one region of the body on equal footing with any other, neither more nor less sensitive, and with no particular social status. Likewise, the mechanical structure of the limbs is not a particularly outstanding feature of the body as felt, while the notion of the felt body as a corpse is a contradiction in terms. Thus the body, which on Descartes's line of reasoning could be part of a dream while Descartes himself continues to exist, is in fact a visual one. The visual body is the body of which Descartes claims he conceivably could exist independently. The felt body is quite clearly ignored in Descartes's skeptical and conceptual operations.

Just such a reproach is addressed to Descartes by a number of French philosophers who identify the self with the body as it is for oneself, or, as it has been variously characterized, with 'the subjective body', 'the felt body', 'the tactile-kinesthetic body'. Early nineteenth-century French philosopher Maine de Biran, for example, is emphatic in denying that the self is Descartes's thinking being. He identifies the former with one's own body as it is for oneself, and in particular with the feeling of willed effort.[14] Jean-Paul Sartre in *Being and Nothingness* likewise draws a sharp distinction between two "irreducible" bodies, one's body as it is for oneself and one's body as it is for others. He identifies the self with the former, a body which is lived, not known, a center of orientation which cannot be an object for oneself.[15] He furthermore argues against the Cartesian notion of a pure thinking being on the ground that it leads to paradox, the paradox of an unoriented perceiving subject, and of an immaterial soul handling a physical instrument that is the body.[16] Maurice Merleau-Ponty takes up the theme in turn, and makes a valiant effort to show that the perceiving self must be one's felt body. He argues in particular that if the self were a pure thinking being of the sort envisaged by Descartes, then for such a self all orientations should be equivalent; a face seen upside down should not have the unnatural appearance it does have, and in George Stratton's experiment in which the subject is outfitted with lenses that invert the visual field, the perceiver should not experience the field as inverted.[17]

While Maine de Biran along with Sartre and Merleau-Ponty are right to identify the self with the felt body, the arguments they present fail to establish the point. Sartre, for instance, gives very fine descriptions of the experience of one's own body in adult perception and action, but, while the descriptions are quite suggestive, they do not in themselves establish the claim that the perceiving subject and author of action must be a body rather than an immaterial thinking being. His characterization of one's body as an unknowable presence on which there can be no point of view, for instance, is apt enough when one is involved in everyday object-directed perception and action, that is, when one's felt body is part of the background, but the characterization does not hold for introspectively examined movement. His claim regarding the necessity of a center of orientation in perceptual experience shows at best that for perception to be possible it is necessary to *have* a body, a point with which Descartes would willingly agree: it does not show that for perception it is necessary for the subject to *be* a body. In the end, his claim that the construal of the body as a tool handled by an immaterial soul leads to an infinite regress and to inextricable problems remains unelucidated and simply echoes the puzzlement voiced at an earlier time by Elizabeth.

Merleau-Ponty presents a case which although initially more plausible is ultimately equally inconclusive. At the crux of his case is the dubious claim that the sensuous items given in perception are themselves devoid of orientation—or, as he states the matter, "both experience and reflection demonstrate that no content is in itself oriented."[18] The reasoning is that the vertical orientation found in perception must be supplied by the perceiver, which state would be impossible if the latter were a pure thinking being, hence a being devoid of vertical orientation. Merleau-Ponty's central claim is false, of course, since the tactile-kinesthetic field of felt experience contains a vertical orientation due to the perpetual pull of gravity: immobility finds the body pressed in one particular direction (down), and movement of one's body requires the deployment of a quite different effort depending on the direction of the movement. The vertical orientation of visual phenomena is consequently explicable as a feature automatically acquired from the tactile-kinesthetic field when the two fields are coordinated to form an integrated world. It should be added that Merleau-Ponty is also mistaken in his claim that it is inexplicable that Descartes's immaterial perceiver should see an inverted visual world upon the application of inverting lenses, as in Stratton's experiment. On Descartes's representational account of perception, the impression made on the mind is a direct function of a brain state; since an inverted retinal image would produce an altered brain state while the brain state relating to tactile-kinesthetic phenomena would remain unchanged, visual items should be perceived as inverted—which is exactly what the experiment finds. Merleau-Ponty's case against the Cartesian self thus also fails. If a sound case is to be made for the claim that the felt body is an essential constituent of the thinking self, then fresh grounds must be uncovered. Let us see whether these grounds may be found in any of the various activities of the thinking self.

A WORD ON INTROSPECTION

In what follows extensive reliance will be placed on introspective findings. Introspection may be roughly described as the observation of a person's experience by that person. The aim of such observation, at least insofar as it is of philosophical interest or service, is to provide an accurate description of particular experiences of a particular type had by the observer, and to do so with a view to formulating generalizations about the essential structures of any experience of that type. Since introspection is much maligned in present-day Western philosophy (whether by linguistic disciples, lab-coated analysts, or relativistic conversationalists), there is some need for a few words to be said in its defense.

One source of aversion to introspection is simply the fact that it deals in experience, and hence, to a large extent at least, in items private to one person. The complaint is that two observers cannot observe the same object; at most they can compare like experiences. This awkward situation provides little warrant for a very serious objection to introspection, however. If any information at all about private objects is to be had, then those private items must be introspected since introspection is the only tool available. The alternative is to dismiss the private objects altogether from any account of the world, a procedure which not only would accord poorly with the spirit of empirical inquiry, but also would amount to the questionable espousal of a revised Socratic injunction of the sort, "Ignore thyself."

A more serious objection to introspection is that it is an enterprise which cannot possibly succeed in the task it sets itself. It
proposes to give an accurate account of some particular experience
in which the observer is involved. Yet any observation of that experience while it is going on, requires a shift in the focus of attention (or
at least a shift in interest or purpose), which shift alters the original
experience so that the experience actually observed is no longer the
one that is to be described. The objection is fair enough. Any introspective observation must to some ill-defined degree involve an inference from what is actually observed of the altered experience to
what must have been the structures of the original experience, and
hence to some extent involve operations other than observation.
Attempts to capture the experience by reliving it in memory hold
little promise of overcoming the difficulty (and incidentally are
more aptly termed 'retrospection', as in William Lyon's terminology).[19] However, while the difficulty is real enough, its import
should not be overestimated. It is not as if the introspective attention shift removed huge chunks of reality from the original experience, converted reds into blues, cramps into itches, or played general
havoc with the putative object of observation, and furthermore did
so in such a way as to preclude the change being noticed by the
observer. The fact is that there are substantial continuities between
the two experiences despite attention shifts, and these continuities
allow important observations to be made. The discontinuities occasioned by the shift certainly do require that some appeal be made
to inference and to memory to flesh out an account of an experience. Nevertheless it hardly seems to follow that as a result, all
descriptions of experience, however cautious, must be radically
vitiated.

A less serious objection sometimes felt is that an introspective
report is invariably skewed by personal and cultural beliefs, and is in
fact what Lyons terms "a stereotyped 'folk psychological' account,"
or a "culture-tinged model" of what is believed to be going on.[20] Yet
while it is true that the skewing of observation is a danger, a similar
danger threatens any empirical inquiry. If the threat of culture-
tinged accounts constituted a sufficient reason to condemn introspection, by parity of reasoning all empirical enquiry should be con-
demned. The question with which we are concerned has to do with
rather rudimentary structures of experience, with whether there is
experiential evidence for considering thinking (in Descartes's sense)
to be bodily or spatial. It should be possible to reach a careful and
accurate answer to this question, one which is not skewed to the

point of falsification by the influence of cultural models or folk psychology. After all, accurate introspective reports are made when people admit to experiencing color, pain, joy, anger, or dreams. Such simple admissions cannot be plausibly dismissed as hopelessly skewed by folk psychology or culture. If proper care is taken to record the evidence actually perceived rather than some interpreted or structured version of it, there seems little reason to think our question may not be satisfactorily answered.

Finally, objection is often made to the practice of formulating generalizations about other people's experience from one's own introspective findings. The claim is that it is quite presumptuous and unwarranted to generalize from the particular case of one's own experience to that of other selves generally, and that the generalization can be drawn with assurance only within the context of a statistical study involving a random or representative set of experiencing selves. It is true that ideally it would be preferable to base generalizations about private items on a statistical study involving a large random sample of introspecting selves. Unfortunately, however, psychologists have not seen fit to undertake studies on the topics of interest, and philosophers lack the financial means to do so. Given the present state of the art, one is obliged to rely on one's powers of self-observation for information on the relevant issues. In generalizing from one's own experience one must place trust in the far from implausible assumption that other human beings are not so constituted that the essential structures of their experiences differ in important ways from those of one's own. In what follows this assumption will be made. The reader is invited to test for himself or herself the veracity of the conclusions drawn.

THE CORPOREALITY OF THE FEELING SELF

In *The Principles of Philosophy*, Descartes distinguishes two modes of thinking: perception and volition. In the first, Descartes classes the more properly cognitive activities such as "sensory perception, imagination, and pure understanding"; in the second, he classes two groups of activities or states, on one hand, willing proper, which he labels "desire" and "aversion," and on the other, doxastic phenomena such as "assertion, denial and doubt."[21] Since phenomena in the three groups differ considerably in nature, we shall have to examine all three to determine in each case whether Descartes is right in his claim that the thinking in question is conceivable apart from anything bodily. For reasons that will be clearer later, we shall begin with the sticky case of willing proper. Although for Descartes desire and aversion are paradigm cases of willing, it is best to approach the topic through what is perhaps at first glance a side entrance, namely, those other forms of willing of concern to Elizabeth: the emotions and feelings generally.

Descartes terms emotions and feelings "passions of the soul," rather than forms of willing, and classes them with perceptions. The particular location Descartes attributes to such perceived entities is crucial to his mistaken conception of the self. On Descartes's account of perception, colored shapes are perceived as if in an external world; pains, hunger, warmth are perceived as if in the body, while (curiously enough) joy and anger are perceived as if in the soul itself.[22] The locating of feelings in the soul is a mistake heavy with consequences, since it takes feelings out of the body and allows them to be characterized as noncorporeal.

Descartes is not alone in his assessment of where feelings are located. Emotions or feelings generally are often viewed as a nebulous mental accompaniment to one's particular involvement in the world, something on the order of a pervasive and subjective atmosphere enveloping and permeating events in the world. Yet the view is mistaken, and may be readily dispelled by a minimal appeal to introspective evidence. The widespread espousal of the view would seem due largely to the fact that one's attention is generally centered on something out in the surrounds, if not some person, then some task to be accomplished; it is not focused on bodily feelings, which as a result, become part of a background atmosphere. Feelings are, however, primarily a specific state of one's tactile-kinesthetic or felt body. To convince oneself of the fact, one need only cast a quick introspective glance at one's felt body in any emotional situation. Instead of a putative atmosphere, one invariably finds some modification of one's felt body, that same body in which are located one's pains, one's hunger, and one's feelings of warmth.

The point is most readily substantiated in the case of emotions. Let us briefly consider what might be found with regard to one emotion, anger, and flesh out the evidence from there. When one is in the throes of a vigorous rage, a furtive glance at the feelings involved encounters a wealth of newcomers on the normally benign scene of one's tactile-kinesthetic body: a choking, seething throat, congestion in the face, a tingling in the scalp, a coursing thumping in temples and chest, a tension in the brow and round the eyes, a pent up energy in thorax and arms, a churning in the abdomen, shaking in the knees, and gripping in the toes. Each of these various feelings is a modification of the tactile-kinesthetic body. Each occupies a certain vaguely defined volume of tactile-kinesthetic space; it has a location with respect to the others—it is adjacent to, between, or distant from the other feelings; it is not simply a discrete qualitative presence but is also a certain felt dynamics continuous with the tensions elsewhere in one's tactile-kinesthetic complex. For this reason, it is nonsensical to ask where one is angry, not because anger is nowhere, but because it is everywhere throughout one's felt body. Together the various feelings make up the substance of the felt body. Likewise they constitute the substance of the anger. Short of these tactile-kinesthetic feelings, the tensions and dynamics specific to felt anger, one would not be angry.

It is of course true that feelings are not the only constituents of the anger. There is also an awareness of grievances, an awareness of the person (or situation) toward whom (or which) the anger is directed. The anger is also in part a modification of one's mode of reasoning, as also of one's mode of perceiving, since one's seeing and hearing are altered by the tactile-kinesthetic commotion. Nevertheless, the feelings are the essential constituent of the anger in the sense that they are the determining constituent: if the feelings specific to anger were removed, the remaining state of awareness would qualify rather as indifference or calm. The point is quite forcefully made by William James in the following passage: "*If we fancy some strong emotion, and then try to abstract from our consciousness of it all the feelings of its bodily symptoms, we find we have nothing left behind,* no 'mind-stuff' out of which the emotion can be constituted, and that a cold and neutral state of intellectual perception is all that remains."23

The situation is analogous for any emotion or sentiment. In the case of love, for instance, the bubbly lassitude, the warmth, the tingling delight and rapt fascination, each pervade the felt body and may be characterized as modes of the tactile-kinesthetic body. Similarly the awe and delight experienced in watching a sequence of graceful movements is not some ethereal mental aura attached to the event. It is a lightness centered about one's eyes and radiating through one's body, a captivation of one's gaze that rivets attention so strongly to the movement as to lead one to hold one's breath. It would be quite possible to run through the various emotions in turn—fear, grief, hate, joy. Each would be found in the same way to involve necessarily a particular mode of the tactile-kinesthetic body, to be a specific complex of localized feelings and tensions, which could with time and patience be described in detail, and distinguished from other affective modes.

The above remarks might well be thought too sanguine. In an experiment some twenty years back, Stanley Schachter and Jerome Singer found that subjects injected with the stimulant, epinephrine, tended to construe the resulting physiological disturbances either as anger or as euphoria depending upon the emotional tenor of the social context in which they found themselves.[24] Since presumably the physiological reactions caused by the drug are the same or very similar whatever the construal, the conclusion is sometimes drawn that physiological reactions are insufficient to differentiate emotions. Yet surely such a conclusion is unwarranted. It is clearly in contradiction with the introspective evidence that may be gathered quite freely from one's own experience. While anger and mirth are grossly alike in that they both involve a spastic or explosive tension, they show considerable difference in finer detail—a difference which might be succinctly summed up as that between a growl and a howl. Unless one is prepared to take the courageous and ultimately self-defeating step of denying the evidence of one's own experience, one must conclude that it is rather the subjects in the experiment who were mistaken in their reports about their experience. It is significant in this regard that the experiment took place in an emotionally charged social context, and furthermore that those subjects told what to expect from the drug did not experience the drug-induced physiological reactions as an emotion. The most plausible interpretation of the experimental results is that the unwary subjects experienced certain tensions, congestions, and tremors grossly like those typical either of anger or of mirth, and that the social atmosphere, as is often the case, empathically induced like feelings of anger or mirth of which the unsuspecting subjects assumed the drug-induced reactions to be an integral part. In the final analysis, the experiment is evidence not of the ambiguity of the physiology of emotions but rather of a tendency in experimental psychology to insensitivity toward physiological niceties.

A more relevant experimental finding is one uncovered by a researcher, George Hohmann, who interviewed some twenty-five paraplegics, and found that for them the intensity of their emotional reactions was significantly diminished in proportion to the extent of their neurological damage.[25] This finding is exactly what might have been predicted in view of the corporeal nature of feeling as revealed by introspection. Any diminution in the capacity to feel is a diminution of the tactile-kinesthetic body, and hence of the capacity to have emotions.

The corporeal nature of emotions has grave implications for Descartes's account of the self. The embarrassing fact for Descartes's account is that one identifies with one's emotions. When, for instance, I declare, "I am furious!" I do not regard myself as a mere thinking being, an intellect which happens to have at its disposition a tactile-kinesthetic body that is furious. I identify with the seething, volatile configuration of tensions which defines my tactile-kinesthetic body (illuminated of course by awareness). Its turmoil and agitation are my own turmoil and agitation. When I cease to identify with the tensions and dynamics, I cease to be angry, and become a spectator to fast-fading feelings.

The case is similar with any other emotion. To be in love is to have feelings of a certain sort, to act on them, to identify with their warmth and energy. If a tactile-kinesthetic body were merely something an incorporeal thinking subject had at its disposition, then the thinking subject would be divorced from the being who was in love. The appropriate description of the situation would be not that one was in love, but that one's body was. Analogous remarks apply in the case of other feelings such as surprise, or excitement, or uneasiness. If a body was something one has rather than something one is, it would simply happen to be the case that one was conjoined to a body that was surprised, or excited, or uneasy. A pure, thinking spirit would have at its disposal, as it were, a body charged with feeling—whether rage or terror, delight or despair—like a ship with engines throbbing and an immaterial pilot at the helm.

THE CORPOREALITY OF THE SELF THAT WILLS

Let us now turn to desire and aversion which Descartes classes as forms of willing. Since, on Descartes's account, willing is a form of thinking, desire and aversion, like other modes of thinking, must be immaterial or incorporeal states or activities. On the experiential evidence, however, the account encounters two apparently insurmountable difficulties. On one hand, an examination of experience fails to turn up any such thing as an *act of willing* distinguishable from a *corporeal doing.* On the other hand, willing involves motivation, and a careful scrutiny of experience finds that most (perhaps all) motivation essentially involves feeling and/or emotion, hence something that is spatially extended. Let us examine these two points more closely.

It should be stressed at the outset that for Descartes the willing of an action is not and cannot be the actual doing of the action. Descartes takes great pains to draw a distinction between an operation of the will and the voluntary movement which follows from it.[26] Indeed, he must draw this distinction if he is to claim that willing and the subject that wills are incorporeal. Any voluntary movement of a body is qua movement something corporeal, something a body does. If willing were identical with the actual execution of the movement, then willing would be a corporeal operation, and the subject who wills would have to be a corporeal being rather than the immaterial thinking being of Descartes's account.

The difficulty is to make sense of the concept of willing as an operation distinct from the actual performing of an action. What might such willing be? One initially promising approach is to attempt to identify willing with some one or more of the many processes often found to precede the execution of the action—with a prior wish or longing, for example, with the choosing of one possible course of action from among a number of options, with a prior resolution to act at some particular future time, with the nursing of one's determination to so act. Yet willing cannot properly be equated with any of these operations. Many actions apparently fail to involve operations of the sort—actions done on impulse, for instance. More importantly, there is the fact that prior to the actual performance of an envisaged action, the agent is in principle free not to act. Consequently, the willing of an action can only be an operation that takes place at roughly the same time as the performance of the willed action.

Now, on Descartes's account, willing is an operation of a thinking being, hence one that should in principle be accessible to introspection. Consequently careful introspective investigation of one's experience of one's own actions should turn up an operation of willing contemporaneous with the physical movement being effectuated but distinguishable from it. Since the willing is allegedly something distinct from the physical activity, it is presumably the intentional component of the action, the motivation or desired goal with implicit awareness of means. Yet an account of willing that restricts the operation to the intentional component will not do as a general account. It is apparently quite possible to find cases of experienced action where the intentional component is identical in nature with the intentional component of an experience where no action takes place. Otherwise stated, it is apparently possible to have two experiences, one in which there is desire without action and one in which there is desire with action, and for the sole relevant difference between the two experiences to be simply the performing of the action or the directing of the appropriate tactile-kinesthetic commotion (the consequent monitoring and perceptual differences being irrelevant). The difference between willing and not willing in such cases is simply the actual doing or the voluntary physical activity itself. Thus, the willing cannot be simply the intentional component but must include the physical activity. Any reader who is unconvinced should consult his or her own experience, and attempt to uncover the putative acts of willing which allegedly make the difference between intending and doing and intending and not doing, the putative acts being not simply the doing of the action. It should be a fairly easy matter to undertake a search for such entities since, after all, willing is something we all do incessantly. The repeated failure to find any acts of willing of the alleged kind is strong evidence that there are none to be found.

One might be tempted at this point to attempt to save Descartes's account by postulating an incorporeal act of willing over and above the intentional component, but a postulated entity of the sort would be a gratuitous addition devoid of experiential support. There would be no more warrant to postulate such an entity than to postulate the existence of any of an indefinitely great number of possible hypothetical entities, each devoid of any experiential support.

Descartes is thus clearly mistaken in his account of willing as an operation independent of the actual execution of the action. Even if he were not, he would be faced with the further apparently impossible task of squaring his account with the nature of motivation. It is certainly true, as Descartes maintains, that awareness and cognition are an indispensable constituent in any willing or doing. An activity is never the fruit of a mere undirected impulse, but always involves some awareness of the situation or environment in addition to expectations of various sorts including consequences of certain courses of action. It is also true that the awareness and cognition are not something sensuously present in the experience and hence properly characterizable as extended or spatial in nature. It should immediately be added, however, that everyday experiences of willing contain not only perceptual and cognitive elements but affective elements as well. The latter may be very complex and involve both motive in the form of various feelings and emotions, and also determination and energy. These affective elements clearly figure in the motivation and effectuation of the willing no less than the cognitive and perceptual ones. Equally clearly they are corporeal, hence a form of extended being, and as such ruin Descartes's doctrine of an immaterial willing self.

The crux of the matter is the fact that *qua* feeling the affective element that motivates any decision, determination, and action (hence willing) is some particular state of the tactile-kinesthetic body. The point is most easily made in cases in which some emotion or other is the motivation for acting. When an action is done from anger, there seems little doubt that the tactile-kinesthetic body is an essential constituent in the motivation and hence in the willing and doing. Without a tactile-kinesthetic commotion of the sort peculiar to anger, the agent would not be angry and so could not act from anger. Similarly, when an action is done from fear, the specific type of tactile-kinesthetic commotion characteristic of fear—the sinking petrification and paralyzed agitation—is essential to the willing and to the action, since without it neither willing nor action would be motivated by fear. Analogous remarks clearly hold for many other actions the motivation of which fails to qualify as an emotion according to usual classificatory standards. Curiosity, for instance, involves a specific state of ordered tensions of the tactile-kinesthetic body—a ceasing of activity and riveting of attention—and does so essentially in the sense that unless a person is in such a state, that person cannot qualify as being curious. A particular state of the felt body is consequently a necessary constituent in any willing or action done from curiosity. Compassion likewise involves a specific complex of feelings in the tactile-kinesthetic body, in particular something on the order of a warm melting feeling in chest and throat, without which complex an action would not qualify as done from compassion.

The situation is not essentially different if the motivating feeling is geared into an envisaged situation rather than into a presently perceived one. A particular option may sound attractive, or be judged worth pursuing on the basis of expected similarity with some satisfying past experience, or a series of options may be run through and, as it were, tried out emotionally before the choice of one is made, or some past experience may be relived in memory and awaken a present yearning. Motivation comes in a variety of modes, and may be a quite complicated phenomenon involving layers of considerations. Yet, when feeling enters the picture, as apparently it must at some point, that feeling is not some nebulous mental stuff proper only to an immaterial thinking being. Invariably, it would seem, feeling may be found to be located outside the major focus of attention in some region of the tactile-kinesthetic body. A claim of the sort is of course an experiential one, and as such it is one which the reader can verify for himself or herself. For the present purposes of showing Descartes's account of willing to be mistaken, it suffices to find that in many cases the affective element in motivation is part and parcel of the tactile-kinesthetic body.

It should be emphasized that the affective constituent in willing is *not* dispensable. In any willing and doing, there is espousal and identification of self with the affective motive. When one decides or acts out of anger, one identifies with the anger. Such identification is most clearly the case with emotions, but takes place in any of a multitude of less passionate affective states: surprise, disgust, curiosity, disappointment, pride, sympathy, boredom, contentment, excitement, interest, irritation. When one acts from curiosity or from discomfort, one identifies with the curiosity or with the wish to terminate the discomfort. In his fine analysis of sexual desire, Sartre characterizes such desire as "consciousness making itself body," or as "incarnation."[27] Something similar might be said of all desire and emotion that is acted upon; there is identification of oneself with the feeling in question, hence incarnation. If some objection may be made to the use of the expression 'incarnation' in this context, it is based not on the spurious notion that feelings somehow fail to be bodily, but on the dubious implication that a self that becomes incarnate was previously disincarnate.

It should be noted in fairness to Descartes that he is not completely unaware of the implausible position on affectivity to which his metaphysical dualism leads. In the *Meditations* he repeatedly recognizes that the relationship of the self to affectivity is not a mere extraneous one when he characterizes the union of a thinking self with its body as a "very close" one, as an "intermingling" and "a substantial union," or again, when he denies that the soul is in the body like a pilot in a ship.[28] Yet, bare declarations of the sort amount in the end to mere verbal concessions which serve to paper over the difficulty. The root of the problem is that an allegedly immaterial and incorporeal self nevertheless insists on identifying itself with corporeal affectivity, and that inasmuch as it does so, it cannot be an incorporeal thinking being.

In further fairness to Descartes, it should be recognized that elsewhere in his writings, in his correspondence and in *The Passions of the Soul*, he draws a distinction with regard to desire and emotion which, if defendable, would make his thesis of a mind/body (thought/body) dichotomy more plausible. His claim is not just the hardly debatable one that willing or desiring is inconceivable without thinking,[29] but that desire is to be equated with the embracing of a judgment of worth. Perhaps the clearest instance of such equating is to be found in a long letter to Pierre Chanut in 1647[30] in which Descartes attempts to answer questions from Christine of Sweden about love. He first distinguishes between two sorts of love, a "sensual or sensuous" love that is a passion, and a "purely intellectual or rational" love, subsequently stating that the two are in fact found together in most cases of love. According to Descartes, rational love "consists simply in the fact that when our soul perceives some present or absent good, which it judges to be fitting for itself, it unites itself to it in volition, that is to say, it considers itself and the good in question as forming two parts of a single whole."[31] The function of sensuous love apparently is simply to *dispose* the soul to rational love. Descartes uses the case of thirst to illustrate the distinction (which presumably might be extended to any instance of motivation), and claims that "the sensation of the dryness of the throat is a confused thought which disposes to the desire for drink, but is not identical with that desire."[32] Apparently the essential element of desire, according to Descartes, is the embracing of a value judgment as to what is good or bad. The view that desires are value judgments surfaces often enough elsewhere in Descartes's reflections: it is suggested in his comment in *Meditations*, "For if I always saw clearly what was true and good, I should never have to deliberate about the right judgment or choice,"[33]—as if all choice was choice between goods; it lies behind his remark to Father Mersenne that "to do what is good, it suffices to see what is good"[34]—as if a pure intellect alone were involved in the espousal of motives; it seems presupposed in his claim to Father Denis Mesland that if one clearly sees what is good, then unless one's attention gets directed elsewhere, it is impossible to stop the course of desire.[35]

Descartes's account of willing receives considerable moral support from his further views on a class of emotions, 'internal' pleasures or emotions that are to be distinguished from passions in that they are occasioned by judgment or reflection. He claims that some of these pleasures of the mind (e.g., love of perfection) as opposed to pleasures of the body may be "immortal" as the soul itself is, and that they include rational love in addition to emotions related to such love—for example, joy in the knowledge that the soul is united in fact to the object of love, sadness that it is not, or desire to be so united—and could exist in the soul even if the soul were not united with a body.[36]

Yet, if the thought/body dichotomy defended by Descartes is to be taken seriously, then the 'internal' pleasures and emotions allegedly capable of existing in a bodiless soul must be thoughts, that is, immaterial entities devoid of spatial extension. Fairly obviously this is not the case. A feeling of joy occasioned by the thought of gaining the object of one's love is an elation and buoyancy, a bodily expansion and opening, while the feeling of disappointment occasioned by the awareness of one's loss is a deflation and listlessness, a pained contraction and closing in on oneself. Both feelings are complex dynamic states located in and throughout one's tactile-kinesthetic body. Doubts on the matter are readily dispelled by consulting one's own experience. When Descartes draws a distinction between 'internal' pleasures and passions, he does so on the basis of the criterion of causal origin, of whether the feelings are occasioned by a thought or by a perception. For present purposes of classification according to ontological nature (thought or body), causal antecedents are irrelevant. Observation of the experience of the feeling finds it to be spatially extended.

There remains Descartes's equation of willed desire with the embracing of a judgment of worth. The illustration offered by Descartes, thirst and the desire to drink, might seem at first glimpse to have considerable weight to it. The feeling of thirst is itself a mere feeling of dryness and discomfort in the mouth and throat, and suggests nothing as to what if anything should be done about it. Indeed, a person who had never experienced thirst before might simply react to the feeling with puzzlement. There is clearly a huge gap to be bridged between the bodily discomfort and a proposed course of action or desire to drink. But while the presence of the gap is undeniable, it does not follow that only a judgment of worth can do the bridging. An awareness of thirst-quenching techniques gained from past experience of similar situations would play a necessary role in any desire to drink experienced by normal human beings. Once this technical competence is added, it becomes a debatable issue what further elements must be added to arrive at a desire to drink. In some cases, the desire to drink seems to contain merely the physical discomfort elucidated by an awareness of how the discomfort may be alleviated; no judgment of worth is to be found in the experience. In many others (perhaps even the majority given the pervasiveness of social grooming), the desire to drink becomes a second level desire:

the feelings of thirst are felt to be a hindrance to the continued execution of one's activity, to be bothersome, to be something to be rid of, to be an affront. It would seem inaccurate to claim that these various acquired reactions to the feelings of thirst always involve a judgment of worth. Very often too the desire to drink (as a willing to drink) may involve a weighing of options, and the election of the option of quenching one's thirst as opposed to continuing to have feelings of thirst. Here too it runs counter to a straightforward reading of the experiential evidence to claim that opting always takes place on the basis of the judgment that one option is better than the other. Choices are often made on the basis of what one would describe as mere personal preference, and what one would be disinclined to defend as in any sense better or as having more worth. The freedom to do or not to do, including what for Descartes is in the last resort the freedom to avoid an evident good by shifting attention to some other topic, is itself for the most part not to be construed as a value judgment. The shifts of attention are themselves motivated by feeling, by discomfort or apprehension or regret or sudden impulse to enjoy, all of which require the participation of the tactile-kinesthetic body.

Finally, it should be noted that even if it were the case that a value judgment was involved in all desire, Descartes's view of the self as a pure thinking being would remain problematic. It is highly questionable that the judgment of worth may be properly construed as the work of a pure intellect. Any appreciation of worth and resulting judgment of worth or comparative worth would seem to involve affectivity, and hence the participation of the tactile-kinesthetic body at least in the function of indispensable research assistant. In these circumstances, it is difficult to see how an appeal to judgments of worth could rescue Descartes's immaterial desiring self from the implications of the fact of the bodily nature of feeling.

Thus, Descartes's account of the self that wills will not pass muster. It flies in the face of the evidence to consider feeling an essentially superfluous item in desiring or willing, and to attempt to identify the agent, or self which wills, with an intellect making a value judgment. Quite clearly in most cases (at least most) the self identifies with the feeling giving rise to the willing and doing, and if the feeling were removed from the experience, that is, if the discomfort or fear or anger or fascination or curiosity were removed from the scene, the action would simply collapse (and the willing along with it). Descartes, of course, does not in fact attempt to exclude all feeling from the self. The main point on which he goes astray is, as noted earlier, his unexamined assumption that emotions or feelings are perceived as if in the mind, unlike pains and pleasant bodily feelings that are perceived as if in the body. On the basis of this assumption, he is able to claim that the feelings occasioned by thoughts, as distinct from the feelings occasioned by something bodily, may exist in a soul separated from the body. The assumption is, however, confounded by the experiential evidence. The incorporeal thinking self of Descartes's account would reduce, qua immaterial being, to a being devoid of feeling, and hence to a being devoid of motivation.

THE CORPOREALITY OF THE THINKING SELF

Descartes's failure to appreciate the key role played by the tactile-kinesthetic body has consequences extending far beyond his belittling of the role of affectivity in motivation. It vitiates his account of all other modes of thinking, both the operations of affirming, doubting, and denying that Descartes classes as forms of willing, and the properly intellectual modes of thinking: perception, understanding, and imagination. Let us look briefly at both these modes.

The opinion of the average person would undoubtedly be that attitudes such as assent, denial, doubt, or conviction require affective involvement. The view is corroborated by introspective observation. Careful attention to experiences of conviction or doubt or refusal to believe invariably finds affective involvement in the more dramatic cases at least, and finds, too, that the affective involvement is a mode of the tactile-kinesthetic body. To test the plausibility of the claim, consider the perceptual judgments made in some concrete everyday situation. Let us suppose that one hears a peculiar sort of noise at the window, and thinks, "a bird." One's subsequent attitude may take a number of forms. It may be one of conviction equivalent to "That *must* be a bird." It may be more detached, a mere entertaining of an hypothesis, somewhat equivalent to "Maybe it's a bird." Then again, it might be an attitude of doubt or even of strong disbelief—"That *couldn't* be a bird." In each case the same two words "a bird" might be uttered, although with a quite different tone of voice.

Now, let us ask in what consists the difference in attitude in the various cases. The difference in attitude is not reducible to a verbal difference. The words, "a bird," are the same in each case. One might attempt to equate the difference in attitude with the difference in the tone in which the words are uttered, but such an account of the matter would be doubly mistaken. First of all, if one is thinking to oneself, the thought could well involve a sound or auditory image quite neutral in tone, or again, the thought could well be nonverbal, and involve instead a visual image of a bird. In such cases there is no difference in tone of voice. Rather the difference between conviction, doubt, and mere possibility is quite clearly a difference in affective state: conviction is assurance, readiness to act, while doubt is hesitation and absence of commitment. A particular affective state is present, and it is what motivates any tone of voice indicating sincere belief or disbelief. Second, even in cases where tone of voice is a factor, it should be noted that the practice of using a certain tone of voice to indicate conviction, another to indicate doubt, is not a purely arbitrary convention. An emphatic utterance is appropriate as an indication of conviction precisely because it reflects the speaker's assurance, determination, and willingness to act, as opposed to the hesitation engendered by uncertainty, or to the absence of involvement specific to the mere entertaining of an hypothesis. Assurance, hesitation, and deliberation are all dynamic states of the tactile-kinesthetic body. If the state of the body were removed from the experience, there would be no conviction, no doubt, no hypothesizing, and hence no reason to adopt one tone of voice rather than another. No less than the emotions considered earlier, an attitude of judgment clearly and necessarily involves a tactile-kinesthetic body.

It is true enough that the above reflections leave out essential elements of the situation: the awareness of the evidence provided by the type of sound heard, one's knowledge of sound production, of environments and their possible residents, and so on. The belief or doubt or lack of commitment are obviously to some degree a function of the available evidence. It would be a mistake, however, to attempt to construe belief and doubt as essentially intellectual operations of 'evidence-evaluation', operations accompanied by affective overtones which are in fact dispensable. Descartes is quite right to class belief and doubt, assertion and denial, as modes of willing. In the average case, the adoption of belief is not a mere seeing of what the evidence is, or a mere evaluating of the likelihood of truth. Belief goes beyond the evidence; it is the embracing of an envisaged state of affairs, a treating of that state of affairs as fact, and doing so moreover on the strength of evidence which falls short of being compelling. The same is true of denial; it is a rejection which goes beyond a mere evaluation of evidence. The evaluating intelligence has finished its work once the likelihood of truth of the envisaged state of affairs is established. A pure intelligence has no cause to assert or to deny. Only a being endowed with feeling has any reason to leap beyond the evidence, whether driven by the exigency of action in the world or by any of a multitude of desires, hopes, and preferences. Only a tactile-kinesthetic body may believe or disbelieve, affirm or deny.

Feeling is operative, of course, not merely in the leap from evaluation to belief. Often it intrudes to skew the evaluation itself. In the general course of human activities, evidence is more or less wittingly misread or distorted rather than considered impartially. Since certain considerations are found to counter one's own opinions or interests, to be unflattering, uninteresting, or disagreeable, they are belittled or ignored while others are accorded attention or emphasis. In point of fact the range of emotions, desires, and fears capable of collusion in the distortion of evidence is more or less coextensive with the range of possible human feelings. These judgment-distorting feelings are not countered by pure value judgments, as Descartes would have it, but by a variety of other factors: respect for the truth and impartiality, a sense of fairness, perhaps a desire to be seen as impartial. All of these are surely modes of affectivity, so it would seem that both the deceiver and the watchdog turn out to be modes of the tactile-kinesthetic body.

Even the more properly intellectual modes of thinking—perceiving, reflecting, imagining—involve the tactile-kinesthetic body in a variety of roles. Among the most important are those providing the motive and the means for thinking, whether the energy or the vehicle. Any concerted thinking, any enterprise of inquiry or exploration requires a motive, and a motive involves the tactile-kinesthetic body at some level. Curiosity, for instance, is not a property of an immaterial, incorporeal intellect. The openness and directedness of the eyes, the eagerness or impatience to see, to feel, or to understand, the compelling attractiveness of the object of curiosity, the mild wonder or puzzlement or awe—these are all essential aspects of the curiosity. In their absence there would be no curiosity. Clearly too all are locatable as specific modifications of the tactile-kinesthetic body. The same is true of anticipated delight or the enjoyment adherent to the exercise of one's thinking faculties. It is still more clearly true of the ambition or pride, desperation or insecurity which might be prompting the exercise from the wings. A pure thinking being would in fact have no reason to bother to think. It might contemplate ideas flushed up by the passing show, but it would be incapable of initiating any concerted, thoughtful activity.

Serious thinking also involves a mobilization of resources, again a patently bodily phenomenon. The activity of thoughtful reflection is aptly captured in Auguste Rodin's statue, *The Thinker*, which features a man seated and immobile, his chin cupped in his hand, his gaze vacant, his brow heavily cast. Quite obviously the statue is a representation, not of a pure spirit or bodiless thinking being, but of a mindful body in a pose and state of tension typical of concentrated thinking. If thinking were an activity specific to an incorporeal spirit, then what would Rodin's statue be a statue of? If it does not represent thinking, the only remotely plausible alternative interpretation is that it represents the activity of striving or of trying to think: the fixed gaze, heavy brow, and clenched jaw are all part of an effort to clear extraneous matters from the field of attention, and hence allow the pure intelligence to engage in its characteristic activity.

Now this answer is correct insofar as it places striving in the body. Any striving one does, including the effort required for serious thought, is some configuration of tactile-kinesthetic feelings located in one's felt body. Indeed, the very notion of a mental effort is nonsensical if *mental* is taken to mean *non-bodily*. The point is easily verified by making the alleged mental effort and subjecting it to a long introspective fish-eyed gaze. The mental effort in fact turns out to be some complex of tensions in the felt body. Making an effort, including an effort to think, is something a body does. Now this fact creates serious problems for the claim that thinking is the activity of a pure spirit. If a pure spirit does the thinking, then since the body makes the effort, the striving and the thinking are the work of two distinct subjects. Surely this cannot be the case. Effort is one's own doing; it is the measure of one's engagement in a particular course of action; it is the measure of one's tenacity, one's sincerity, one's devotion, or alternatively of one's stubbornness or vindictiveness. To view one's self as a pure intellect dissociated from all striving would be no more warranted than to view one's self as a striving body dissociated from all intelligence. One is both, which is to say, one cannot be an incorporeal thinking being, any more than an unthinking force of nature.

Finally, a word should be said about the vehicle of thinking, the perceptual processes, images, and words which provide the structural support for thinking. Activities of various sorts are indispensable constituents in many of the processes of thinking. Bodily activity is required for the actual manipulation of objects, for the imagined transformation of a given perceived situation, for the calling up of images. For instance, bodily movement, particularly eye movement, is indispensable to the planning of moves in chess, not only when the position studied is that of real pieces on a board, but when the board is called up in imagination and fleshed out with remembered verbal instructions. Verbal thinking itself requires the generation of verbal symbols. In general, the latter arise only concomitantly with various fluctuations of tensions in the throat, mouth, and lips, a point on which one may convince oneself by attempting to think verbally without any contractions of the sort. The important point in the present context is the very need for words and images to serve as vehicles for an associated meaning, the fact that thinking independently of any sensuous vehicle whatsoever is apparently unfeasible.

In sum, the purely intellectual activity of thinking is not a possible pursuit apart from a corporeal being. In itself, it has neither the motive, nor the energy, nor the vehicle necessary for its own thinking activity. A human intelligence bereft of a body would be an intellectual cripple. Certain sights might be familiar, certain collections of sounds or squiggles might have meaning. Yet for such an intelligence there would be no reason to inquire or pursue any question or issue, no energy to do so, no vehicle to act as support for any thought. No remotely plausible case can be made for identifying oneself with this derelict intelligence.

THE INVALIDITY OF COGITO, ERGO SUM

The conclusion to which we are driven is that Elizabeth was quite right to protest against the account of the self proposed by Descartes, and that Descartes was mistaken in the reasoning that led him to his account of the self as an incorporeal thinking being. Descartes's central contention was that one may clearly and distinctly conceive of oneself as a thinking being independently of any notion of body or spatial extension. As we have seen, this claim is simply untrue. The thinking being which loves or spurns, which believes or denies, which desires to understand and strives to reflect, is a tactile-kinesthetic body, and cannot be clearly and distinctly conceived as an incorporeal being. Certainly it may be claimed that each of the acts of thinking contains an indispensable incorporeal element, whether intention, goal, perception, cognition, or meaning. Yet whatever the correct position to take on this claim, it is nevertheless true that many of the acts of thinking (perhaps all of them) also contain an indispensable corporeal one in that each involves the tactile-kinesthetic body.

It follows as a corollary from the above conclusions that Descartes's well-known dictum, "I think, therefore I am," must be fallacious. Since the subject who thinks must be a tactile-kinesthetic body (whatever else it is), that subject's existence is no more indubitable than the existence of any other sensuous element in the flux of experience. If the existence of an ostensibly present sheet of paper cannot be affirmed with certainty since it may be a hoax or one of the constituents in a dream, then by parity of reasoning the existence of one's tactile-kinesthetic body cannot be affirmed since it may equally be a hoax or dream constituent. The thinking in which Descartes finds himself indubitably engaged might well be, along with Descartes himself, an integral part of some nonreal occurrence. The feelings involved in his thinking and doubting have no better claim to be real than has anything else that is spatial. Hence the word 'I' in the premiss "I think" refers to a possibly unreal thinking self, that is, to a possible hoax. Since the conclusion "I am" is based on the premiss, the word 'I' it contains consequently must also refer to a possibly unreal self. As a result the argument, "I think, therefore I am," is fallacious.

In point of fact, Descartes's argument actually runs somewhat as follows: I, who am possibly a hoax, think; therefore, I, who am possibly a hoax, am. If the expression "I am" is taken to mean "I exist" (and this is what Descartes takes it to mean), then the conclusion does not follow from the premiss: to exist is not to be a hoax, and the possession of such a property as existence cannot be deduced from the fact that a possible hoax is thinking. What is more, if the conclusion did follow, it would be a self-contradictory statement; it would be the statement that I, who am perhaps a hoax, am not a hoax. Thus, Descartes's argument fails, and with it the main reason he offers for the claim that he cannot be a body and must be a pure thinking being.

Descartes's incorporeal thinking being must then cede its position to a thinking tactile-kinesthetic body. Curiously enough, a few of the claims which Descartes makes regarding the thinking being also hold *mutatis mutandis* for its successor. In particular, instead of the certainty of the existence of the thinking being, we find what might be characterized as the certainty of the non-illusory nature of the self. The affection one feels, the effort one makes, the fear one experiences, each contributes to define who one is. These defining characteristics cannot subsequently be found to be illusory or unreal in the manner of perceptual illusions, that is, to be in fact something other than what they appear to be. The violet hue of the distant hills, the plump red sun at sunset, the bent shape of an oar dipped in water, are each illusions in this latter sense of appearances that are not to be taken at face value as definitive of the perceived object. One's feelings, however, cannot be illusions of the sort: one cannot, for instance, after being moved with affection for a particular person, subsequently discover that one's true feeling was disdain and that the affection one felt was an illusory appearance of that disdain. One may, of course, misread one's feelings or be mistaken as to what they are. Nevertheless an involvement cannot turn out to be an illusory appearance of reluctance, any more than a burst of anger can be an illusory appearance of calm. The reason is not that such illusions are inconceivable in principle, but that one identifies with one's phenomenal nature, and cannot subsequently be found to have been in fact something quite different. The phenomenal and hence non-illusory nature of the self could serve as the ground for a revised version of *cogito, ergo sum*, one in which, as it were, the certainty of one's existence is replaced by the certainty of one's essence:

I feel such and such; therefore, I am such and such.

What the revised *cogito* says is simply that if I feel angry, then unless I am making some stupid mistake such as being inattentive to my feelings, or careless in my observations, or grossly misusing language, I am angry. Similarly, if I feel hesitant, then unless I am making some very silly mistake in reading what my feelings are, I am hesitant.

In the revised scheme of things an equivalent of sorts is also found for Descartes's notion of a thinking being which may conceivably exist independently of a body. A felt body could conceivably exist apart from its visual counterpart as well as apart from the physical brain which figures in the second mind/body dichotomy, the mind/brain dichotomy. It is unclear whether this more concretely conceivable immortal soul would have met with Elizabeth's approval. Be this as it may, Elizabeth would undoubtedly have found the revised account of the thinking self more accommodating of her reservations regarding the version of the self proposed by Descartes.

NOTES

1. Such a defense is one of the aims of my book, *Rationalized Epistemology: Taking Solipsism Seriously* (Albany, New York: State University of New York Press, 1991).

2. Charles Adam and Gerard Milhaud, *Descartes. Correspondance publiée avec une introduction et des notes,* Vol. VI, (Paris: PUF, 1936–63), 1.

3. René Descartes, *Meditations on First Philosophy* in *The Philosophical Writings of Descartes,* trans. John Cottingham, Robert Stoothoff, Dugald Murdoch, Vol. II (Cambridge: Cambridge University Press, 1984), 19. Unless otherwise indicated, all subsequent references to Descartes's writings will be to translations in the above collection.

4. René Descartes, *Descartes Philosophical Letters,* trans. Anthony Kenny (Minneapolis: University of Minnesota Press, 1970), 105.

5. Descartes, *Meditations,* II, 50–51.

6. Descartes, *Objections and Replies,* II, 113.

7. Descartes, *Philosophical Letters,* 106.

8. David Hume, *A Treatise of Human Nature,* ed. L. A. Selby-Bigge (Oxford: Clarendon Press, 1897), 252.

9. Descartes, *The Search for Truth,* II, 412.

10. Descartes, *Meditations,* II, 54.

11. Adam and Milhaud, *Descartes. Correspondance,* Vol. V, 287–288, 313–317; Vol. VI, 1–2.

12. Descartes, *Meditations,* II, 15.

13. Descartes, *Meditations,* II, 17.

14. M. F. P. Maine de Biran, *Essai sur les fondements de la psychologie et sur les rapports avec l'étude de la nature, Oeuvres de Maine de Biran,* edition Tisserand, VIII (Paris: Alcan, 1932), 127, 177, 207.

15. Jean-Paul Sartre, *Being and Nothingness,* trans. Hazel E. Barnes (New York: Philosophical Library, 1956), 305, 310, 318, 324.

16. Ibid., 318–321.

17. Maurice Merleau-Ponty, *Phenomenology of Perception,* trans. Colin Smith (London: Routledge and Kegan Paul, 1962), 247–252.

18. Ibid., 248.

19. William Lyons, *The Disappearance of Introspection* (Cambridge, MA: The MIT Press, 1986), 11.

20. Ibid., 127, 152.

21. Descartes, *Principles of Philosophy*, I, 204.

22. Descartes, *The Passions of the Soul*, I, 337; see also Descartes's letter to Elizabeth of October 6, 1645 in *Philosophical Letters*, 178.

23. William James, *Principles of Psychology*, Vol. II (New York: Dover Publications, 1950), 451.

24. Stanley Schachter and Jerome Singer, "Cognitive, Social and Physiological Determinants of Emotional States," *Psychological Review* 69 (1962), 379–399.

25. George W. Hohmann, "Some Effects of Spinal Cord Lesions on Experienced Emotional Feelings," *Psychophysiology* 3 (1966), 143–156.

26. Descartes, *Objections*, II, 113.

27. Sartre, *Being and Nothingness*, 389, 391.

28. Descartes, *Discourse on the Method*, I, 141; *Meditations*, II, 56, 160.

29. Descartes, *Principles*, I, 211.

30. Descartes, *Philosophical Letters*, 208–211.

31. Ibid., 208.

32. Ibid., 209.

33. Descartes, *Meditations*, 40.

34. Adam and Milhaud, *Descartes. Correspondence*, Vol. I, 351.

35. Descartes, *Philosophical Letters*, 149.

36. Descartes, *Passions*, 356, 361, 381; *Philosophical Letters*, 170, 208–209.

3

An Eastern Concept of the Body: Yuasa's Body-Scheme[1]

INTRODUCTION

I should like to give a brief account of how the Japanese have traditionally understood the body in its long cultural, historical tradition, particularly in its intellectual (or philosophical) dimension. I will approach this inquiry not by examining the historical sources, but by articulating the subject matter from a contemporary perspective. I have chosen Yasuo Yuasa's concept of *body-scheme* as it is developed in *Ki Shugyō Shintai* (Ki-Energy, Self-Cultivation and The Body)[2] for this purpose because Yuasa's analysis is suited particularly to a theoretical elucidation of a Japanese concept of the body, and more importantly because Yuasa offers a comprehensive and deeper analysis of the body than most philosophers, East or West, have thus far provided. Yuasa's concept of body-scheme purports to explicate the inseparability and the oneness of the lived body-mind as it is achieved through the *prāxis* of personal self-cultivation. This achievement, then, is the theme of this inquiry.

YUASA'S BODY-SCHEME[3]

The concept of body-scheme was introduced by philosopher Maurice Merleau-Ponty in his book *Phenomenology of Perception*. He incorporated neurologist Henry Head's idea of "body-image" as a way of giving a structure to the functions of the lived-body.[4] Following this lead, Yuasa proposed his own "body-scheme" drawing on Eastern and depth-psychology insights. His concept of body-scheme is comprised of four circuits of interrelated information systems.[5] Yuasa analyzes the four circuits to determine how we live our bodies from within, that is, live our subject-body, and at the same time correlates these circuits, as far as possible, with neuro-physiological structures of the body—our object-body. In so doing, he attempts to capture the dynamic and whole function of the lived and living body.

THE EXTERNAL SENSORY-MOTOR CIRCUIT

Yuasa calls the first circuit the "external sensory-motor circuit" (*gaikai kankaku undō kairo*). This is a circuit connecting the body to the external world through the sensory organs of the body via stimuli received from the external world. The term "sensory" in external sensory-motor circuit refers to the function of the sensory organ which *passively* receives information about the external world via sensory nerves attached to the sensory organ; the term "motor" in external sensory-motor circuit designates an *active* motor response on the received information, that is, an execution of a response through the various limbs.[6] The whole is called a "circuit" because information received by the sensory organ goes to the central nervous system (the brain) via sensory nerves to form a centrifugal path; the brain in turn conveys the information to the distal motor organs through the motor nerves to form a centripetal path. The circuit explicates the experiential process, for example, of seeing a tree and walking toward it.

THE CIRCUIT OF COENESTHESIS

The second circuit in Yuasa's body-scheme is called the "circuit of coenesthesis" (*zenshin naibu kankaku kairo*) and deals with the information system that pertains to the *internal* sensations of the body. Yuasa recognizes two subdivisions in this circuit of coenesthesis: the first one is called the "circuit of kinesthesis" (*undō kankaku kairo*), and the second the "circuit of somesthesis" (*taisei naibu kankaku kairo*).

The circuit of kinesthesis deals with kinetic movements of the body which function in close conjunction with the motor-nerves of the first circuit, the external sensory-motor circuit. This second circuit is formed between the motor nerves and the sensory-motor nerves attached to the muscles and tendons of the limbs. In this circuit, each sensory-motor nerve functions as a centripetal path, conveying information about the condition of a distal motor organ (e.g., a hand or a leg) to the brain. The motor nerve, just as in the first circuit, functions as a centrifugal path, conveying the received information back to the limbs. Those who excel in the performing arts or in sports have a well developed "circuit of kinesthesis"; they can rapidly convey information about a condition of their limbs and coordinate this information skillfully with bodily movement. Yuasa notes that the circuit of kinesthesis supports "from below" the working of the first circuit. It is "from below" the first circuit because the experiential correlate to the circuit of kinesthesis is found in the *periphery* of the so-called ego-consciousness in functions such as thinking, willing, feeling, and imagining.[7] Yuasa acknowledges that philosopher Edmund Husserl had already taken note of this kinesthesis in terms of "passive syntheses," "acts" prior to the active meaning-bestowing functions of consciousness.[8] In general, this circuit is an information system ready to activate the body toward an action in the external world.[9] Together with the first circuit, the second circuit explains how in our everyday life we engage our immediate environments through perception and action. When philosophers deal with the dichotomy of mind and body, they focus on the problems arising from the division of these two circuits.

The second subdivision within the circuit of coenesthesis, the circuit of somesthesis, is concerned with the condition of internal organs via the splanchnic nerves, which are attached to the internal organs.[10] Splanchnic sensations convey the condition of a distal organ (e.g., a stomach) to the brain, forming a centripetal path. Under normal and healthy conditions, these sensations are vaguely perceived (i.e., they are protopathic sensations) and are thus unlike the clear localization of motor sensations. This is because the region in the cortex connected to the splanchnic nerves is small compared to the region regulating the sensory-motor nerves. However, when there is an abnormal condition in an internal organ, a person may experience pain (i.e., an epicritic sensation). This suggests that the circuit of somesthesis in a normal healthy condition recedes into the background, first behind the circuit of kinesthesis, and then behind the external sensory-motor circuit. Significantly, Yuasa points out that though no philosophers in the West have taken note of the importance of the issues arising from this circuit, some psychoanalysts in the Freudian and Jungian schools have paid attention to the circuit of somesthesis in light of their clinical experience, and in connection with Eastern methods of meditation.

Yuasa likens the circuit of coenesthesis to a biofeedback system. Changes that take place within this system are conveyed to the central nervous system and the latter in turn sends out responses to cope with changes in particular organ experiences. This self-contained system suggests that the body embodies a self-controlling mechanism. Yuasa says that generally, the circuit of coenesthesis is translated experientially into an awareness of the self "grasping the body," or simply an awareness of one's body. Insofar as it can be experienced, however vaguely, the circuit of coenesthesis belongs to consciousness.

Important in this connection is Yuasa's observation that the circuit of coenesthesis, particularly its somesthesis, maintains a close link between movements of the body and motile memory. When one learns to play the piano, for example, he/she acquires a knack for the placement of fingers through repeated practice. Once the technique is learned, however, the body *knows* in an instant how to respond to the next move that is required, that is, unconsciously or without forming an intellectual judgment. From this observation, Yuasa reasons that:

> [T]here is *an automatic memory system* at the base of consciousness for judgment, which stores past data, and checking a failed datum, it directs the datum in order for it to be a successful [execution] next time. The repetition of this process is a training. In other words, training is to *habituate* the body in a definite direction. For this purpose, the capacity of the memory system must be enhanced.[11]

A point to keep in mind regarding the "automatic memory system" is that it is situated below the external sensory-motor circuit and the circuit of kinesthesis, both of which belong to consciousness. What is more important in this connection is that the automatic memory system does not require a conscious effort of recall: *the body* learns and knows. This idea seems to be derived from a combination of Merleau-Ponty's concept of "habit-body" (*le corps habituel*) and philosopher Henri Bergson's "learned memory" (*souvenir appris*), both of which designate an internalization of bodily movement for the utility of life. Yuasa admits, however, that the mechanism of biofeedback for this automatic memory system is not clearly understood because the relationship between the psychological function of (motile) memory and the corresponding physiological mechanism of the body is not yet known sufficiently.[12]

THE EMOTION-INSTINCT CIRCUIT

The third of the information systems in Yuasa's body-scheme is called "emotion-instinct circuit" (*jōdō honnō kairo*). This circuit has never been incorporated within concepts of body-scheme so far articulated. Yuasa's insight derives from his knowledge of depth-psychology and Eastern self-cultivation methods. He gives the following reason for the designation of this circuit:

> This circuit has a very close relationship with human instincts such as sexual desire and appetite. For this reason, I call it emotion-instinct circuit.[13]

First, he observes that this circuit is correlated with the autonomic nervous system, which controls and regulates the function of various internal organs such as the respiratory organs (lungs), the circulatory organ (heart), and the digestive organs (stomach and colon). All of these functions are necessary to maintain the life of the body. If the function of any of these organs fails, an individual body cannot sustain its life. For this reason, "this circuit is fundamental for maintaining not [the motor-function of] the body but its life."[14] A healthy condition of the body is maintained when an appropriate balance of tension and laxity obtains between the sympathetic and parasympathetic nerves which comprise the autonomic nervous system. If an excessively tense condition is prolonged, it will offset the balance between the sympathetic and parasympathetic functions. The experiential correlate of the imbalance is stress. However, only cumulative stressful conditions make us aware of the condition of our body.

How, specifically, does Yuasa account for an occurrence of stress using the emotion-instinct circuit? The autonomic nerve, which controls and regulates the emotion-instinct circuit, carries within its fibre both the centrifugal and centripetal information paths, unlike the previous two circuits which have independent centrifugal and centripetal paths. The centripetal information system of this emotion-instinct circuit conveys the information concerning the condition of an internal organ to the brain, the central nervous system. However, Yuasa points out that this centripetal circuit does *not* reach the cortex (neoencephalon). This means that the activities of the internal organs are performed usually below the conscious level.[15] In other words, we do not have a conscious awareness of their functions under normal and healthy conditions. They function independent of our will. In contrast, the centrifugal path of this circuit sends out to the distal internal organs those stimuli which the brain receives from the external world vis-à-vis the sensory organs, converting them into an *emotional response* (i.e., pleasure or pain), which may turn into stress or a stressful response.

Yuasa notes that emotion generated out of this emotion-instinct circuit has a special significance compared to perception and thinking. Although both perception and thinking can be mapped approximately onto corresponding sensory organ or onto physiological counterparts,[16] emotion when experienced is not localized in any particular organ. Yuasa interprets this to mean that emotions such as anger and sorrow take over the entire body, that is, they are holistic in nature.[17] They affect the whole body.

THE SUMMARY OF THE THREE CIRCUITS

Yuasa explains how the preceding three circuits are interrelated. He says:

> The relationship among [them] . . . may be summarized as follows. The sensory stimulus [received] from the external world enters the first "external sensory-motor circuit" that is in the uppermost surface layer, and passing through the second circuit of coenesthesis, reaches the third emotion-instinct circuit that is the lowest layer where the emotional response of pleasure or pain is generated. This response returns to the second circuit, and eliciting its movement, it further activates the first circuit, which is expressed as a bodily movement in the external word.[18]

As may be evident, one of the characteristic features of Yuasa's three-circuited body-scheme is that he conceives the scheme as forming a multilayered information system: starting with the external sensory-motor circuit, he recognizes underneath it the circuit of coenesthesis and at the lowest layer the emotion-instinct circuit. This schematization suggests that the control which one can exercise on these circuits decreases as one recedes from the first external sensory-motor circuit and progresses to the third emotion-instinct circuit. The difference in control correlates with an awareness of the body, which decreases in opacity, or increases in transparency, as one moves from the first to the third circuit. For a visual presentation of this point, the following diagram may be helpful.

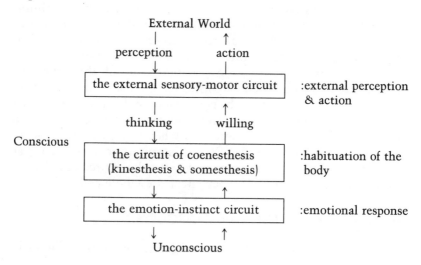

According to Yuasa, there is no direct and immediate relationship between the first external sensory-motor circuit and the third emotion-instinct circuit. For example, the fact that one cries does not immediately impair the capacity for visual perception. However, the capacity of the first circuit is dependent on the second circuit of coenesthesis. As noted earlier, this is because the second circuit is closely connected with the motile memory, which assists the habitualization of the body. Therefore, an athlete who has mastered a set of certain techniques for moving his/her body through training, for example, embodies an enhanced capacity of the second circuit, which in turn heightens the level of activity in the first circuit. In fact, this is the goal of Western sports, perhaps symbolically represented by the phrase "muscle man.[19] It suggests to Yuasa that the goal of Western sports is not conceived in connection with, and in consideration of, the organs governed by the autonomic nervous systems. Psychologically this means that the training method of Western sports does not take into account the idea of controlling the emotion-instinct circuit.[20]

Since the goal and training method of Western sports are mentioned, it is appropriate here to contrast them with those of Eastern self-cultivation methods, which have influenced various Japanese cultural activities such as martial arts, tea-ceremony, *ikebana*, and so forth, and which seem not to require the same discipline as sports. The methods Yuasa has in mind in this regard are represented by "*samādhi* through constant motion" or "*samādhi* through continual sitting,"[21] both of which are an ideal to be achieved in self-cultivation methods. In contrast to the goal of Western sports, Yuasa sees one of the goals in personal cultivation to be that of "control[ling] the patterns of emotional response," or more broadly, controlling the function of the emotion-instinct circuit. He states:

> The goal of personal cultivation is to change the patterns of emotional response [i.e., complexes in personality] by controlling emotions and integrating the power of the unconscious within consciousness.[22]

There are two concepts to be clarified and elaborated in this quote: (1) "controlling emotions," and (2) "integrating the power of the unconscious within consciousness." Since the second concept concerns the last and fourth circuit of Yuasa's body-scheme, I shall reserve it for later. For now, our concern is the concept of "controlling emotions." What does "controlling emotions" mean within the Japanese cultural tradition of personal self-cultivation and how does Yuasa interpret it? He does not mean an exercise of conscious will to suppress emotions, as is suggested, for example, in Immanuel Kant's ethical theory.[23] Concurring with Aristotle's concept of virtue as a habit-formation, Yuasa interprets "controlling emotion" to be a process of habit-formation that works on the third emotion-instinct circuit.[24] He explains the process of habit-formation within his theory of body-scheme as follows:

> The information entering the first external sensory-motor circuit reaches the third emotion-instinct circuit, and an emotional response to this information ricochets back to the second circuit which *habitualizes* the body, forming a definite

passage among the three layers of these circuits.[25] [emphasis added]

This process is an instance of conditioned reflex which otherwise is not functional in our "natural attitude." Initially, the passage among the three circuits is a temporary conjunction, but through repeated practice, it becomes a *definite* conjunction.[26] Since Yuasa conceives of controlling emotions as a process of habit-formation, that is, repeated training, the control in question is developed naturally. The process depends largely on the body, not on the mind, in other words, not on the exercise of conscious will to suppress the emotion. An assumption in Yuasa's understanding of controlling emotions is that it is possible to correct the modality of the mind by correcting the modality of the body—emotion being the modification of the body as Spinoza has it.[27]

In the process of discussing habituating the second circuit of coenesthesis as a way of controlling emotions, Yuasa takes note of the importance of breathing exercises, which are emphasized in all forms of Japanese training and cultivation methods.[28] Physiologically, the respiratory organ is regulated and controlled by the autonomic nerves and motor-nerves; the respiratory organ has an ambiguous character of being linked both to the voluntary and involuntary muscles. This means that one can consciously control the rhythm and pattern of breathing, and in turn affect the physiological functions governed by the autonomic nervous system. More importantly still, one can affect the emotion-instinct circuit since, as Yuasa observes, the autonomic nervous system is closely connected to emotion:

> The function of autonomic nerves is deeply linked to emotions (both positive and negative emotions such as anger, sorrow, hatred, joy, love and peace, i.e., pleasure and pain). If the negative emotion is always stressed, a pathological state will result, but on the other hand, if the positive emotion is always strengthened, it will nurture more mature psychological traits (i.e., the pattern of emotion as a habit of the mind/heart).[29]

The goal of the Eastern method of training and self-cultivation is then designed to habituate naturally the emotion-instinct circuit through breathing exercises that conscious will can control. What is implicit here is the Eastern discernment of the correlativity between state of mind and state of body in the rhythms and patterns of breathing. For example, when one is angry, the pattern of breathing is irregular and its rhythm rough. When this insight is generalized, it means that controlling emotions in personal self-cultivation:

> enhance[s] *the degree of correlativity* between the movements of mind and those of the body, thus producing a closer relation of unity between the mind and body. Ultimately, it pursues a spiritual goal of developing an all-round personality.[30] [emphasis added]

We witness in this quote an important thesis of the Eastern mind-body theory, namely, that the relationship between mind and body is originally one of unity or oneness that a practitioner restores through *prāxis*.

Having touched on the subject of controlling emotions, I would now like to investigate the point that was left unattended, namely, Yuasa's point that the goal of Eastern methods of training and personal self-cultivation is to "integrate the power of the unconscious within consciousness." An examination of this point will in turn enable us to understand more concretely the meaning of unity or oneness that is said to obtain through *prāxis* between mind and body in the Eastern, particularly Japanese, tradition.

THE CIRCUIT OF UNCONSCIOUS QUASI-BODY

The "circuit of unconscious quasi-body" (*muishikiteki jun shintai*) articulates the fourth and the last circuit in Yuasa's body-scheme. The term "unconscious" used in this designation indicates that this circuit is not accessible to our everyday consciousness. The term "quasi" qualifying "body," on the other hand, indicates that the body at this level does not conform to the idea either of the subject-body or of the object-body which phenomenologists have thus far investigated and elucidated. It defies our ordinary understanding, and yet is in some fundamental sense connected to the body.[31] Yuasa characterizes this fourth circuit of unconscious quasi-body as follows:

> This fourth circuit is an *invisible circuit,* insofar as we examine it anatomically, and so it cannot be perceived by means of external perception. And when it is viewed psychologically, it is *a potential circuit below consciousness,* which consciousness in an ordinary circumstance cannot detect.[32] [emphases in the original]

According to Yuasa, this quasi-body does not have an anatomical counterpart because our sensory perception cannot detect it; hence it is "invisible" for external perception. Yet Yuasa claims that it is psychologically "a potential circuit below consciousness." This suggests that although the quasi-body is potentially invisible to us, and hence unknown to the everyday consciousness, the practice of various self-cultivation methods can render the "invisible" circuit "visible," that is, bring its function into awareness. If it can become actual, we should understand the "unconscious quasi-body" as only *relatively* invisible—in other words, as potentially visible.

Yuasa incorporates the circuit of unconscious quasi-body within his concept of body-scheme in consideration of the *ki*-meridian system, which acupuncture medicine has recognized for thousands of years in the Far East. The connection of unconscious quasi-body with *ki*-meridian is explicit in Yuasa's statement: "I shall call the system of *ki*-meridian 'unconscious quasi-body.'"[33] According to acupuncture medicine, the *ki*-meridians form an invisible network beneath the surface of the skin which covers the entire body, and which serves as a grid through which the *ki*-energy flows. *Ki*-energy can be detected only in a living body, not in a corpse. Yuasa describes the nature of *ki*-energy as it is presently understood:

> [T]he substance of the unknown energy *ki* is not within our [present] understanding. It is a flow of a certain kind of energy unique to the living organism which circulates in the body, although it is uncertain yet what generates such a function. To be more specific, when the flow of *ki* is examined psychologically, it can be perceived as an extraordinary sensation, as a lived body's self-grasping sensation in a unique situation on the surface of the circuit of coenesthesis. (e.g., a case of a *ki*-sensitive person.) Furthermore, when it is seen physiologically, it can be detected on the surface of the skin which is a boundary wall between the body and the external world.[34]

When Yuasa refers to the experiential detection of *ki*-energy as it flows through the body, he has in mind the medical application of the acu-points that are distributed on the twelve major *ki*-meridians. He mentions, for example, that stimulation applied by an acu-needle on the acu-point called "*san-li,*" located roughly on the outer side of the shin within the stomach-meridian, produces a change in the stomach, which can be verified by X-ray. Of course, there is no anatomical connection between the point on the shin and the stomach in terms of the nervous system. Yet with respect to the medical use of the acu-points, the existence of the *ki*-meridians is uncontestable. They have proved a source of successful medical treatment of the living human body for many hundreds of years.

For our present concern, Yuasa's reference to the psychological detection of the *ki*-meridians by *ki*-sensitive persons as a "lived body's self-grasping sensation" is significant in that this psychological experience is based upon experimental research performed by Yoshio Nagahama. Nagahama discovered that a *ki*-sensitive person could detect "vibrations" when an acu-needle was inserted at a point on the body.[35] The tracks along which the vibrations are felt correspond, according to Nagahama, to the *ki*-meridian system that charts the distribution of the acu-points as they are recorded in the old Chinese treatises.[36] It is important to emphasize here that in Yuasa's body-scheme the unconscious quasi-body circuit lies deeper than the circuit of coenesthesis (especially the circuit of somesthesis), for *ki*-vibrations in the *ki*-sensitive person are generated "on the surface of the circuit of coenesthesis," suggesting that the effect of the unconscious quasi-body circuit surfaces from below the circuit of coenesthesis. Furthermore, when Yuasa mentions the physiological detection of the "*ki*-vibrations," he has in mind the difference in conductivity of *ki*-vibrations as compared to the conductivity of nerve-impulses. The movement of *ki*-vibrations is said to be much slower than the movement of nerve-impulses.[37]

In the case of a *ki*-sensitive person, *ki*-energy is said to be felt or intuited as a sensation of power from below the circuit of coenesthesis. In light of the previous three circuits then, this unconscious quasi-body mediates between the first two circuits and the third emotion-instinct circuit. The first two circuits at least in part belong to consciousness and the third as Yuasa has noted has a close connection with the unconscious. Thus, the unconscious quasi-body mediates between consciousness and the unconscious through the flow of *ki*-energy.[38] The philosophical consequence that Yuasa draws from this observation is enormously important. Yuasa states:

> The *ki*-meridian system is related closely to both mind and body, both spirit and matter, and is a middle system that influences them. For this reason, it is a third term which cannot be explained by Descartes' mind-body dichotomy, but it forms a mediating system that links the mind and the body. Herein lies, it seems, a *break-through* point that reforms the paradigm

of empirical science [established] since Descartes.[39] [emphasis added]

Given this observation that the *ki*-meridian system, and hence Yuasa's circuit of unconscious quasi-body, is a mediating third term between mind and body, the question naturally arises if this claim is empirically verifiable. For an answer, Yuasa refers us to the practice of meditation and its conceptual analysis within the framework of his concept of body-scheme.

Yuasa notes that meditation "bring[s] the activity of the third emotion-instinct into awareness."[40] In order to see why this is the case, we must first understand what meditation is. Here, Yuasa draws our attention to the status of the external sensory-motor circuit in seated meditation. He says:

> To meditate in a sitting position means to stop the muscular movements of the limbs while cutting off the sensory stimuli of the external world. By means of this, the external sensory-motor circuit is brought to a state of standstill.[41]

The circuit of kinesthesis is by implication rendered inoperative, because this circuit functions in close conjunction with the first external sensory-motor circuit. In seated meditation, then, both the external sensory-motor circuit and the circuit of kinesthesis are rendered inoperative. Yet the circuit of somesthesis, which has a close connection with automatic memory system, and whose experiential correlate is a self-grasping awareness of one's body, is still functional. Yuasa continues:

> When we meditate, we assume a posture of looking into our body (e.g., the interior of the abdominal cavity inside the skin). However, nothing is seen in the interior of the body since it is dark. The condition of the activity of various internal organs is in most parts buried in the unconscious, except that we are aware of it in a limited degree as a vague sensation of the internal organs as a whole. What is felt in this case is only the condition of the activity of the circuit of coenesthesis as a *self-grasping sensation of one's body*, that is, as an *awareness* of the whole of one's body.[42] [emphases in the original]

This is a description of meditation in its initial stage, but as meditation deepens, Yuasa notes that:

. . . [O]ut of this self-grasping sensation of one's body, emotional complexes gradually start appearing in the form of wandering thoughts and delusions. To use the terminology of Gestalt's psychology, meditation can be regarded as a training where emotional complexes surface as images (figures) whose canvas is the self-grasping sensation of one's body as its background (ground). According to the view of the body [espoused] by Eastern medicine, emotion in this case is understood as a flow of *ki*-energy.[43]

Important in this regard is Yuasa's observation that emotion is identified with the flow of *ki*-energy.[44] What Yuasa means then by "bringing the emotion-instinct circuit into awareness" is that the *ki*-energy *qua* emotion appears during meditation as "wandering thoughts and delusions" against the background of self-grasping awareness of one's body. The meditator incorporates and assesses the meaning of these images. Since "wandering thoughts and delusions" are referred to as "patterns of emotional response" or "emotional complexes," we may ask why "patterns of emotional response" or "emotional complexes" are experienced as "wandering thoughts and delusions." Yuasa seems to be echoing C. G. Jung's idea that the unconscious has an autonomous function with creative power. When the level of activities of the first external sensory-motor circuit and the circuit of somesthesis is lowered in meditation, the autonomous function of the unconscious surfaces into awareness as "wandering thoughts and delusions," that is, *ki*-energy appears as images. Once the "wandering thoughts and delusions" are all cleared, that is once they no longer appear in the course of the meditation practice, creative energy begins filling the meditator. It is in recognition of this experiential fact, Yuasa says, that meditation is a way of "integrat[ing] the power of the unconscious within consciousness." Interpreted philosophically, this means an achievement of a higher degree of correlativity between movement of mind and movement of body.

We have just observed how *ki*-energy *qua* emotion can be brought into awareness in seated meditation. A question naturally arises if the same result obtains in moving forms of meditation such as Japanese archery[45] or recitation of *nembutsu*[46] while constantly walking. The principle involved in these practices, Yuasa claims, is the same as that of seated meditation. Both seated and moving forms of meditation are the "practice of entering into a quiet and immovable state by relaxing the mind and the body."[47] In martial arts, in particular, this principle is expressed as "letting the mind and *ki*-energy accord with each other" (*shinki icchi*). Yuasa interprets this to mean that:

> the mind appropriates the flow of *ki*-energy through its feeling-awareness. That is, *ki*-energy is not the function which the ordinary, everyday consciousness can perceive, but is a new function which the consciousness (mind) becomes gradually capable of perceiving.[48]

It is here that we can appreciate the fact that the circuit of unconscious quasi-body, initially characterized as the "invisible," "potential" system below consciousness, proves visible and becomes actualized in awareness.[49] When this occurs, oneness of body and mind is experienced. Traditionally, this state is expressed as "Oneness of the body and mind" (*shinshin ichinyo*) by Eisai (1141–1215), as "Casting off the body and mind" (*shinshin datsuraku*)[50] by Dōgen (1200–1253), and as "Crystallization of the mind and body" (*shinjin gyōnen*) by Myōe (1173–1232).

CONCLUDING REMARKS

I would like to conclude this brief exposition of Yuasa's concept of body-scheme with a few philosophical observations. Yuasa's concept of body-scheme is epistemologically dualistic and ontologically non-dualistic. The dual aspect is present in Yuasa's concept of body-scheme because he recognizes an existential transformation in the practice of personal cultivation. The concept of lived body that emerges from Yuasa's body-scheme is one of *achievement*.

The dualism with which Yuasa starts his investigation must be distinguished from Cartesian dualism.[51] Descartes's dualism is an ontologically *disjunctive* dualism, admitting no interaction between two separate realities, the mind and the body. Yuasa's body-scheme, on the other hand, suggests an epistemologically *provisional* or *correlative* dualism. It is provisional because the third and the fourth circuit of Yuasa's body-scheme are separated epistemologically in our "natural attitude"[52] but, as Yuasa has demonstrated, dualism can change into non-dualism through the *transformative* practice of self-cultivation. Yuasa accepts that this transformation is an empirical fact, tested through long historical and cultural traditions in Japan. Theoretically, this means that there is a functional correlativity between mind and body, that is, the functions of both mind and body can be enhanced through *prāxis*. Yuasa has elucidated the correlativity in his analysis of the third emotion-instinct circuit and the fourth unconscious quasi-body circuit. In his final analysis, correlativity is demonstrated in the experience of body-mind oneness. Ontologically, then, the original relationship of mind and body is non-dualistic in nature. In fact, Yuasa's provisional dualism and non-dualistic position presuppose one another: unless mind and body were provisionally dualistic in our "natural attitude," it would be impossible even theoretically to conceive of their oneness. Were this not the case, the practice of self-cultivation, with its transformative dimension, would be meaningless. Generally, this conception of mind and body is in accord with the implication of traditional Eastern concepts such as *nirvana, tao, satori,* that is, with the implication that there is a higher epistemological perspective achievable through the process of self-cultivation.

What this achieved epistemological perspective suggests, among other things, is that knowledge thus gained is somatic in character. The nature of knowledge that obtains through the achieved mind-body is "somatic knowledge." Somatic knowledge does not simply mean "knowledge of the body" but knowledge gained *through the body.* Such knowledge may be contrasted with "intellectual knowledge." Intellectual knowledge is that mode of cognition which results from objectifying a given object, which propositionally takes a subject-predicate form, and which divorces the somaticity of the knower from "the mind" of the knower. For these reasons, intellectual knowledge circumscribes its object; it is incapable of becoming one with the object. Somatic knowledge in its immediate, everyday occurrence, lacks this objectification. There is a "feeling-judgment" operative in somatic knowledge. In feeling-judgment, "knowing that" and "feeling that" are one and the same in the constitutive *momentum* of forming a judgment. In this experience, there is an attunement of mind and body, of "I" and other, and of human nature *qua* microcosm and physical nature *qua* macrocosm.

NOTES

1. Ruth Tonner, a friend at Temple University, kindly went over this paper to make sure that my English is intelligible, and Professor Maxine Sheets-Johnstone, the editor of this book, put a superb finishing touch on this paper. My appreciation goes to their selfless efforts.

2. YUASA Yasuo, *Ki Shugyō Shintai* (Tokyo: Hirakawa shuppan, 1986). I have given a brief biographical account of Yasuo Yuasa in David E. Shaner, Shigenori Nagatomo and Yasuo Yuasa, *Science and Comparative Philosophy* (Leiden, Holland: The Brill Publishing Co., 1989), 1–11.

3. I have given an account of Yuasa's "body-scheme" in relation to the concept of somatic self within the Japanese intellectual tradition in Ibid., 126–192.

4. An historical predecessor to the concept of "body-scheme" was the concept of the lived body (*leib*) that Max Scheler analyzed. See Stuart F. Spicker, ed., *The Philosophy of the Body* (Chicago: Quadrangle Books, Inc., 1970), 159–86. Also in relation to Bergson's concept of "motor-scheme," see Yasuo Yuasa, *The Body: Toward an Eastern Mind-Body Theory*, trans. Shigenori Nagatomo and T. P. Kasulis, ed. T. P. Kasulis, (Albany, New York: SUNY Press, 1987).

5. What follows concerning Yuasa's "body-scheme" is my summary presentation.

6. YUASA, *Ki Shugyō Shintai*, 73.

7. This peripheral ego-consciousness is exemplified by the experience of double sensation that Aristotle talks about, in which there is an active-passive ambiguity felt between the pointing finger and middle finger. (Aristotle, *Metaphysics*, 1010a.) Hiroshi Ichikawa provides a phenomenological description and meaning of this double sensation. See Shigenori Nagatomo, "Ichikawa's View of Body," *Philosophy East and West*, 36, No. 4, Oct., 1986, 375–391.

8. Husserl's "passive synthesis" seems to be resurrected as the body's intentionality (*le corps intentionel*) in Maurice Merleau-Ponty's *Phenomenology of Perception*. The body casts an invisible intentional arc prior to its comportment. Thus, in Merleau-Ponty, it is not a passive function but is an active readiness of the body to comport itself in the world.

9. YUASA, *Ki Shugyō Shintai*, 74.

10. In addition to the splanchnic sensation, Yuasa includes in the circuit of somesthesis a dermal sensation, and the sensation of balance. Ibid., 75.

11. Ibid., 77.

12. Yuasa points out a need to study the unconscious in this respect, because memory connects consciousness to unconsciousness, that is, to a storage of the past data of experience. Ibid., 77.

13. Ibid., 78.

14. Ibid.

15. I use the word "usually" here to suggest that there are yogins who can control the function of the autonomic nervous system, for example, the heart beat.

16. Visual perception will be correlated with the eyes and thinking roughly with the frontal lobe of the brain, for example.

17. One may recall in this connection Sartre's characterization of emotion as a magical power to transform the world. See Jean-Paul Sartre, *Esquisée d'une théorie des émotions*, 41 ff.

18. YUASA, *Ki Shugyō Shintai*, 81.

19. Eliot Deutsch characterizes aptly the ideal of the body cherished in the Western culture as "muscle man." See Eliot Deutsch "De Corps." (Unpublished paper, University of Hawaii, Honolulu, 1983.) This generalization, I believe, still holds, although recently there have been attempts to incorporate Eastern meditation techniques into a theory of sports. See, for example, James F. Brandi, "A Theory of Moral Development and Competitive Sports." Ph.D. diss., Loyola University, 1989.

20. YUASA, *Ki Shugyō Shintai*, 93.

21. The cultivation methods of "*samādhi* through constant motion" and "*samādhi* through continual sitting" were first introduced by T'ien T'ai Master Chih I (538–597) in his *Maho Chih Kuan*. The goal of these methods is to reach the state of *samādhi*, a completely unified state, through either sitting meditation or walking meditation. Yuasa mentions several cultivation methods such as *kaihōgyō* and recitation of mantras such as *daimoku* and *nembutsu*. *Kaihōgyō* is a method of *prāxis:* namely, walking through mountains for so many miles a day for a thousand days over a ten year period, while holding in mind an image of a buddha or reciting a mantra.

22. YUASA, *Ki Shugyō Shintai*, 85–84.

23. Robert C. Solomon, in *The Passions: The Myth and Nature of Human Emotion*, (South Bend, Indiana: University of Notre Dame Press, 1976). This work aptly uses the metaphor "hydraulic" to refer to the exercise of conscious will as a way of "controlling emotions."

24. Having made this comparison, I would like to point out that Yuasa's account is advantageous in that he not only specifies the emotion-instinct circuit as that which is habitualized but also how it can be habitualized. Yuasa elaborates on the second point in terms of personal self-cultivation.

25. YUASA, *Ki Shugyō Shintai*, 88.

26. Here a relationship between the first external sensory-motor circuit and the third emotion-instinct circuit is indirectly established. Cf. p. 12.

27. De Benedict Spinoza, *Ethics,* trans. R. H. M. Elwes (New York: Harper and Row Publishers, 1966), Part V, Prop. XVI, Proof.

28. A few practical applications of breathing exercises are pertinent to note here for those people in American society who might not be aware of them. Currently, it appears that our society is troubled by prison over-population. From a Jungian perspective, it is a shadow cast from the bright day world. Instituting breathing exercises in prisons would change the emotion-instinct circuit of the shadows. The same consequence would obtain if breathing exercises were utilized by drug users, another shadow. It is clear that we need both light and shadow at a societal level. I would like to remind the reader of the man who sold his shadow and the miserable consequences he undergoes. Those consequences are depicted in A. Chamisso, *Peter Schlemihls Wundersame Geschichte* and discussed in KAWAI Hayao, *Kage no genshōgaku* [A Phenomenology of Shadows], (Tokyo: Shisaku sha, 1976). See the latter also for a full discussion of shadows.

29. YUASA, *Ki Shugyō Shintai,* 92–93.

30. Ibid., 86.

31. Yuasa's "unconscious quasi-body circuit" roughly corresponds to the "subtle body" (*sūkṣma śarīra*) of which Yogic tradition speaks. This "subtle body" is believed to support the gross body (*sthūla śarīra*) in its psychophysiological function and is the object on which a healer works. Yogic tradition recognizes one more "body" beyond this subtle body, the "causal body" (*kārana śarīra*). This "causal body" probably corresponds to *shen* of Taoist tradition.

32. YUASA, *Ki Shugyō Shintai,* 168–169.

33. Ibid.

34. Ibid., 167–168.

35. NAGAHAMA Yoshio, *Harikyū no Igaku* (Acupuncture Medicine) (Osaka: Sōgen sha, 1982), 159 ff.

36. For a detailed examination of this point, see Shaner, Nagatomo and Yuasa, *Science and Comparative Philosophy.*

37. According to Nagahama, the vibration of *ki*-energy is measured to be 15–50 cm/sec. while nerve-impulses travel 5-80 m/sec. See also MOTOYAMA Hiroshi, *Ki no nagare no sokutei shindato chiryō* [The Treatment, Diagnosis and Measurement of *Ki*-flow], (Tokyo: Shukyō shinri shuppan, 1985), 1–23, and "Electrophysiological and Preliminary Biochemical Studies of Skin Properties in relation to the Acupuncture Meridian," in *Research for Religion and Parapsychology,* Vol. 6, (2) (June, 1980), 1–36.

38. YUASA, *Ki Shugyō Shintai,* 161.

39. Ibid., 168.

40. Ibid., 161.

41. Ibid.

42. Ibid.

43. Ibid.

44. This should not suggest that the *ki*-energy is reducible to emotion. Acupuncture medicine maintains that the *ki*-energy "activates the physiological functions in close contact with the object-body while connecting the body to the external world." Although it is not treated in this paper, the second point in this quote, namely, that the *ki*-energy intermingles with the external world through the body is extremely important. See YUASA, *Ki Shugyō Shintai*, 168–169.

45. To understand how Japanese archery is a form of meditation in motion, see Eugen Herrigel's *Zen in the Art of Archery* (New York: Vintage Books, 1971).

46. *Nembutsu* is a short phrase consisting of *namu amidabutsu* ("to entrust oneself to Amida Buddha"), which is recited by the practitioner of Shin Buddhism.

47. YUASA, *Ki Shugyō Shintai*, 120.

48. Ibid.

49. We might compare this conception with Aristotle's hierarchical theory of soul as expressed in *De Anima*. Aristotle places the vegetative soul at the bottom and the intellectual soul at the summit of his hierarchy. In contrast, Yuasa attempts to see in the vegetative soul and the region below it a source for achieving ideals such as tao, nirvana, and satori—ideals cherished in the Eastern philosophical traditions. Aristotle's theory is an upward-moving transcendence, progressively eliminating the somatic dimensions of a person to reach the active mind, and in which process we can detect Plato's influence, while Yuasa's theory is a downward-moving transcendence, increasingly appropriating the somatic dimensions of a person. It is a trans-descendence from the perspective of everyday consciousness toward the regions below it. This should not, however, suggest that the experiential correlate to "trans-descendence" is simply a downward movement: there are both ascents and descents of the psyche in this process. I wonder if the Platonic and Aristotelian models, insofar as their theories of the body are concerned, might not be causing people in the West to soar up too high on the wings of reason and speculation when what is needed is first a proper launching pad.

50. I have given an analysis of Dōgen's experience in "An Analysis of Dōgen's Casting off Body and Mind," *International Philosophical Quarterly*, Vol. XXVII, No. 3, September 1987, 227–247.

51. Here I am excluding Descartes's position advanced in *The Passions of the Soul*. The union of the body and soul that was guaranteed by the "sincerity of God" is for now disregarded.

52. Aside from the provisionality suggested by the tentative opposition between the first two and the last two circuits of Yuasa's body-scheme, we can take a few examples for maintaining provisional dualism first by way of citing the broader existential situation of human existence, namely, that no historical person can escape sickness, aging and dying. This fact suggests that the human living body functions independently of the mind. If it were otherwise, one's mind, for example, should be capable of preventing him/her from dying. The second situation is the modest one of learning a new performative skill or technique, such as karate or playing the violin. When one learns karate, for example, one's mind cannot freely control the movements of the body. If it were otherwise, a new karate learner would be an instant master of self-defense!

DANIEL E. MOERMAN

4

Minding the Body: The Placebo Effect Unmasked

COMPONENTS OF THE HEALING PROCESS

Healing has three basic components. The first component is autonomous healing: many things (indeed most things) "heal by themselves," sooner or later. More precisely, human bodies (more generally, living things) have an extraordinary repertoire of immunological and inflammatory processes which promote healing. The second and third components fall under the heading of *treatment* which has two dimensions: the specific and the general. None of the components is always effective: there are chronic conditions beyond any kind of healing—we are ultimately mortal; this is the price we pay for sexual reproduction.

To reiterate, medical treatments usually have two dimensions, the specific and the general.[1] Examples of specific treatments might include these:

1. giving *acetylsalicylic acid* (or perhaps acetaminophen) for a headache.
2. Participating in *psychoanalysis* (or perhaps Jungian therapy) for neurosis.
3. performing a *coronary artery bypass* (or perhaps angioplasty) for angina.
4. or, among Iroquois, using a tea of *wild geranium roots* (or perhaps of burdock roots) for fever sores.

Some examples of general treatment might include:[2]

1. taking a *pill*, regardless of its contents, for a headache (or for some other illness).
2. using *psychotherapy*, regardless of theoretical persuasion, for neurosis (or for some other psychological problems).
3. doing *surgery* for heart (or some other) problems.
4. or, among Iroquois, using *plants*, regardless of species, for treating illnesses (be they cold sores or arthritis).

Much of medical research is devoted to understanding the effects of specific therapy, for example, how aspirin affects pain; this paper is focused on the general effects of therapy, for example, how pills affect pain.

Both dimensions can affect the outcome of the treatment.[3] Taking a pill (regardless of its contents) can, in the Western world, be an effective medical treatment. This can be demonstrated in a number of ways. The best demonstration is to compare the outcome in two groups diagnosed as having the same condition where one is given inert drugs while the other is given nothing. Few such studies exist in the medical literature; even when there is little effective treatment available, the ethos of American medicine is to treat anyway. A study at the National Institutes of Health showed that postsurgical pain was significantly reduced in patients who received placebo injections compared to untreated patients.[4] In a more complex situation, two French studies of drugs compared several treatments for ulcer disease (ultimately proven ineffective) with placebo and with no treatment at all. The 108 placebo treated patients experienced disappearance of pain after an average of 8.76 days; 30 untreated patients experienced disappearance of pain after an average of 19.5 days.[5] Other studies, which can be similarly interpreted, are those where placebos are given to patients with severe postoperative wound pain, angina, acute common cold, or seasickness, among whom we might expect very few to experience any substantial relief in the short-term without some medication. In studies like these, inert pills taken orally regularly relieve such conditions in from 20 to 55 percent of cases.[6]

Most of the medical literature recognizes that the placebo effect does not always occur; research has largely been aimed at finding a way to identify "placebo responders" in terms of some personality characteristic so such individuals can be excluded from drug trials, thus, obviating the need for complex double-blind protocols. Of course, very few drugs are always effective (if they were, medicine could presumably offer surcease from death itself).

The standard medical research study in this area has been to divide a group of patients into responders (placebo reactors) and nonresponders (placebo nonreactors), and then try to differentiate them on range of personality measures. This work has shown at least the following:

1. In one study, reactors were more neurotic and extroverted than nonreactors;[7]
2. In another study, reactors were more acquiescent than nonreactors;[8]
3. In another, reactors were "outgoing, verbally and socially skilled and generally well adjusted" while nonreactors were "belligerent, aggressive, and antagonistic to authority";[9]
4. And in another, reactors tended to exhibit "higher anxiety and lower ego strength and self-sufficiency" than nonreactors.[10]
5. And so on.

In summary, placebo reactors are neurotic yet well-adjusted, extroverted yet with low ego strength, and acquiescent yet antagonistic to authority. Generally, it seems that the least significant variable in the equation is the personality of the patient. I want to be very careful here: the implicit assumption underlying all of this work, as is probably necessarily the case in a bourgeois science like Western biomedicine, is that we can understand these matters in terms of psychological variables of personality or character. I do not argue that individuals are not important in understanding these matters, only that there is more to people than psychology!

More significant than the psychological characteristics of the patient are a number of elements in the form of the treatment. Among others, things such as color and number are important.

1. In an Italian study of placebo influence on sleeping, women tended to sleep better with blue placebo tablets, while men slept better with orange ones.[11]

2. In a British study, the tranquilizer oxazypam improved symptoms of anxiety more effectively in a green tablet and improved
   symptoms of depression better in a yellow tablet.[12]
3. In another British study, medical students were told they were
   testing either stimulants or sedatives:
   (a) Red placebo pills tended to act as stimulants while blue
       placebo pills tended to act as sedatives.
   (b) Two pills (of whichever sort) had more effect than one. (One
       student who received two inert blue pills had to be admitted
       to the student clinic after suffering a major depression.)[13]
4. Several additional studies have shown in a variety of ways that
   two placebo tablets are more effective than one.[14]
5. Another study has shown that patients receiving different
   placebos in three consecutive two-week periods improved more
   than a group receiving one placebo for a six-week period.[15]

These results show that what is central in the placebo process
is not the personality of patients but their *knowledge*. We know that
blue is down/low/cool and that red is up/high/hot. We know that
two is more than one. These are not matters of personality, but of
epistemology. And so a central role is played in these general dimensions of healing by physicians and healers, surgeons and shamans,
specialists who seem universally to display their power and knowledge with intensity and drama.

Indeed, I argue that by far the most significant element in this
process is the character of the physician and the display (I usually
think of it as a dance) he or she produces for the patient. This
follows from comparative studies of placebo response rates and is
nicely illustrated by a more detailed look at the French studies of
ulcer treatment mentioned earlier. Neither of these two double
blind studies showed that the drugs tested had any influence on
ulcer healing; both showed substantial placebo effectiveness compared with an untreated control group. But there were substantially
and significantly different outcomes in placebo effectiveness in the
groups treated by different physicians. For 30 untreated patients,
the mean days of pain following first consultation was 19.5. For
several groups of patients treated with placebos, outcome varied as
a function of the physician: 12 days of pain for one physician's
patients, 7 days for two others, and 3.5 days for a fourth. In all cases,
placebo treatment was effective, but one physician was three times
more effective than another in alleviating pain using inert treatment.[16]

Similarly, I have shown substantial differences in placebo healing rates in different situations for the same condition. I compared thirty-one highly controlled studies of four- or six-week healing rates of patients with ulcer disease treated either with cimetidine (Tagamet) or with placebo. The first remarkable finding was that the placebo healing rate of this very serious condition in 776 patients was 48 percent; even more striking was the fact that, in individual trials, these endoscopically verified placebo healing rates ranged from 10–90 percent.[17]

Exactly what is involved in causing differences of such magnitude is not clear but there is reason to imagine that a significant factor is the things that people understand, or *know* about their medicines and treatment. Consider another fascinating study carried out in England. Four groups were constructed to compare the effectiveness of aspirin and of placebo for headache. One group received generic aspirin. One received placebo looking like generic aspirin. One group received aspirin with a highly advertised brand name. The last group received placebo labeled with this highly advertised brand name. On a 6-point scale from -1 (worse) to 4 (completely better), mean pain relief after one hour as reported by unbranded placebo users was 1.78, by branded placebo users 2.18, by unbranded aspirin users 2.48, and by branded aspirin users 2.7.[18] "Knowing" as they did from watching the telly that this particular brand of aspirin was "better" than others apparently made it better, even improving the effectiveness of the placebo formulation.

This is a particularly interesting study because we can see that the kinds of knowledge involved are multiple and, in simple situations, analytically separable.

I have also demonstrated that there may be cultural factors which influence the effectiveness of placebo treatment. Six of the thirty-one studies of treatment of ulcer disease described above were carried out in Germany. These six studies show a higher rate of cure than the remaining twenty-five—63.6 percent *vs.* 41.4 percent; this difference is statistically significant ($T = 2.85$, $p < .01$). What might differentiate German placebo effectiveness rates from those obtained by neighboring Danes (23 percent in two Danish studies) is unknown.

We have a whole series of ideas about what makes medicine *work*, a metaphor we derive from physics or business. Various treatments have various amounts of *power* associated with them. Generally, shots are more powerful than pills; colored pills are more powerful than white ones. Large pills (containing a lot of medicine) and very tiny pills (containing very concentrated medicine) are more powerful than medium sized pills. Capsules are more powerful than tablets, and multicolored capsules are more powerful than single colored ones. More expensive medicines are more powerful than cheap ones. Liquid medicines should be pink or red but not green or blue. Ointments should look like petroleum jelly, and should *not* be colorful while antiseptics should be blood-colored. Prescribed medicines are more powerful than over-the-counter medicines. (Medical text books frequently recommend that, when the appropriate treatment for an illness is not a prescription drug, the physician should prescribe it anyway—with his prescription pad—to convince the patient of its efficacy.) There is no particular scientific evidence for the validity of most of these ideas, but they *are* our ideas. As such, it is reasonable to believe that they are in a very important sense *true*.

Certain kinds of knowledge have been shown to have a strong influence on the healing process. In a study at Massachusetts General Hospital, abdominal surgery patients were randomly divided into two groups; the first received standard care while the second received, in addition, a short talk with the anesthetist the evening before surgery where he described frankly the pain they would experience after surgery, what would be done about it, and how to minimize it by simple breathing and relaxing techniques (think of this as a dance to teach a dance). Following surgery, the anesthetist visited with the patients regularly, assuring them that the pain they were experiencing was normal. Patients receiving these talks (participating in these *pas de deux*), who knew some different things than other people, experienced significantly less pain than controls, and used significantly less treatment with narcotics. More interesting still, attending surgeons, "unaware of the care each patient received, sent the special-care patients home an average of two and seven-tenth days earlier than the control group (p less than 0.01)."[19]

A similar study at Yale showed that a five-minute talk with the mothers of children about to undergo a tonsillectomy, describing postoperative course, resulted in the children having a significantly easier and quicker recovery on both subjective and objective measures (including blood pressure, pulse rate, body temperature, postoperative emesis, etc.).[20] Children know their mothers' dances well.

It is interesting that such effects have been noted for an enormous range of medical problems: inert treatments of some sort or other have been shown to relieve acne,[21] warts,[22] insomnia,[23] asthma,[24] anxiety,[25] and, of course, pain.[26] In a case which I may consider myself, placebo has been shown to increase hair growth in men with male pattern baldness.[27] The generalization I would offer is that general or placebo effects can be demonstrated for any condition for which any treatment can be shown effective. Thus, the one area of contemporary medicine where it is hard to find clear evidence of such effectiveness is in oncology (note that I do not say "no evidence" but rather no "*clear* evidence.")

There is also evidence which indicates that in at least some situations, placebo healing may be "better" than drug healing.[28] Several studies have indicated that ulcer patients treated with placebos have substantially lower relapse rates than patients treated with the (highly effective) drug cimetidine. For example, in an analysis of 7 patient groups, there was a 0.9 correlation between the placebo healing rate and the time until relapse (*Halbwertszeit: rezidivfrei mit Placebo*); the higher the placebo healing rate, the longer patients remained ulcer-free.[29]

How are we to account for such phenomena? The first attempt that people usually make involves some variation on Cartesian dualism which often sounds quite scientific: Well, it is psychosomatic, they say. What does "psychosomatic" mean? It has something to do with the mind and the body, but it is not clear what. Once a student explained it to me quite simply: "Well, the mind just tells the body what to do," she said. This kind of individualistic simplemindedness is not, I assure you, confined to students. The level of explanation in the medical community is not any more compelling. Indeed, the medical approach is generally not to *explain* or *understand* these processes at all (let alone to optimize them), but to attempt to escape or avoid them. A typical tactic is to suggest that the processes involved are really not very complicated at all, indeed, the explanations are obvious. A recent Los Angeles Times story about the effectiveness of certain Mexican folk treatments (usually referred to as "cleaning") demonstrates this approach very neatly. The reporter summarized the account of her physician sources this way:

> The cures sometimes seem magical, but experts say the explanation is mundane. While the dimensions of the human brain remain largely uncharted, the power of faith appears to have tremendous curative value. If a person believes that an amulet will help, it just might. If someone thinks it's hogwash, the amulet might as well be a lump of coal.[30]

I beg to differ. The notion that people can heal one another of lesions of the gut by sharing meaningful performances is *not* mundane. This is one of those "facts" that remind us of Ludwig Fleck's definition of a fact: "a stylized signal of resistance in thinking."[31] A fact is a social agreement to stop thinking, and in this case, that resistance has set in very early. It becomes clear that people are walling themselves off from important insights.

Consider one last statistic on the "effectiveness" of placebo treatment. Although I surely do not recommend it, a recent review shows that placebo treatment can suppress lactation in 67 percent of cases.[32] This, of course, immediately reminds us of the epigram in Ashley Montagu's wonderful book *Touching: the Human Significance of Skin*, in the chapter on breast feeding: "I will lift up mine eyes unto the hills, from whence cometh my help" (Psalm 121).[33] From those hills comes not simply milk, but *help*. Never was there a better example of the general and the specific. Here is the source of the moral foundation of human knowledge. When the desperate crying child is quieted at the breast, his mother croons "Good baby. What a good baby." And the baby knows, in the most fundamental, belly-warm way, that he *is* good, that morality is good. And when he is six and responds that one and one is two, he will be told "Good, Johnny! That's right" in the same language of morality and ethics, and his belly will feel good again. How can we separate the milk from the help of those hills? And if Johnny is as lucky as I was, he will learn somehow to generalize from morality to aesthetics; he will see his first demonstration of long division and he will be awed at its beauty.

We know that placebo analgesia can be blocked by the opiate antagonist naloxone.[34] This means that as the physician does his dance and injects me with a vial of morphine, or a vial of saline solution, in anticipation of the proffered relief, I can somehow generate pain-killing and even euphoria-producing endorphins in my brain (whose action is blocked by the naloxone). This does not account for all of placebo analgesia,[35] but then there are other pain control mechanisms than the endorphin system, notably the one which seems to involve the prostaglandins, the manipulation of which accounts for the analgesic quality of aspirin. But we have no evidence for such an effect (just my guess).

The centrality of these processes to human life can be seen in the cases reported in the literature of people addicted to placebos. Here is one of a handful of such reports.

The patient was a 38-year-old married schizophrenic woman with three children who was being treated three times a week in psychotherapy for a severe depression and multiple suicide attempts. . . . A previous physician had prescribed methylphenidate [e.g., Ritalin] for her depressions; when I saw her, she was addicted to the medication and usually took between 25 and 35 10-mg pills a day—when she was upset she took 4 or 5 at a time. After taking the medication, she became toxic and confused, and her husband would then decrease the medication by withholding her pills. . . . During the years I treated her, I never prescribed methylphenidate. She was incredibly adept at persuading pharmacists to refill old prescriptions written by local physicians and maintained her addiction in this fashion. The patient's husband noted that on more than one occasion she seemed to develop a euphoria from the drug as soon as she swallowed it, almost before it passed into the stomach. Because of her severe and intractable difficulties, including bizarre suicide attempts, he proposed that he substitute increasing numbers of placebos for the methylphenidate. In a graduated fashion, and with the help of the drug company, the patient was ultimately changed to a daily dose of two 10-mg tablets of methylphenidate and 25–30 placebos. The husband doled out her medication daily, and she took it in divided doses. This procedure continued for more than a year. The patient felt satisfied with the "medication" and never reported the need for any increase in the "dosage." The pharmaceutical company was extremely cooperative and made up special shipments that were sent to her pharmacy. During that year she took approximately 10,000 placebos.[36]

This woman "knew" that taking these pills would ease her suffering. And she was right.

The origins of this knowledge are deep in the human past. We have been involved with specific therapeutic activity, with the treatment of diseases, at least since the Middle Paleolithic. The famous Neanderthal burial at Shanidar described by Ralph Solecki is a case in point. Pollen analysis shows that a body deep in the cave at Shanidar was buried with a garland of spring flowers: blue cornflowers, St. Barnaby's thistle, groundsel, grape hyacinth, yarrow and joint fir, or ephedra. While all of these remain part of the popular medicine of the contemporary peoples of the Middle East today, only ephedra remains part of ours: one of the constituents of that plant—the alkaloid ephedrine—is used in a variety of allergic syndromes and as a central nervous stimulant in narcolepsy, and elsewhere as well; the synthetic stereoisomer pseudoephedrine hydrochloride has slightly different properties and is a common ingredient in cold tablets, like Sudafed.[37]

So medicine is a human tradition with an ancient and effective lineage. But people have rarely been content to rely solely on chemistry in medicine. Over these thousands of years, people have not only found thousands of effective specific medical agents, but have attempted as well—knowingly or otherwise—to optimize the general dimensions of therapy as well.

Here is an example. Perhaps my favorite medicinal plant (tough choice, that) is the wild geranium or cranesbill, *Geranium maculatum*. This lovely spring wildflower is a favorite remedy of the Iroquois. They class it with a number of plants which have "hook-like, ensnaring qualities." Some other such plants are *Geum* and *Anemone*. These plants, because of their hooks, are known and believed to be useful for capturing, ensnaring, and enfolding. Therefore, they are used for retrieving straying wives, for "basket medicines"—various concoctions, sprinkled on baskets, which will compel shoppers to buy them—and they are also useful for healing cold sores, boils, pimples, bee stings, and the like. The roots of two or three wild geranium roots are boiled in a quart of water until it is down to about a pint. The sores are then washed with the liquid several times a day. The hook-like, ensnaring qualities of the plant will enfold the sore in new skin. Moreover, the high tannin content of geranium roots means that this wash is an excellent astringent. The general and specific effectiveness of this remedy is, for the Iroquois, undoubtedly substantial. The plants are "natural symbols," "natural metaphors," meaningful to the Iroquois, and hence capable of constructing effective truths. Medicines like the wild geranium are not only good to take but "good to think."

Suppose I, not an Iroquois, went to the doctor complaining of a cold sore. How would my treatment differ? I might be told that I had "primary acute herpetic gingivostomatitis," and that this was the result of a local injury or more general stress activating a quiescent strain of *Herpes simplex*, a virus that I probably first contracted as an infant. In our culture, it seems most reasonable to treat such an illness not with the roots of capturing and ensnaring plants, but with an ointment. Our idea generally is that wounds should be covered to protect them from "germs," or from "bad air" or "mal-aria." We have, of course, a long history of concern with the air; we all "know" for example that one can "catch a cold" from sitting in a "draft." Since it is usually impractical to bandage a sore on a lip to protect if from air, the next best thing is an ointment, preferably with an oil base. So, my physician will write some words in a secret code on a little piece of paper. I will take the paper to another professional (similarly attired in a white coat) who, in addition to selling liquor, newspapers, hardware, and outdoor furniture, has been trained to decode the secret message; he will sell me a petroleum based ointment containing some astringent and a mild anesthetic. This scenario, so much more right for us than the wild geranium cure, contains precisely the same elements, the two dimensions of the general and the specific, the epistemological and the biological.

Among the most interesting and challenging cases which show the effect of knowledge on the body, are those that come from surgery. I briefly summarize an episode from the history of the surgical treatment of heart disease:

> The internal mammary (or thoracic) arteries arise from the aorta and descend just inside the front wall of the chest, ultimately supplying blood to the viscera. Following anatomical research by Fieschi, an Italian surgeon, which indicated connections between various ramifications of these arteries and the coronary circulation, several other Italian surgeons developed a procedure in which the arteries were ligated below the point where these branches presumably diverged to the myocardium in order to enhance this flow and supplement the blood supply. The bilateral internal mammary artery ligation (BIMAL) was first performed in the United States by Robert Glover and J. Roderick Kitchell in the late 1950s.[38] It was quite simple, and, since the arteries were not deep in the body, could be performed under local anesthesia. The physicians reported symptomatic improvement (ranging from slight to total) in 68 percent of their first sample of fifty patients, in a two to six month follow up. The operation quickly gained some popularity.

The procedure, a simple technique requiring only local anesthesia to treat a grave disease, laid the basis for a remarkably and nearly unique scientific study. Two research teams independently carried out double-blind studies comparing the BIMAL with a sham procedure where the entire operation was carried out except that the arteries were not ligated.[39] In both studies, patient follow-up was carried out by cardiologists unaware of which patients had undergone arterial ligation and which had not. In both studies, the sham-procedure patients reported the same substantial subjective relief from angina as BIMAL patients. Most patients, with ligation or without, reported substantially reduced need for nitroglycerin. Both studies concluded that the results of the operation could be accounted for by placebo effects, and therefore the operation should be discontinued. It was. Dr. E. G. Dimond reported subsequently that his paper was "generally credited with the successful burial of internal mammary artery ligation."[40]

In sum, the surgery did not work for the reasons that it was performed and it quickly disappeared from the surgeon's repertoire. The question for *us* is, how *did* it work, how did it relieve severe systemic pain?

Curiously analogous information exists for coronary artery bypass surgical patients who have no patent grafts yet who nonetheless "experience impressive symptomatic improvement regardless of completeness of revascularization."[41]

How can cutting two little incisions over the second intercostal space alleviate the pain of angina pectoris? How can coronary bypass patients with occluded grafts experience this profound relief? The logic of these procedures is persuasive, if incomplete. And it is this logic that is propounded to patients by surgeons who rarely seem compelled to describe as well the unremitting controversy in the medical profession about the place and value of these procedures. The biological consequence of this knowledge for the patient is a compelling remaining portion of the explanation of the effectiveness of the procedures. Bypass surgery, especially, is, from a patient's point of view, a cosmic drama following a most potent metaphorical path. The patient is rendered unconscious. His heart, source of life, fount of love, racked with pain, is *stopped*. He is, by many reasonable definitions, dead. The surgeon reconstructs his heart, and the patient is reborn, reincarnated. His sacrifice (roughly $20,000) may hurt as much as his incisions. Why does it work: "I feel better because I have more blood in my heart muscle and because I have a restructured heart," a less Cartesian patient might assert.

Anthropologist Claude Lévi-Strauss long ago articulated in general terms the character of the process by which meaningful, symbolic action could stimulate what he called "organic transformation." In his comparison of the psychoanalytic and the shamanistic cure, he noted that either would "induce" the patient to "live out a myth—either received [in the shamanistic case] or created by himself [in the psychoanalytic]—whose structure would be, at the unconscious level, analogous to the structure whose genesis is sought on the organic level." "The effectiveness of symbols," he wrote, "would consist precisely in this 'inductive property' by which formally homologous structures, built out of different materials at different levels of life—organic processes, unconscious life, rational thought—are related to one another."[42] As geraniums provide a good metaphor for the Iroquois, "induction" provides a good one for us, but it is, of course, only a metaphor.

How does knowledge get transformed into physiological action? How does receiving a placebo pill heal ulcers? How does receiving an injection of sterile saline stop pain? How does a Navaho Beauty Way ceremony relieve rheumatism? Are all forms of knowledge equally "effective" at healing? How can we optimize the overall healing process? How can we heal ourselves? How are we to understand these processes in the context of our animal mortality? What are the limits of healing action? These are all very difficult and challenging questions; they cannot be addressed by trivializing or denying them. Most important, they can never be answered if, before the fact, the symbolic and biological processes involved are placed on different planes of discourse. In answering them, we will learn a great deal about the very nature of what it means to be human beings, *Homo faber*, constructing our dances of life, building the lives we lead.

NOTES

1. Some medical treatments have no or very little general effectiveness in that they are not generally "experienced," for example, fluoride in the water supply; some have little or no specific effectiveness in that their "active ingredients" are, indeed, inactive, for example, xanthines, khellin, or vitamin E for angina; see Herbert Benson and David P. McCallie, "Angina Pectoris and the Placebo Effect" *New England Journal of Medicine* 300(25) (1979):1424–29.

2. For a discussion of another kind of general treatment, see A. A. Nareff, "Therapeutic Values of Cognac" *Current Medical Digest* (July 1966): n.p.

3. I will focus here on some consequences of internal medicine and on some aspects of surgery. Otherwise, for an introduction to the general

effects of psychotherapy, see L. Luborsky, B. Singer, and L. Luborsky, "Comparative Studies of Psychotherapies: Is It True That 'Everyone Has Won and All Must Have Prizes'?" *Archives of General Psychiatry* 32 (1975):995–1008. For more on the general effects of surgery, see H. K. Beecher "Surgery as Placebo," *Journal of the American Medical Association* 176 (1961):1102–1107; and Daniel Moerman "Physiology and Symbols: The Anthropological Implications of the Placebo Effect" in Lola Romanucci-Ross, D. Moerman, and L. Tancredi eds., *The Anthropology of Medicine: From Culture to Method* (So. Hadley, MA: Bergin Publishing, 1983) 156–168. For a recently demonstrated case of effective placebo surgery, see J. Thomsen, P. Bretlau, M. Tos, and N. J. Johnsen, "Placebo Effect in Surgery for Meniere's Disease: Three Year Follow Up" *Otolaryngology—Head and Neck Surgery* 91 (1983):183–6. For Iroquois plant use, see J. E. Herrick, *Iroquois Medical Botany* (Ann Arbor: University Microfilms 1977), and Daniel Moerman, *Geraniums for the Iroquois* (Algonac, MI: Reference Publications, 1982).

4. R. H. Gracely, W. R. Deeter, P. J. Wolskee *et al.*, "The Effect of Naloxone on Multidimensional Scales of Pain in Nonsedated Patients," *Society for Neuroscience Abstracts* 5 (1979):609.

5. H. Sarles, R. Camatte, and J. Sahel, "A Study of the Variations in the Response Regarding Duodenal Ulcer When Treated with Placebo by Different Investigators," *Digestion* 16 (1977):289–92.

6. For the classic review, see H. K. Beecher, "The Powerful Placebo," *Journal of the American Medical Association* 159 (1955):1602–1606.

7. M. A. Gartner, Jr., "Selected Personality Differences between Placebo Reactors and Non-Reactors," *Journal of the American Osteopathic Association* 660 (1961):377–378.

8. S. Fisher and R. L. Fisher, "Placebo Response and Acquiescence," *Psychopharmacologia* 4 (1963):298–301.

9. B. P. Muller, "Personality of Placebo Reactors and Nonreactors," *Diseases of the Nervous System* 26 (1965):58–61.

10. B. C. Walike and B. Meyer, "Relation between Placebo Reactivity and Selected Personality Factors" *Nursing Research* 15 (1966):119–123.

11. A. D. Cattaneo, P. E. Lucchelli, and G. Filippucca, "Sedative Effects of Placebo Treatment," *Journal of European Pharmacology* 3 (1970):43–45.

12. K. Shapira, H. A. McClelland, N. R. Griffiths, and J. D. Newell, "Study of Effects of Tablet Color in Treatment of Anxiety States," *British Medical Journal* 2 (1970):446.

13. B. Blackwell, S. S. Bloonfield, and C. R. Buncher, "Demonstration to Medical Students of Placebo Responses and NonDrug Factors," *Lancet* 1 (1972):1279.

14. Blackwell, "Placebo Responses" p. 1279; K. Rickels, P. T. Hesbacker, C. C. Weise, *et al.*, "Pills and Improvement: A Study of Placebo Response in Psychoneurotic Outpatients, *Psychopharmacologia* 16 (1970): 318–328.

15. K. Rickels, C. Baum, and K. Fales, "Evaluation of Placebo Responses in Psychiatric Outpatients Under Two Experimental Conditions," in *Neuropsychopharmacology* Vol. 3 (1963):80–84. Excerpta Medica Foundation, Amsterdam.

16. Sarles, Camatte and Sahel, "A Study."

17. Daniel Moerman, "General Medical Effectiveness and Human Biology: Placebo Effects in the Treatment of Ulcer Disease," *Medical Anthropology Quarterly* 14 (1983):3.

18. A. Branthwaite and P. Cooper, "Analgesic Effects of Branding in Treatment of Headaches," *British Medical Journal* 282 (1981):1576–1578.

19. L. D. Egbert, C. E. Battit, C. E. Welch, *et al.*, "Reduction of Postoperative Pain by Encouragement and Instruction of Patients: A Study of Doctor-Patient Rapport," *New England Journal of Medicine* 270 (1964): 825–827.

20. J. K. Skipper and R. C. Leonard, "Children, Stress and Hospitalization: A Field Experiment," *Journal of Health and Social Behavior* 9 (1968): 275–287.

21. R. G. Crounse, "The Response of Acne to Placebos and Antibiotics," *Journal of the American Medical Association* 193 (1965):906–910.

22. D. Hyman, "Plantar Warts, Newer Treatments," *New York State Journal of Medicine* 63 (1963):1680–1.

23. Cattaneo *et al.*, "Sedative Effects."

24. S. Schwank, K. Kyd, and M. Scherrer, "Exercise-Induced Asthma and Placebos," (English translation of German), *Schweiz. Med. Wochenschrift* 108 (1978):225–8.

25. K. Solomon and R. Hart, "Pitfalls and Prospects in Clinical Research on Antianxiety Drugs: Benzodiazepines and Placebo—A Research Review," *Journal of Clinical Psychiatry* 39 (1978):823–83.

26. Beecher, "The Powerful Placebo."

27. J. T. Headington and E. Novak, "Clinical and Histological Studies of Male Pattern Baldness Treated with Topical Minoxidil," *Current Therapeutic Research* 36 (1984):1098–1106.

28. Moerman, "General Medical Effectiveness."

29. A. Sonnenbert, K. Keine, and W. B. Weber, "Prevention of Duodenal Ulcer Recurrence with Cimetidine," *Deutsche Medizinische Wochenschrift* 104 (1979):341.

30. A. O'Shaughnessy, *Ann Arbor News* Oct 23, 1989.

31. Ludwig Fleck, *Genesis and Development of a Scientific Fact*, Reprint, 1935 (Chicago: University of Chicago Press, 1979), 98.

32. N. K. Kochenour, "Lactation Suppression," *Clinical Obstetrics and Gynecology* 23 (1980):1045–59.

33. Ashley Montagu, *Touching: The Human Significance of Skin*, 3rd ed. (New York: Harper and Row, 1986), 69.

34. J. D. Levine, N. C. Gordon and H. L. Fields, "The Mechanisms of Placebo Analgesia," *Lancet* September 23 (1978):654–7.

35. R. H. Gracely, R. Dubner, P. J. Wolske, and W. R. Deeter, "Placebo and Naloxone Can Alter Post-Surgical Pain by Separate Mechanisms," *Nature* 306(5940) (1983):264–5.

36. I. Mintz, "A Note on the Addictive Personality: Addiction to Placebos" *American Journal of Psychiatry* 134 (1977):327.

37. R. S. Solecki, "Shanidar IV, A Neanderthal Burial in Northern Iraq" *Science* 190 (1975):880–81.

38. See for example J. F. Kitchell, R. P. Glover and R. H. Kyle, "Bilateral Internal Mammary Artery Ligation for Angina Pectoris," *American Journal of Cardiology* 1 (1958):46–50.

39. L. A. Cobb, G. I. Thomas, D. H. Dillard, K. A. Marendino, and R. A. Bruce, "An Evaluation of Internal Mammary Artery Ligation by a Double Blind Technic," *New England Journal of Medicine* 260 (1959):1115–8; E. G. Dimond, C. F. Kittle, and J. E. Crockett, "Comparison of Internal Mammary Artery Ligation and Sham Operation for Angina Pectoris," *American Journal of Cardiology* 5 (1960):483–86.

40. E. G. Dimond, Personal communication, 1978.

41. M. Valdes, B. D. McCallister, D. R. McConahay, W. A. Reed, D. A. Killen, and M. Arnold, "'Sham Operation' Revisited: A Comparison of Complete vs. Unsuccessful Coronary Artery Bypass," *American Journal of Cardiology* 43 (1979):382.

42. Claude Lévi-Strauss, "The Effectiveness of Symbols," in *Structural Anthropology*, trans. Claire Jacobson and Brooke G. Schoepf (Garden City, N.Y.: Doubleday, 1967), 197.

5

The Body as Healer:
A Revisioning of Trauma
and Anxiety

SOMATIC EXPERIENCING

The wind shifts. The grazing impala are poised to a hair trigger of acute alertness. They smell, listen, and look. Danger is in the air. It is in the form of a few molecules of a new, but familiar scent, diluted minutely in millions of parts of air. The impala will flee, or, if they find no further cues, return to their grazing. In this same split second, the cheetah, hidden and waiting, also knows that the moment must be seized. It leaps from behind the bush. The herd of impala spring together as one organism. They flee for the cover of the thickets at the perimeter of the wadi.

One juvenile, separated from the rest, trips and then recovers its footing, but the critical second has been lost. The cheetah, now a blur, is on top of it. The young impala falls to the ground, appearing to be dead. Remarkably, it is not injured, nor is it "feigning" death. It has so changed in its physiology though, that it lies motionless in a profoundly altered state of consciousness.[1] If the cheetah is not too hungry or has cubs at home to feed, the impala's life may be temporarily spared. The cheetah may drag its prey back to the lair where it could possibly escape in an unguarded moment. And if the cheetah does make the kill, the young impala, in this altered, analgesic state is at least spared, in nature's parsimony, the pain of its demise.

An exploration of the relationship between active escape and paralytic freezing in the survival strategies of animals illuminates a neglected key in the understanding and treatment of diverse anxiety reactions as well as of certain depressive and psychosomatic conditions. In particular, "post-traumatic" and other panic and dissociative reactions show striking similarities to the behaviors and physiology of prey animals when they perceive themselves to be trapped by predators. Normally, with animals in the wild, these freezing responses are acute, terminating in hours or even minutes; the animal escapes or is eaten. In humans, however, fear potentiates immobility and these reinforcing effects may persist, often for years or indefinitely, unless treated effectively. The post-traumatic Vietnam veteran or the molestation survivor who *only* relives, or understands, or re-evaluates, or expresses his or her anger, fear, and sorrow about an event without also terminating residual immobility reactions, remains fixated in these primitive, evolutionary holdovers. Unable to complete these responses, humans become fixed in partial immobility states. They continue to orbit around them like moths around a flame. Their constricted behaviors, physiology, and disturbing emotions, moods, and perceptions continue to reflect these compelling atavistic responses to inescapable threat.

Somatic Experiencing (SE) is a biological, "body-oriented" approach that alters these fixated immobility reactions. It is based upon the study of normal instinctive behaviors as a model for treating various traumatic anxiety symptoms and syndromes. SE facilitates the resolution of human panic and post-traumatic reactions by neutralizing fear-potentiated freezing. It accomplishes this by uncoupling an individual's immobility response from internally generated fear. This allows the immobility (post-traumatic) reactions to complete as they do normally with animals in the wild.

As an experiential-educational "body-mind" approach, SE utilizes the transformative value of body awareness (somatic feeling) in the healing of post-traumatic impairment and in the resolution of various anxiety reactions. It examines the individual's developmental history of (mal)adaptation to psychophysiologically over-whelming, inescapable events. SE "tracks" the neuromuscular, autonomic, and perceptual resources which are necessary to meet potentially life-threatening situations. It considers particularly an individual's present survival pattern as a reflection of resources that were lacking at the time of traumatic activation. SE is based upon the *reworking* of traumatic responses, from paralytic-maladaptive to active-adaptive. It accomplishes this by restoring those (biological) resources in the form of orientation and defensive responses that were missing or insufficient at the time of life-threatening activation, and that resulted in post-traumatic immobility. These responses still exist, latently, in the form of "genetic potential." *Orienting* responses involve those sensory-motor mechanisms that allow animals to localize and identify novelty (and therefore potential sources of danger or utility) in their environments. *Defensive* responses include the survival mechanisms of fight or flight, of ducking, dodging, retracting, stiffening, contracting, and so forth. "Genetic potential" represents those patterns of orientation and defense which exist, structurally, as neuromuscular organization.

TREATMENT STRATEGIES

The various positions that have been taken in the psychological treatment of trauma reflect five different viewpoints: (1) The individual is considered scarred for life; the damage is irreparable and the best thing that one can do is offer support, reassurance, drugs, and coping skills; (2) Unconscious traumas can be uncovered by analytic methods and removed by reliving, by catharsis, and by abreaction; (3) The patient is exposed and desensitized to elements of the traumatic experience; the approach is behavioral; relaxation and biofeedback training may be used; (4) The working through of trauma is a lifelong, psychodynamic process; and (5) Healing is seen to arise through transforming the "meaning" of the traumatic event; in this Ericksonian type approach,[2] the client's (unconscious) resources are developed.

The first position, essentially a resignation to traumatic impairment, recognizes the importance of support, of social networks, and the use of psychoactive drugs for symptom management. The consequences of post-traumatic injuries are seen in the last analysis to be permanent. The most that can be hoped for is that the symptoms will abate over time and that there will be a gradual restoration of function. The approach is unfortunately, too often, the last resource of the resourceless.

The second view, that of uncovering and of catharsis, represents an approach that has its historical roots in Sigmund Freud's early work, in the pre-Freudian work of Josef Breuer, Jean-Martin Charcot, Franz Mesmer, and, even further back, in the writings of Aristotle. Traumas were seen to be lodged deep within the 'unconscious' mind and exerted their harmful effects because they were repressed. Accordingly, cures were sought by uncovering and releasing these repressed, dammed up energies through reliving and catharsis. Although such abreactive, "hydraulic discharge" views have lost favor, abreactive techniques still are significant in the treatment of trauma. In reliving traumatic events, however, patients often find themselves uncovering other traumatic episodes or caught in an endless reliving of a particular event. Thus, rather than "surgically" extirpating their traumas, patients can find themselves in bottomless pits of terror and despair.

Behavioral approaches to trauma are generally milder than abreactive techniques and deal more with specific phobias and stimuli. In exposure treatment, for example, patients are made to confront (related) unpleasant situations until their responses have "habituated" or "extinguished." Abreaction is less emphasized, though strong autonomic discharge and catharsis can occur. In addition, other behavioral methods such as biofeedback and relaxation training are employed to help deactivate the patient's high arousal responses.

With its emphasis on uncovering innate biological resources, and on the "renegotiation" of habitual response from paralytic freezing to active defense, SE is quite different from either behavioral/exposure or abreactive approaches. SE also offers some useful insight as to why some exposure paradigms and treatments are more effective than others. In particular, it suggests that exposure is effective to the degree that it evokes *restructuring* in the form of psychophysiological resources which were not previously available at the time of a traumatic episode. In addition, because survival-regulatory systems operate complexly through (inter)reaction, traumatic responses are only indirectly addressed with linear methodologies like desensitization, biofeedback, and relaxation. The maladaptive (biological) organization of paralytic freezing remains essentially unchanged with relaxation procedures, though the latter's ameliorative effects may be valuable.

SE differs from cathartic and behavioral approaches in general in that it examines in a specific way how a (post-)traumatic reaction was originally patterned in the body and perceptual systems. Rather than reliving and releasing so-called repressed affect and ideation, SE seeks to "renegotiate" the client's maladaptive responses to overwhelming threat. It does this by gradually and progressively *destructuring* a particular traumatic response such as chronic freezing, and then *restructuring* the maladaptive neuromuscular patterns as flexible, defensive, and orienting responses.

With respect to all of the above-outlined positions, the approach taken by SE in treating anxiety and post-traumatic responses is most similar to Erickson's view (5) of "healing through transformation." SE, however, offers a much wider, developmental appreciation of the catalytic role played by motoric responses and body sensations as latent (genetic) potential. SE is a naturalistic approach that charts the functional role played by bodily experience in organizing behavior and affect. It acknowledges instinctual behaviors and feelings as the wellspring of the organisms capacity for self-regulation and healing.

The type of traumatic reactions treated by SE include, but extend beyond, those ordinarily considered by psychological therapists. The sensitizing and eliciting stressors underlying trauma include emotional, physical, and sexual abuse: disaster, intrauterine (maternal-fetal) distress, difficult birth, severe abandonment and neglect, surgery, near drowning, illness, poisoning, prolonged immobilizations, physical injury (e.g. automobile accidents), physical attack, abduction, extreme physical pain, and mutilation of self and others. SE also examines the effects of chronic stress. All of these occurrences have the potential for initiating, sensitizing, and augmenting post-traumatic (shock) reactions. The seeds of traumatic impairment are sewn where an individual's bio-developmental resources are insufficient to resolve successfully a source of (extreme) threat by removing the threat, or by escaping (actively) from it.

SE compliments and extends the psychological treatment of abuse and other trauma through a refined use of body awareness; it depotentiates post-traumatic dysfunction by precisely identifying and restructuring the motoric and other psychophysiological patterns underlying a wide variety of traumatic responses.

THE SUBSTITUTE TIGER

My interest in the essential role played by bodily responses and motoric patterns in the genesis and treatment of anxiety began quite accidentally about twenty years ago when a young woman was referred to me by a psychiatrist. Nancy had been suffering from panic attacks for two years. She had not responded to psychotherapy, and tranquilizers and antidepressant drugs gave her only minimal relief. The referring psychiatrist asked me to do some massage and relaxation training with her. My attempts were equally unsuccessful. She resisted; I tried harder. We got nowhere. Since I knew almost nothing about panic attacks and agoraphobia at the time, I asked her one day out of frustration for more detailed information about her attacks. She revealed that the onset of her first attack occurred while she, along with a group of other students, was taking the Graduate Records Examination. Becoming suddenly terrified, she forced herself to complete the test and then ran out, frantically pacing the streets for hours, afraid to enter a bus or taxi. Fortunately, she met a friend who took her home. During the following two years her symptoms worsened and became more frequent. She was unable to leave her house alone and could not enter graduate school even though she had passed the exam and was accepted by a major university.

Nancy recollected the following sequence of events. She felt expectant but confident on the bus ride to the exam. (As she recalled this, I was surprised to note that her chest elevated and expanded in contrast to its habitual collapsed, sunken attitude.) Arriving early, she went to the canteen to have a coffee and to smoke a cigarette. A group of students was already there, talking about how difficult the test was. Nancy became agitated, lit another cigarette, and drank another coffee. She remembered feeling quite jittery upon entering the room. (I noticed her neck pulse increasing slightly as she described this.) She remembered that the exam was passed out and that she wrote vigorously. (She stopped speaking momentarily at this point, and became quite still. I noticed that her neck pulse was increasing rapidly. Her chest collapsed. I asked her to lie down and try to relax. Her heart beat accelerated further to almost 130. We had rather unfortunately discovered, some years before it was reported in the literature, "relaxation-induced panic syndrome.") The session continued as follows:

Nancy replies, "I don't know . . . I can't think . . . I . . . I don't know."

Her eyes develop a stuporous drifting gaze. To focus her attention, I ask if she was writing with a pen or pencil.

"With a pencil I think . . . yes, it's a pencil."

"Can you feel it?"

"Yes, I can . . . it's a blue pencil . . . I mean it makes blue marks on the page."

Her breathing and pulse rate start to decrease. I am relieved, but only momentarily. Her pulse continues to drop precipitously to about fifty beats per minute. Her face pales and her hands begin to tremble.

"I'm real scared . . . stiff all over . . . I feel like I am dying . . . I can't move . . . I don't want to die . . . help me."

She continues to stiffen, her throat becoming so tight that she can barely talk. She forces the words, "Why can't I understand this . . . I feel so inferior, like I'm being punished . . . I must have a character flaw . . . I feel like I'm going to be killed but there's nothing . . . it's just blank."

"Feel the pencil," I demand, without knowing why.

"I remember now. I remember what I thought," she replies. "My life depends on this exam."

Her heart rate increases now, moving up into the eighties, it continues to increase.

At this point, a dream image of an attacking tiger jumping through the African bush flashed before me. I was quite startled. A fleeting thought about a zoological article I had recently read on "tonic immobility" or "death feigning" in predator-prey behaviors prompted me to announce loudly: "You are being attacked by a large tiger. See the tiger as it comes at you. Run towards that tree, climb it, and escape!"

Nancy let out a piercing, blood curdling yell—a scream which brought in a passing police officer (fortunately my office partner took care of the situation). Nancy began to tremble, shake, and sob in waves of full body convulsions. I held her for almost an hour while she continued to shake. She recalled a terrifying memory from her childhood: the experience of a tonsilectomy with ether anesthesia; the experience surfaced in images and feelings. We talked about this and she left feeling "like she had herself again." We continued relaxation including assertion-training for a few more sessions. She was taken off medication, entered graduate school, and completed her doctorate in physiology without relapse.

Motivated by my own subconscious image processes, I had introduced to Nancy a "substitute tiger" as the specific and localized stimulus accounting for her persistent arousal. This previously unexplained arousal (augmented by caffeine, nicotine, and the excitement of taking the exam) had become associated with her perceived inability to survive a "life and death situation" (derivative from an actual earlier life and death situation, the tonsilectomy). Being trapped in a closed room had triggered her intense panic reaction. The evoking of running-escape in our session, at a heightened level of activation, allowed for some completion of the previously aborted escape response (in the exam and the operating room). By orchestrating an appropriate, and critically timed defensive escape, Nancy learned an appropriate response which allowed her to alter her earlier freezing response. This learning is not a learning in the usual cognitive sense, but rather in the bodily-perceptual sense of restructuring primitive brain stem/bodily responses all the way from freezing (like the cornered impala) to active escape (away from the substitute tiger).

When the psychiatrist, astonished by Nancy's dramatic recovery, asked me what I had done with her, I was without an adequate explanation. I did not, at the time, realize the critical and unitary importance of restructuring activation responses in completing previously thwarted defensive responses. Bridging somatic resource states from habitual, collapsed, frozen attitudes to open, supported, expanded ones was an essential clue that kept repeating itself again and again in my Body Work practice in the early 1970s. Over the next few years, I was referred several more clients with anxiety and panic symptoms. I began to comprehend that the central axis in the resolution of post-traumatic and various anxiety responses was the bridging of previously thwarted motor acts to active defensive orienting responses. It was readapting the biological body-mind into less limited ways of responding.

Maladaptations can be seen in clients' habitual postures and movement patterns, and give clues for working through strategies. The abreaction which occurred with Nancy was, as I soon came to realize, neither an essential or even desirable component in the resolution of anxiety states. While abreaction and catharsis may sometimes occur, it is the emergence of *genetic potential* in the form of specific patterns of defense activation that is the critical catalyst for therapeutic success.

GIVING THE BODY ITS DUE

Aaron Beck and Gary Emery, in their important book, *Anxiety Disorders and Phobias*,[3] make the point that to understand fear, anxiety, and panic, the person's appraisal of a situation is most important. In the chapter "Turning Anxiety on its Head," the authors consider cognitive appraisal to be a critical fulcrum in anxiety reactions. They argue that because anxiety has a strong somatic-emotional component, the more subtle cognitive processing which occurs may be neglected both in theory and in clinical practice. By focusing narrowly on the cognitive aspects of anxiety, however, they overlook the fundamental role played by body responses and sensations. It is because anxiety has such a strong and compelling somatic component that the subtlety and range of somatic sensations are often overshadowed by the urgency and meaning of the experience. In addition to recognizing the importance of cognitive factors, systematic study of bodily reactions, of body sensation, and of sensate experience is not only important, it is essential. This study must occur conjointly with the recognition and exploration of cognitive and perceptual factors. Appreciating the role of bodily experience illuminates the complex web called "anxiety" and connects many threads in understanding and modifying its physiological and experiential basis. In addition to turning anxiety on its head, we need to return the body to the head. The intrinsic psychophysiological unity that welds body and mind together is otherwise compromised.

Cognitive theorists believe that anxiety serves primarily to signal the brain to activate a physical response that will dispel the source of anxiety. The role of anxiety is likened in this way to that of pain. The experience of pain impels us to do something to stop it. The pain is not the disease. It is merely a symptom of fracture, appendicitis, and so forth. Similarly, according to Beck, anxiety is not the disease but only a signal: "Humans are constructed in such a way as to ascribe great significance to the experience of anxiety so that we will be impelled to take measures to reduce it." He notes that: "The most primal response depends on the generation of unpleasant subjective sensations that prompt a *volitional* intentional action designed to reduce danger. Only one experience of 'anxiety' is necessary to do this"[4] [emphasis added]. As examples, Beck mentions the arousal of anxiety when a driver feels that he is not in complete control of the car and which prompts him to reduce his speed until he again feels in control. Similarly, a person approaching a high cliff retreats. What is the wisdom of an involuntary, primitive, global, somatic, and often immobilizing brain stem response? Is it exclusively for calling the individual's attention to making varied and specific voluntary responses? Such an inefficient arrangement is highly questionable.

A lack of refinement in appreciating the essential nuances played by bodily responses and sensations in the structures and experience of anxiety is typical of cognitive approaches. Beck, for example, flatly states that "a specific combination of autonomic and motor patterns will be used for escape, a different combination for freezing, and a still different pattern for fainting. However, the subjective sensation—anxiety—will be approximately the same for each strategy." In the following paragraph of this same article he adds: "An active coping set is generally associated with sympathetic nervous system dominance, whereas a passive set, triggered by what is perceived as an overwhelming threat, is often associated with parasympathetic dominance . . . as in a blood phobic. In either case the subjective experience of anxiety is similar."[5]

These statements of Beck's reveal a significant glitch in the phenomenology of anxiety and highlight its paradoxical nature. According to Beck's reasoning, the same body signal is relayed to the brain's cognitive structures for all forms of threat. The "head" structures are then somehow expected to decide on an appropriate course of action. This top-heavy, Cartesian holdover goes against the basic biological requirements for an immediate, precise, and unequivocal response to threat. It is a view that is quite confusing because it requires that distinctly different proprioceptive and autonomic feedback be experienced as the same signal. We have tended, in the Cartesian view of the world, so much to identify with the rational mind that the wider role of instinctive, bodily responses in orchestrating and propelling behavior and consciousness has been all but ignored.

Animals possess a variety of orientation and defensive responses which allows them to respond automatically to different, potentially dangerous, situations rapidly and fluidly. The sensations involving escape are profoundly different from those of freezing or collapse. Beck is correct, however, in describing panic and post-traumatic anxiety states as having in common the experience of dread with the perception of inescapability. The singular experience of anxiety that Beck talks about occurs *only* where the normally varied and active defensive responses have been unsuccessful, that is, when a situation is *both* dangerous *and* inescapable. Anxiety, in its pathological panic form (as distinguished from so-called signal anxiety), represents a profound failure of the organism's innate defensive structures to mobilize and thus allow the individual to escape threatening situations, actively and successfully.

Where escape is possible, the organism responds with an active pattern of coping. There is the continuous experience of danger, running, and escape. When, in an activated state, escape is successfully completed, anxiety does not occur. Rather a fluid (felt) sense of biological competency is experienced. Where defensive behaviors are *unsuccessful* in actively resolving severe threat, anxiety is generated. It is where active forms of defensive response are aborted and incomplete that anxiety states ensue. *The monolithic experience of anxiety camouflages a wealth of incomplete underlying and identifiable somatic responses, sensations, and bodily feelings. These body experiences represent the individual's genetic potential or resource of underlying defensive capabilities.* The recognition that these instinctive orientation and defensive behaviors are organized motor patterns, that is, prepared motor acts, helps to return the body to the head. Anxiety derives ultimately from a failure to complete motor acts successfully. Jean Genet, in his autobiographical novel, *Thief's Journal,* states this premise in bold prose: "Acts must be carried through to their completion. Whatever their point of departure, the end will be beautiful. It is (only) because an action has not been completed that it is vile."

When orienting and defensive behaviors are carried out smoothly and effectively, anxiety is not generated. Instead, there is the complex and fluid sensate experience perceived perhaps as curiosity, attraction, or avoidance. It is only when these instinctive orientation and defensive resources are interfered with (thwarted) that the (incomplete) experience of anxiety is generated: "I am not afraid of snakes or spiders, but of my inability to respond effectively to these creatures. . . . Ultimately, I have only one fear, the fear of not being able to cope, of my own uncopability."[6] Without active defensive responses, we are unable to deal effectively with danger and so we are anxious.

ORIENTATIONS, DEFENSE, AND FLIGHT

A scene from an uplands meadow illustrates the motor act concept. Suppose you are strolling leisurely in an open meadow. A shadow suddenly moves in the periphery of your vision. Instinctively, all movement is arrested; reflexively you crouch in a flexed posture; your autonomic nervous system is activated. After this momentary arrest response, your eyes open wide and your head turns, automatically, in the direction of the shadow or sound in an attempt to localize and identify it. Your neck, back, legs, and feet muscles coordinate so that your whole body turns and then extends. Your eyes narrow somewhat, while your pelvis and head shift horizontally giving you an optimal view of the surroundings and an ability to focus panoramically. This initial two-phase action pattern is an instinctive orientation preparing you to respond flexibly to many possible contingencies. The initial arrest-crouch flexion response minimizes detection by possible predators and offers some protection from falling objects. Primarily, though, it provides a convulsive jerk that interrupts any motor patterns which were already in execution and then prepares you, through scanning, for the fine-tuned behaviors of exploration or defense.

If the shadow was cast by an eagle taking flight, a further orientation of tracking-pursuit occurs. Adjustment of postural and facial muscles occurs unconsciously. This new "attitude of interest," when integrated with the contour of the rising eagle image, is perceived as the feeling of excitement. This aesthetically pleasing sense, with the meaning of enjoyment, is affected by past experience, but may also be one of the many powerful, archetypal predispositions or undercurrents which each species has developed over millennia of evolutionary time. Most Native Americans, for example, have a very special, spiritual, mythic relationship with the eagle. Is this a coincidence, or is there something imprinted deep within the structures of the brain, body, and soul of the human species that responds intrinsically to the image of eagle with correlative excitement and awe? All organisms possess dispositions, if not specific approach/avoidance responses, to moving contours. A baby chick, without learning from its mother, flees from the moving contour of a hawk. If the direction of movement of this silhouette is reversed, however, to simulate a goose, the baby chick shows no such avoidance response.

If the initial shadow in the meadow had been from a raging grizzly bear rather than from a rising eagle, a very different preparedness reaction would have been evoked; the preparation to flee. This is *not* because we "think bear" and then evaluate it as dangerous, and *then* prepare to run. It is because the contours and features of the large, looming, approaching animal cast a particular light pattern upon the retina of the eye. This stimulates a pattern of neural firing which is registered in phylogenetically primitive brain regions. This pattern recognition triggers defensive responding. These responses derive from genetic predispositions as well as from the outcomes of previous experiences with similar large animals. Nonconscious circuits are activated, triggering preset patterns or tendencies of defensive posturing. Muscles, viscera, and autonomic nervous system activation cooperate in preparing for escape. This preparation is sensed kinesthetically and is internally joined as a gestalt to the image of the bear. Movement and image are fused, registered together, as the feeling of danger. Motivated by this *feeling* we continue to scan for more information—a grove of trees, some rocks—

at the same time drawing on our ancestral and personal memory banks. Probabilities are nonconsciously computed, based on such encounters over millions of years of historical evolution, as well as by our own personal experiences. We prepare for the next phase in this unfolding drama. Without thinking, we orient toward a large tree with low branches. An *urge* is experienced to flee and climb. If we run, freely oriented toward the tree, it is the feeling of *directed running*. The urge to run is experienced as the feeling of danger, while successful running is experienced as *escape* (and not anxiety!).

If, on the other hand, we chance upon a starved or wounded bear, and moreover find ourselves surrounded on all sides by sheer rock walls, that is, trapped, then the defensive preparedness for flight concomitant with the feeling of danger is "thwarted" and will change abruptly into the fixated emotional states of anxiety. The word *fear*, interestingly enough, comes from the old English term for danger, while *anxious* derives from the Greek root meaning to "press tight" or strangle. Edward Munch's compelling painting, *Angst*, is a graphic portrayal of anxiety. Our entire physiology and psyche become precipitously constricted in anxiety. Response is restricted to non-directed desperate flight, to rage, counterattack, or to freeze-collapse. The latter affords the possibility of diminishing the bear's urge to attack. (From the bear's point of view, and in contradiction to common propaganda, if it is not cornered or hurt, and able to identify clearly the approaching human being, the bear usually will not attack the intruder. It may even remain and go on with business as usual.)

In summary, when the normal orientation and defensive escape resources have failed to resolve the situation, life hangs in the balance with non-directed flight, rage, freezing, or collapse. Rage and terror-panic are the *secondary* emotional anxiety states which are evoked when the *preparatory orientation processes* (*feelings*) of danger-orientation and preparedness to flee are not successful, when they are blocked or inhibited. It is this blockage which results in freezing and anxiety-panic.

TONIC IMMOBILITY-FREEZING

Anxiety has often been linked to the physiology and experience of flight or fight. Ethological analyses of distress behaviors suggest that this may be quite misleading. Ethology points to the "thwarting" of escape as the root of distress-anxiety.[7] When an antelope is attacked by a tiger on the plains, it will first attempt to escape through directed oriented running. If, however, the fleeing animal is cornered so that escape is diminished, it may run blindly, without a directed orientation, or it may attempt to fight wildly and desperately against enormous odds. Abruptly, when trapped, or at the moment of physical contact, often before injury is actually inflicted, the antelope then appears to go dead. It not only appears dead, but its autonomic physiology undergoes a widespread alteration and reorganization. The antelope is in fact highly activated internally, even though outward movement is almost nonexistent. Prey animals are immobilized in a sustained (cataleptic-catatonic) pattern of neuromuscular activity and high autonomic and brain wave activity.[8] Sympathetic and parasympathetic responses are also concurrently activated, like brake and accelerator, working against each other.[9] Nancy, as she re-experienced the examination room, exhibited this pattern when her heart rate increased sharply and then plummeted abruptly to a very low rate. In tonic immobility, the animal is either frozen stiff in heightened contraction of agonist and antagonist muscle groups, or in a continuously balanced, hypotonic, muscular state exhibiting what is called "waxy flexibility." In the hypotonic state, body positions can be molded like clay, as is seen in catatonic schizophrenics. There is also analgesic numbing.[10] Nancy described many of these behaviors as they were happening to her. She was, however, not aware of her physical sensations but rather of her self-depreciating and critical judgements about those sensations. It is as though some explanation must be found for profoundly disorganizing forces underlying one's own perceived inadequacy. Psychologist Paul G. Zimbardo has gone so far as to propose that "most mental illness represents, not a cognitive impairment, but an (attempted) interpretation of discontinuous or inexplicable internal states."[11] Tonic immobility, murderous rage, and nondirected flight are such examples.

Ethologists have found wide adaptive value in these immobility responses: freezing makes prey less visible and nonmovement in prey appears also to be a potent inhibitor of aggression in predators, often aborting attack-kill responses entirely.[12] The park service, for example, advises campers that if they are unable actively to escape an attacking bear (such as by climbing a tall sturdy tree), they should lie prone and not move. Such a response was dramatically portrayed in the recent and wonderful film, *The Bear.*

The family cat, seemingly on to nature's game, bats a captured, frozen mouse with its paws, hoping to bring it out of shock and continue in the game. Immobility can buy time for prey. The predator may drag a frozen prey to its den or lair for later consumption, giving it a second chance to escape.[13] In addition to these aggression-inhibiting responses, freezing by prey animals near a predator may provide a signaling and decoy effect allowing con-specifics, who are farther away, a better chance for escape in certain situations. Loss of blood pressure may also help prevent bleeding when injured. An immobile prey animal is, in sum, less likely to be detected by a predator and if detected, it is less likely to be attacked. Further, if attacked, it is less likely to be killed and eaten, increasing its chances of escape and reproduction. In a world where most animals are both predator and prey at one time or another, analgesia is a "humane" biological adaptation.

Tonic immobility demonstrates that anxiety can, at one and the same time, be both self-perpetuating and self-defeating. Freezing is the last ditch, cul de sac, bodily response where active escape is not possible. Where flight and fight escape have been (or are perceived to be) unlikely, the nervous system reorganizes to tonic immobility. Both flight/fight and immobility are adaptive responses. Where flight or fight is appropriate, freezing will be relatively maladaptive, and where freezing is appropriate, attempts to flee or fight are likely to be maladaptive. Biologically, immobility is a potent adaptive strategy where active escape is prevented. When, however, it becomes a preferred response pattern in situations of activation in general, it is profoundly debilitating. It becomes the crippling, fixating experience of traumatic and panic anxiety. Underlying the freezing response, however, are the fight/flight, and other defensive and orientation preparations which were activated just prior to the onset of freezing. The depoteniating of anxiety is accomplished by precisely and sequentially restoring the latent flight/fight and other active defensive responses that occurred at the moment(s) before escape was thwarted.

UNCOUPLING FEAR-POTENTIATED IMMOBILITY:
AN EXAMPLE

The key in treating various anxiety and post-traumatic reactions is in principle quite simple: to uncouple the normally acute, time-limited, freezing response from fear re-activation. This is accomplished by progressively re-establishing the pre-traumatic, defensive and orienting responses, that is, the responses which were in execution just prior to the initiation of immobility. In practice, there are many possible strategies that may be utilized to accomplish this uncoupling of the immobility-fear or panic reaction.[14] An extended example of one type of reworking follows:

Marius is a native Eskimo born and raised in a remote village in Greenland. When I asked Marius, a year after working with him, whether I could transcribe his session for a book, assuring him I would disguise his name and identity, his eyes opened wide.

"No, please . . . It would be an honor," he said, "but would you please use my last name, too, so if family and friends from my village read your book, they will know it is me you are talking about."

So this is Marius's story:

Marius Inuusuttoq Kristensen is a slight, intelligent, boyish-looking young man in his mid-twenties. He is shy but unusually open and available. As a participant in a therapeutic training class in Copenhagen, Denmark, he has asked to work on his tendency toward anxiety and panic particularly when he is with a man he admires and whose approval he wants. His anxiety is experienced somatically as a weakening in his legs and a stabbing ache on the lateral midline of his right leg. There are also waves of nausea moving from his stomach to his throat, where the nausea becomes stuck. His head and face feel very warm, and he becomes sweaty and flushed. After talking with him and using some exploratory images, we come to an event that occurred when he was eight. While returning from a walk alone in the mountains, he was attacked by a pack of three wild dogs and bitten badly on his right leg. He remembers only feeling the bite and then waking up in the arms of a neighbor. He remembers, too, his father coming to the door and being annoyed with him. Marius feels bitterly angry and hurt at this rejection. He remembers, particularly, that his new pants were ripped and covered with blood. When he describes this, he is visibly upset.

I ask him to tell me more about the pants. He tells me that they were a surprise from his mother that morning. She had made them especially for him. He is in a transparent moment experiencing pleasure, pride, and excitement similar to that day seventeen years ago. Marius holds his arms in front of himself feeling the fur and feasting on his "magic" polar bear fur pants.

"I feel like I want to jump up and down."

"Marius, are these the same kind of pants that the men of the village, the hunters, wear?"

"Yes," he responds.

"Do they wear them when they go out to hunt?"

"Yes."

Marius becomes more excited. He describes seeing the pants with clear detail and aliveness. I have him feel the pants now with his hand. "Now, Marius," I ask, "can you feel your legs inside the pants?"

"Yes, I can feel my legs. They feel very strong, like the men when they are hunting."

(I am beginning to build, as a resource, a somatic bridge utilizing neuromuscular patterns of the leg.)

Marius's walk into the mountains the day of the attack was an initiation, a rite of passage for him; his pants were power objects on this "walkabout."

I have him describe the sensations and images of walking up into the mountains. His descriptions are bright, embodied with awareness of detail. The experience he describes is clearly authentic and present. He is also aware of being in a group of students, though without self-consciousness. I would call his state of being primarily a state of "presence" and "retrogression" rather than "regression."

As images and kinesthetic perceptions unfold, he sees an expanse of rocks. I ask him to feel his pants and then look at the rocks again.

"My legs want to jump; they feel light, not tight like they usually do. They are like springs, light and strong."

He reports seeing a long stick that is lying by a rock and picks it up. "What is it?" I ask.

"A spear."

"What is it for? What do the men do when they see bear tracks?"

(I am hoping that this "play in dream time" will help stimulate predatory and counterattack behaviors which were thwarted in being overwhelmed by the attacking dogs. This successive bridging is helping to prime required defensive responses that could eventually neutralize the tonic immobility-freeze and collapse which occurred at the time of the attack.)

He goes on, "I am following a large polar bear. I am with the men, but I will make the kill."

Micro flexor and extensor movements can be seen in his thigh, pelvic, and trunk muscles as he imagines jumping from rock to rock in following the trail.

"I see him now. I stop and aim my spear."

"Yes, feel that in your whole body, feel your feet on the rocks, the strength in your legs, and the arching in your back and arms. Feel all that power!"

"I see the spear flying," he says.

Again micro postural adjustments can readily be seen in Marius's body; he is trembling lightly now in his legs and arms. I encourage him to feel these sensations. He reports waves of excitement and pleasure.

"I did it. I hit him with my spear!"

"What do the men do now?" I ask.

"They cut the belly open and take out the insides and then cut the fur off . . . to . . . make pants and coats. The other men will carry the meat down for the village."

"Feel your pants, Marius, with your hands, and on your legs."

Tears form in his eyes.

"Can you do this?" I ask.

"I don't know . . . I'm scared."

"Feel your legs, feel your pants."

". . . Yes, I cut the belly open, there is lots of blood . . . I take out the insides. Now I cut the skin. I rip it off, there is glistening and shimmering. It is a beautiful fur, thick and soft. It will be very warm."

Marius's body is shaking and tremoring with excitement, strength, and conquest. The activation/arousal is quite intense and is approaching a level similar to that during the dogs' attack on him.

"How do you feel Marius?"

"I'm a little scared . . . I don't know if I've ever felt this much strong feeling . . . I think it's okay, . . . really I feel very powerful and filled with an energy. I think I can trust this . . . I don't know . . . it's strong."

"Feel your legs. Feel your feet. Touch the pants with your hands."

"Yes, I feel calmer now, not so much rush, . . . it's more like strength now."

"Okay, yes, good. Now start walking down, back toward the village."

A few minutes pass, then Marius's trunk flexes and his movements hold as in still frame arrest. His heart rate accelerates, and his face reddens.

"I see the dogs . . . they're coming at me."

"Feel your legs, Marius! Touch your pants," I sharply demand. "Feel your legs and look! What is happening?"

"I am turning, running away. I see the dogs. I see a pole, an electricity pole. I am turning toward it. I didn't know that I remembered this."

Marius's pulse starts to drop; he turns pale.

"I'm getting weak," he responds.

"Feel the pants, Marius!" I command. "Feel the pants with your hands!"

"I'm running."

His heart rate increases.

"I can feel my legs . . . they're strong, like on the rocks . . ."

Again he pales. He yells out, "Agh . . . my leg, it burns like fire. . . . I can't move, I'm trying, but I can't move . . . I can't move . . . I can't move! It's numb now . . . my leg is numb. I can't feel it."

"Turn, Marius. Turn to the dog. Look at it."

This is the critical point. I hand Marius a roll of paper towels. If Marius freezes now, he will be re-traumatized. (This would occur if the somatic bridges were not organized and in place.) He grabs the roll and "strangles" it. The group members, myself included, look on with utter amazement at his strength as he twists it and tears it in two. (I have asked weightlifting friends to replicate this and only a few have been able to do so.)

"Now the other one, look right at it."

This time he lets out screams of rage and triumph. I have him settle with his bodily sensations for a few minutes, integrating this intensity. I then ask him again to look.

"What do you see?"

"I see them . . . they're all bloody and dead."

"Okay, look in the other direction. What do you see?"

"I see the pole . . . there are bolts in it."

"Okay, feel your legs, feel your pants."

I am about to say, "Run!" (in order to complete the running response). Before I do, *he* reports, "I am running . . . I can feel my legs, they're strong like springs."

Rhythmic extensor-flexor undulations are now visible through his pants and his entire body is trembling and vibrating.

"I'm climbing . . . climbing . . . I see them below . . . they're dead and I'm safe."

He starts to sob softly and we wait a few minutes.

"What do you experience now?"

"It feels like I'm being carried by big arms; a man has me in his arms, his hands are around my arms. He's carrying me in his arms. I feel safe."

Marius reports now a series of images of fences and houses in the village. Again, he softly and gently sobs.

"He's knocking at the door of my family's house. The door opens . . . my father . . . he's very upset, he runs to get a towel . . . my leg is bleeding badly . . . he's very upset . . . he's not mad at me. He's very worried. It hurts, the soap hurts."

Marius sobs now in waves.

"It hurts but I'm crying 'cause he's not angry at me. I can see he was upset and scared."

"What do you feel in your body now?"

"I feel very peaceful now; I feel vibration and tingling all over. It is even and warm. He loves me."

Again Marius begins to sob and I ask what happens if he feels that in his body, if he feels that his father loves him. There is a silence.

"I feel warm, very warm and peaceful. I don't need to cry now. I'm okay and he was just scared. It's not that he doesn't love me."

In reviewing the session, recall that initially the only image or memory of the event Marius had was the bloody pants, torn flesh, and his father's rejection. Yet here also was the positive seed of the emerging healing nucleus, the "magic pants." The experience of the pants is the thread (no pun intended) by which the altered states, related to the traumatic event, were experienced and progressively renegotiated. In working with several hundred clients, I have never found an instance where there was not this dual aspect of a critical image.[15] Within an initial image are the first stirrings of the motoric plan that a person will develop. The renegotiation processes occur stepwise, from periphery to center; toward a destructuring of the particular anxiety response or thwarting pattern and a restructuring of the underlying defensive and orienting responses.

The image of the ripped and bloodied pants was arousing to Marius, but so was the happiness (his legs wanting to jump for joy) he experienced when he saw the same pants for the first time earlier that morning. He was joyful when presented with this first possibility of manhood. In wanting, literally, to "jump for joy," Marius activated motoric patterns that were essential in the eventual renegotiation of his freezing response. It is necessary to build just such adaptive motor patterns successively, with increasing activation. In moving from the periphery of the experience to the freezing "shock" core, one moves away from maladaptive neuromuscular patterns. The latter are neutralized by adaptive, flexible patterns at similar levels of activation.

As I encouraged Marius to track the initial positive pants experience gradually toward the traumatic, freezing shock core, the joyful extensor-dominated pants experience became linked to support, aggression, and competency, that is, when in somatic experiencing, Marius sees the image of the rock field, the seed begins to sprout. In jumping from rock to rock and finding and picking up the stick, Marius's dynamic body-unconscious propels the motor plan sharply ahead. He is now prepared to meet the impending challenge. He takes the offensive and moves toward mastery of the previously thwarted situation. Like the hunters, he tracks the polar bear as I track his autonomic and motoric responses. Supported by the magical pants and the village men, he makes the find and the kill in a crescendo of high activation approaching ecstasy.

In the next sequence of events, the true test will be made. Empowered and triumphant, he heads back down toward the village. There is expansion in awareness. For the first time, he sees and describes the road and the dogs. (Previously, these images were constricted as in amnesia.) He senses orientation movements away from the attacking dogs and toward the electric pole. Because he now senses his legs moving, the inhibitory freezing response is no longer the exclusive channel of response. The ecstatic trembling from the kill is now bridged into running. This action is, however, only partial; he begins to run but does not escape! I ask him to turn and face his attackers so as not to have him fall back into immobility. This time he counterattacks, first momentarily, with rage, and then with the same triumph that he experienced in the previous sequence of killing and eviscerating the bear. The motor plan has succeeded. Marius is now victorious; he is no longer the defeated victim.

The event, however, is still not yet complete. As the sensations and autonomic responses shift from highly activated sympathetic to parasympathetic resolution, the more primary orienting responses can come into play.[16] Marius not only *sees* the pole, he orients toward the pole and prepares to run. He had begun this maneuver years ago, but until this moment, it had not been executed and completed. He consumates this preparation now with the act of running. Since he has already killed his attackers, this may not make 'left brain' linear sense, but it is completely logical in the biological, reptile (body-brain) language of preparation, defense, and orientation. It is that sequence of activity (somatic experiencing) that alters the basic patterns of an individual's adaptive responses.

When I return to Denmark a year later, I find that Marius's

anxiety reactions are no longer a problem. In all such somatic healing experiences, I hold the position of a guide who allows each
sensate (body) gestalt to unfold in its own ripe moment. My role
seems to be more that of a tracker, teacher, and midwife, rather than
a therapist. The client develops identification with his/her own
bodily sense of self-discovery and mastery. Timing is critical in allowing the client's body-mind to express itself as genetic potential.[17]
"My belief," wrote D. H. Lawrence, "is in the blood and flesh as
being wiser than intellect. The body-unconscious is where life bub-
bles up in us. It is how we know that we are alive, alive to the depths
of our souls and in touch somewhere with the vivid reaches of the
cosmos." Eugene Gendlin also speaks of this innate wisdom in his
development of the psychotherapeutic technique of 'focusing'.[18]

In somatic experiencing, traumatic reactions are addressed by
a wide variety of strategies, ranging from directed touching and gen-
tle manipulation, to the uses of images, movement patterns, and
hypnoidal states. What unifies all of these approaches, however, is
that they are all used in the service of destructuring the thwarted
anxiety response and restoring defensive and orienting resources.
The overall picture shows how each individual's needs and resources
call forth a unique, creatively adaptive solution. Some of the strategies are more linear while others are more richly mythic. Resolution occurs in the creative weaving of both. The transformation is
an integrated psychophysiological process. The elements of the experience are cohesive and organized in their movement toward integration and resolution. The interweaving of mythic with linear
strands was not at all peculiar to Marius because he is an aboriginal.
It occurs with all people and in all the cultures in which I have
worked. All of us grow and develop in the mythic-somatic as well as
the linear-rational world. Joseph Campbell, one of our wise elders,
has fortunately left us with an appreciation of this gift with his
books and with his marvelous television interviews with Bill
Moyers. From *The Power of Myth*, Campbell directs us to the very
mystery of reality and existence of the body:

> People say what we're all seeking is a meaning for life. I don't
> think that's what we're really seeking. I think that what we're
> really seeking is an experience of being alive, so that our life
> experiences on the purely physical plane will have resonances
> within our innermost being and reality, so that we actually feel
> the rapture of being alive in our bodies.

NOTES

1. This reaction, found in almost all prey animals, will inhibit predatory aggression. See G. Gordon Gallup and Jack Maser, "Human Catalepsy and Catatonia", in *Psychopathology: Experimental Models*, ed. Jack D. Maser and Martin E. P. Seligman, (San Francisco: W. H. Freeman, 1977), 334–357.

2. Stephen G. Gilligan, *"Therapeutic Trances,"* in *The Cooperation Principle in Ericksonian Hypnotherapy* (New York: Bruner Mazel, Inc. 1987).

3. Aaron Beck and Gary Emery, *Anxiety Disorders and Phobias; A Cognitive Perspective,* (New York: Basic Books, 1985).

4. Aaron Beck, "Theoretical Perspectives On Clinical Anxiety", in *Anxiety and the Anxiety Disorders,* ed. A. Hussain Tuma and Jack D. Maser, (New Jersey: Lawrence Erlbaum Associated Publishers, 1985), 188.

5. Ibid.

6. Will Schutz, *Profound Simplicity*, 3rd ed. (Muir Beach, CA.: Will Shutz Associates, WSA Publishers, 1988), 39.

7. See Desmond Morris, *Primate Ethology,* (London: Weidenfield and Nicholson, 1969); and A. Eric Salzen, "Social Attachment and a Sense of Security," *Social Sciences Information* 12, (1967): 555–627.

8. Gallup and Maser, "Catalepsy and Catatonia," p. 345.

9. See Ernst Gellhorn, *Autonomic-Somatic Integrations; Physiological Basis and Clinical Implications,* (Minneapolis: University of Minnesota Press, 1967); see also Peter Levine, "Stress", in *Psychophysiology,* ed. Michael G. H. Coles, Emanual Donchin, and Stephen Porges, (New York: Guilford Press, 1986), 331–354.

10. Gallup and Maser, "Catalepsy and Catatonia," p. 337.

11. Paul G. Zimbardo, "Understanding Madness: A Cognitive-Social Model of Psychopathology," invited address at the annual meeting of the Canadian Psychological Association, Vancouver, B.C., June, 1977.

12. Gallup and Maser, "Catalepsy and Catatonia," pp. 350–54.

13. Ibid., p. 354.

14. The mechanisms of *Titration, Expansion,* and *Completion* are developed as basic therapeutic parameters in detail in the author's *The Body As Healer; Transforming Trauma* (work in progress).

15. Akhter Ahsen, *Basic Concepts in Eidetic Psychotherapy,* (New York: Brandon House Press, 1972) refers to this, I believe, as the "Law of Bipolarity."

16. Gellhorn, *Autonomic-Somatic Integration.* This is a major theme developed in Gellhorn's book.

17. Levine, "Stress," pp. 347–48.

18. Eugene T. Gendlin, "On Emotion In Therapy," in *Emotions and the Process of Therapeutic Change,* ed. J. D. Safran and L. S. Greenberg. (New York: Academic Press, in press).

6

Life under Stress: From Management to Mourning

Technology will not be overcome by men. On
the contrary, the coming to presence of technology will be surmounted in a way that restores it
into its yet concealed truth. This restoring sur-
mounting is similar to what happens when, in
the human realm, one gets over grief or pain.
　　　　　　　　　　　　—Martin Heidegger

INTRODUCTION

　　Central to the legacy of Cartesianism in Western thought is the
metaphor that the body is a machine. This metaphor has spawned
countless others, including that of "stress" as used in medicine and
psychology. The metaphor of stress dates roughly from the mid-
nineteenth century, when an engineering mentality began to take
root in medicine. As psychology began to define itself as a science
and a profession in the early twentieth century, it sought to bolster
its prestige in the public eye with the claim that like engineering it
improves the human condition.[1] It comes as no surprise, then, that
"stress" has become a figural metaphor in psychology. Primarily
what are called stresses are "metaphorical stresses," be they crowds,
deadlines, traffic delays, unemployment, or peer pressure. The metaphor is natural in the sense that just as engineering improves machines by designing them with greater and greater precision and

with materials tested to withstand force, so medicine and psychology seek to test, fix, and redesign the body and the person. Hence, the study of the human response to stress, and its only occasional reference to literal stress (temperature extremes, for example).

The questions addressed in this essay are two: if stress is a metaphor, for what is it a metaphor? Second, what are the implications of adopting a metaphor from engineering to describe the burdens of the human condition?

THE METAPHOR OF STRESS

The metaphor of stress names an existential condition characteristic of a world that is constantly shifting, chiefly from the pressures of technological change and the social dislocations that accompany it. Stress happens in a world that is without form or proportion, a time-space of "white noise," in which temporal and spatial boundaries collapse. Because time is scarce, and because there is always work to do, temporal boundaries fail. The future especially floods the present as "things to do" crowd in, eliminating the present as a time to be. Spatial limits disappear because people perpetually find themselves on the go, never dwelling. Speed provides the means to occupy the stressful world. Its occupants experience themselves less as flesh and blood creatures than as sources of energy; they consume time, money, and calories, and swim in a flood of information. They find that they desire stress; in controlled amounts it makes them feel alive, productive, important. It promises to transform them into quasi-immortal beings who cope and prosper—but at a price. They must generate increasing amounts of energy and take in increasing amounts of information to make it through the week. At some point, they find, some of them, that they cannot take it any more. They make lists. They develop symptoms. Stress is costly, since despite their best efforts, their hardiness, their buffers, and their supports, they are not pure energy. They in turn become threatened with a realization that the world to which they have adapted does not nurture or sustain their lives without extraordinary effort and resources on their part. The world is alien and hostile, bombarding them with stimuli, demands, and data as if they were astronauts flung adrift in the reaches of outer space. What can they do?

They can recognize that they are dying of stress. Stress is a modern demon taking its toll on the freeway of life. It has achieved legal status by becoming the basis for workers' compensation claims. In this way and others, stress proves costly to the American economy. Hence, the *management of stress* has becomes a profitable enterprise: stress reduction is good for corporate health. Happy, healthy employees produce better and more efficiently than stressed-out ones. The message has penetrated deep into consciousness as people (primarily the managerial class) take up stress management as a form of self-discipline, as the spiritual exercise of the day. Stress management is a martial art, protecting people from the ravages of white noise.

Terry Monroe, the president of a stress management firm states that "the single most important cause of stress stems from our absolute depressed feelings about our inability to change—a sense of lack of control over our lives."[2] His comment is profound in that it points up the dilemma of stress. On the surface, it might appear that what he says is false: All we do is change, insofar as we constantly adapt to the new, often eagerly. At the least, even those among us who do not idolize progress seek information to help us cope. But all this adaptation is not the kind of change needed to slip from the yoke of stress. At the heart of stress lies a helplessness, a kind of despair over the incessant series of losses whose rapid succession does not leave room for mourning. Despite the energizing effect of going with the changes and the comforts they offer, under stress people do feel helpless, since they must be hooked into systems beyond their control or ken. As the quotation from Monroe suggests, the urge is to change ourselves in order to overcome the lack of control. That is what stress management invites: Change by taking charge.

Because stress is the condition of living in constant and unsettling change, it is a form of grief. More specifically, it names metaphorically a kind of unresolved grief unique to the modern age. Like all grief it has the goal of reconciling past and future by tying them together in the present. Stress, I would hold, is a kind of grief in which losses are not mourned but adapted to. Moreover, the implicit dictate to take control, to adapt to the new and to shed the familiar, shortcircuits the work of grief. Grief is a "work" as Freud observed, of accepting the reality of lost love. Love dies hard, especially when there are mixed feelings toward the lost object. In the course of the grief work, the bereaved undergoes a transformation. The self, which loved the lost love, must itself die in order to live again. "Man is a network of relationships," Antoine de Saint-Exupery wrote in *Flight to Arras,* and when one of those relationships ends, man changes.

Peter Marris, a sociologist who has studied social change in Britain and in Africa, sees in grief two opposing impulses which account for the necessity of a moratorium, a period of stilled time, to heal the wound of loss:

> Grief . . . is the expression of a profound conflict between con-
> tradictory impulses—to consolidate all that is still valuable
> and important in the past, and preserve it from loss; and at the
> same time, to re-establish a meaningful pattern of relation-
> ships, in which the loss is accepted. Each impulse checks the
> other, reasserting itself by painful stabs of actuality or remorse,
> and recalling the bereaved to face the conflict itself. Grieving is
> therefore a process which must work itself out, as the sufferer
> swings between these claims, testing what comfort they might
> bring, and continually being tugged back to the task of recon-
> ciling them.[3]

The resolution, Marris continues, rests upon, "a sense of continuity . . . restored by detaching the familiar meanings of life from
the relationship in which they were embodied, and re-establishing
them independently of it."[4] This gradual "reformulation" of the self
is fraught with danger. Reconciliation is not guaranteed; the grief
may never end but become "chronic."

Grief is the genus, stress a species. Stress like grief entails loss,
loss fundamentally of what was once familiar (body, self, world).
Stress expresses an ambivalence, a particular case of the conflict
that Marris describes for all grief. Grief is an existential condition in
which one's becoming has been placed in question by loss. Death
has gripped what I love, so I must let go in order to live. I am in fact
pulled away by my ongoing living, which refuses to stop entirely
even for death. But in letting go, I face nothing. Thus, like Orpheus I
cannot help but look back; like him, I leave the realm of death for
the sunlight. This existential momentum which sweeps me up in
the passion of grieving is in stress channeled into what feels like
tension, pressure, and energy—by demands that leave no place or
time to let go and reconcile death with a viable future. Instead, since
time is scarce, I divert the passion of grief into productive work and
consumption. These activities appear to fill my emptiness and sati-
ate the desire that springs from loss. This diversion is expected and
enticed in various ways, not the least among them the assumption
borrowed from a technologically driven world that change is natural
and inevitable and good.

Grief, intensely personal, is usually fairly predictable in its course, and resembles a disease or a wound. Cultures ordinarily provide rituals of mourning to give place for the conflict of grief to work itself out. In the West, mourning has been progressively lost as a public custom. We do not know how to deal with loss in the time-honored ways: moratoria and social rituals of mourning. Stress reflects and compounds the dilemma. Grief requires time, and a specific temporality at that. Where time is money, grief cannot occur. Under stress, time as qualitative, as suitable for an activity, does not exist. One constantly adapts to loss and awaits the next blow, leaving one perpetually poised on the threshold of change, being neither here nor there. Losses accumulate, the grief work never done. This vitality of grief has been renamed "energy." It is a vitality upon which we feed. Stress, then, is a kind of grief in which the wound of loss is kept bleeding in order to keep the mourner energized for the work of consumption.

Thus we answer the first question: Stress is a metaphor for grief, for a specific type of grief that could not exist before the modern world of deadlines, skylines, and EEG lines. Stress names, albeit in a distorted manner, the grief of living with the constant loss of the familiar.

THE "IDEOLOGY OF ADAPTATION"

Stress management as a term embraces a large majority of means to reckon with stress. Essentially, it represents an ideology of adaptation.[5] By a series of measures, one comes to have the discipline both to accommodate to the inevitability of change, especially that bred by technological progress, and to gain mastery over the process of change in a variety of ways. The approach is clearly holistic, ranging from dietary measures, exercise, mental techniques of self-development and styles of social interaction, to changes in organizational systems. Stress management programs all have the common end of reducing the toxic effects of stress while maintaining enough tension in the various physiological, psychological, and social systems to provide motivation and interest.

The "management" of stress is a metaphor derived from business management, and it implies that stress is one of the things to be administered. As the scope of management has expanded, the management of employee stress has become part of the mandate. Hence the manifesto-like wording of the following:

> The rapidly changing nature of work presents an unprece-
> dented challenge for today's managers to create conditions that
> will release the power of a work force. For too long this group
> has been constrained by stress associated with change, uncer-
> tainty and insecurity. To release this stress, managers must
> learn to free their employees from such inhibiting forces.[6]

The terms are clear: change and its anxiety generate stress, which
negatively binds the power of the work force. Workers of the world,
relax; you have nothing to lose but your stress.

An ideology of adaptation informs stress management as May
and Kruger admit: "As technology continues to alter and deper-
sonalize the world, people will experience a need to interact more
frequently and effectively with each other, particularly in the workplace."[7] That people must adapt to such a world is beyond question.
That this world is depersonalized does not matter, since "events
have no meaning in and of themselves. Meaning comes from how
the event is viewed."[8] These frank admissions of the hostility and
senselessness of the world and the need to feel comfortable within it
insure that grief over the loss of the familiar and of the meaningful
will never be resolved, since there is ever more change to come.

MANAGING THE BODY

In the midst of white noise, in order to "function" adequately
and even to be happy, we need to feel calm, relaxed, composed. Like
combat pilots winging their way at night to bomb map coordinates,
we need training and morale-boosting to accomplish our tasks, both
on and off the job. Working parents, after a hard day at the office
must learn to be calm when dealing with the children, for example,
for distraught parents may occasionally abuse children out of frustration, or turn to drink in order to alleviate their anxiety. For reasons such as these, we are urged to work on our bodies as a means to
manage stress. Typically, the argument is that because of Cartesian
dualism we are out of touch with our bodies. We do not realize when
we are tense, anxious, out of shape. We need to get in touch with
them for purposes of health and happiness. Stress long endured
makes us ill, but fortunately there are specific things to do to stay or
get healthy. Primarily life-style changes are in order. Dietary
changes, exercise programs, new hobbies, and meditation are typically recommended avenues to calm the Noble Savage. The information about diet and exercise that moves us to do these things

helps get us in touch with our bodies. The terms of this information, such as "cholesterol," "immune system," "coronary arteries," and so forth, have become popular terms that guide the managing actions taken toward the body.

There are more direct measures to use to get back in touch with the body—relaxation and visualization. These measures aim at cultivating a body-image for a stress-filled world. One of these techniques is "body scanning," an elaboration of progressive relaxation:

> Body scanning uses your inner awareness, rather than your eyes, to examine your body. This kind of scanning involves directing your attention quickly and easily to various parts of your body.[9]

The technique works insofar as it calms and centers, while at the same time teaches its practitioners about the location of stresses in their bodies. As an anxiety-reducing method, scanning and its numerous equivalents act as so many Trojan horses, for along with quietude they infiltrate into one's being ever more securely an alienated image of the body:

> when you scan, you will imagine various parts of your body and check to see if they are tense. Some people imagine a picture of their body, others imagine their muscles as they would be drawn in an anatomy book, and still others imagine parts of a stick figure. One individual found it easier to imagine an x-ray machine scanning his muscles.[10]

This activity of dissecting the felt body into its elements of tension and relaxation well exemplifies management techniques of "getting in touch with your body."

Now if I feel better when I relax and scan, why call it a Trojan horse? The answer is in turn a question: What do I get in touch with? What image or set of images does stress management inculcate? I would suggest that what is inculcated is a compound image, a four-layer inscription written into the flesh. The top layer is the "information body" of systems-thinking. Hence the appropriateness of the term "scan," which has acquired the meaning of reading or analyzing patterns of lights and shadows and converting them into electrical impulses for the purpose of information processing. Now information processing is inseparably linked with control or "purposive influence toward a predetermined goal."[11] Hence what one reads or processes exerts an influence on experience and action. A basic insight of the Information Age is that information, tied theoretically to decision theory and to thermodynamics, is not simply "the facts," but particularly in its current usage, carries an implicit coercive force. When we get in touch with the "information body," we experience as "self" what are actually fragments of conceptual schemas that are purveyed by experts on health through the media for the purposes of conforming our behavior to what these authorities have decided is "good."[12] We are told what we *need*.[13] It is illusory to believe that we can "get in touch with" the body without the aid of mediating images. "The soul never thinks without a mental image," Aristotle wrote.[14] The problem with the Information Body of stress management is the tacit coercive force of what is presented simply as data. The information shapes attitudes and behavior in the direction of personal maintenance for the purposes of fitting us into the world of white noise without detrimental impact.

The information "processed" in body-management derives from three scientific areas (at least): the science of thermodynamics, the science of the strength of materials, and the science of anatomy. The sciences have contributed to the development of the discourse on stress, as we have seen. In stress management techniques, they become more fully inculcated in consciousness. These areas actually comprise inscription layers 2, 3, 4. Layer 2 exerts influence by directing consciousness to questions such as: How much energy do I have? How can I get more? Since energy is the ability to do work, the questions help me shape my body to continue to perform with improved efficiency. Layer 3 exerts influence by directing attention to such questions as: How much stress can I take without breaking? How can I strengthen my material? These are engineering questions. Layer 4, the bottom-most layer, the basic text upon which the others are inscribed, is the anatomized body. This body is, as phenomenology has taught us, an alienated body, since it is no-body, no thinking, feeling, willing body. It derives originally from the study of corpses, formerly those of criminals. (The desecration of these bodies in this way was a form of punishment.) Through emblems omnipresent today, courtesy of X-rays, television, and CATSCAN, we come easily to accept the corpse as the real body. Stress management is a form of training which further instills in consciousness a corpse-like body image with its successive layers of inscriptions. To what ends? To the end of molding our behavior and experience, that is, of living with loss of the familiar without getting sick or going crazy.

Nevertheless, the image of oneself as a living corpse—though we do not usually phrase it thus—calms us and reduces anxiety. There are several reasons why the image reduces stress. First, it fosters a sense of control. Since science reveals the inner workings of the anatomical body, to the extent that I live with such a body-image, I participate in the power that knowledge brings. I take up the role of an anatomist, of an X-ray machine, of a physician. Second, knowing my body in these terms allies me with the medical community. I become an active member of the health care team when I can describe myself in such terms. Three, the very anonymity of the image provides a measure of community. As stress isolates me in white noise, so this image of an anonymous body makes me feel that I am not alone. It is an image appropriate for a stressful world, since it is not my body as lived through and familiar; it is a body I can only *have*, not a body I can *be*. Finally, such an image enables me to stay under stress. In no way does it negate stress; in fact, it facilitates being stressed, by making the conditions which produce stress tolerable. The body is but one of the things to manage, and with this image, it becomes quite manageable. But at a price, of course: I must image my flesh as an animated corpse. Stress management strengthens my material, so that I do not break under the strain. The techniques do not call my participation in white noise into question.

THE VAMPIRE IN THE SHADOW OF STRESS MANAGEMENT

Stress management intends a good end, the easing of human suffering and pain. In this effort it is not without success. Yet trailing the good intentions like a shadow is a sinister presence that undoes the good by compounding suffering through miring us deeper in stress. Stress management attempts to construct a rational, powerful, creative, calm being whose body is an animated corpse. For this being suffering, grief, illness, and even death are not inevitable. The changes to which it adapts include medical advances that sustain its life for an increasing length of time and creature comforts that eliminate physical work and the discomforts of nature. The price that this being has to pay for these benefits, however, is enormous. It entails a craving to become the very source of energy that preserves the being in the formless, abstract, bodiless realm of stress. It entails, most fundamentally, not living through the work of grief, never resolving the conflict of grief, but accepting an endless series of hammer blows of loss as the condition for receiving the benefits of stress.

Where have we met such a being? Only in our nightmares and in tales of gothic fantasy. Is it any wonder that this being, whose name is universally known, inspires ever new and increasingly sympathetic treatment in films and novels? This being is the vampire.

Vampires widely occur in myth and legend, but it is less to their archetypal than to their cultural manifestations that I make reference. The same famous evening of story-telling that hatched *Frankenstein* hatched John Polidori's novel, *The Vampyre* (1819). While Polidori did not create the vampire, his book fascinated Western Europe and inspired numerous imitations, the most famous of which is Bram Stoker's *Dracula* (1896). In our own day, countless films have dramatized Stoker's novel and played with the theme. A change in attitude toward the vampire becomes noticeable if we compare the 1979 film *Dracula* with its predecessor of 1933. In the early film, the Count is clearly evil despite his cultivated manners and charm, and good triumphs in the end. In the more recent film, Dracula has become a more sympathetic figure, strikingly erotic, and the melancholic representative of a vanishing race. In the film's ending, good wins out only temporarily, and we are promised, in the language of mass media, sequels. In another recent film, *The Hunger* (1983), beautiful male and female vampires lead a life of quiet charm, teach music, and stalk nightclubs. This film's brilliance is in its making clear that vampires are addicted to the blood of life, that they are hopelessly helpless unless getting their needs filled by transient interpersonal relations. But the most striking re-evaluation of the vampire occurs in Ann Rice's trilogy of novels, *Interview with the Vampire, The Vampire Lestat,* and *Queen of the Damned.* When the novelist was interviewed after the publication of the third book, a reporter asked her if she would like to be a vampire. She answered that she would, in order to go into dangerous parts of cities at night, and to fight crime. To be a vampire is to "take back the night," to make it possible to live without fear in the alien world of stress. Thus, we answer the second question that guides this essay: The implication of adopting the metaphor of stress to describe our sufferings is to make us monstrous creatures who feed on our own suffering and that of others.

A DEATHLESS BODY

To become a vampire, a person must undergo a physical transformation. Louis, the interviewee in Ann Rice's first novel on the topic, recalls what happened after he first drank the blood that initiated the process: "All my human fluids were being forced out of me.

I was dying as a human, yet completely alive as a vampire; and with my awakened senses, I had to preside over the death of my body with a certain discomfort and then, finally, fear."[15] The vampire body, devoid of human flesh, has more acute senses, greater strength and agility, perfect health, and never ages (in some versions). In these qualities it approaches our cultural ideal. What is telling in Louis's account are two aspects of the transition: First, at the moment when he should die, he does not. The death of the old self, essential to the work of grief, has been bypassed in this transformation. Second, his body becomes an animated corpse, over which process of change consciousness hovers in discomfort, fear and finally with equanimity as human feeling drains with the fluids.

Let us imagine the scene again, but in the quotidien: "I" sit at home, tired and frazzled, exhausted from the pressures of the day—from fighting traffic, from stemming the flow from the checkbook, from dealing with the noise, or the heat, or the constant interruptions during the day, and then, from trying to watch television in order to unwind. Sleep eludes "me." What "I" realize, in the typical story of salvation from stress, is that "my" life-style must change, not that "I" will refuse to participate in the noisy world. That choice seems unimaginable. No, "I" take up stress-reducing measures and "I" soon feel better, more relaxed, more in control.

Rather than dying to the stressful world—whatever that could mean at this juncture—"I" take it on in its terms: I become disciplined through stress management. Rather than give in, at the moment of being drained "I" bite back, by becoming the center of the whirlwind, not its victim. Thereby "I" become more in harmony with stress, living on its purchasable substances, that is, energy and information. The desperation that led "me" to embrace stress management is the act that transforms "me" into a vampire. Now stress energizes me rather than drains "me"; "I" do not have to die (or get sick) for "I" have transformed stress into energy.

As Rice depicts it, the critical moment takes this form. The vampire Lestat says to Louis:

> Be still. I am going to drain you now to the very threshold of death, and I want you to be quiet, so quiet that you can almost hear the flow of blood through your veins, so quiet that you can hear the flow of that same blood through mine. It is your consciousness, your will, which must keep you alive.[16]

At the moment of death, when Louis accepts the blood from the vampire's wrist, he experiences a wholeness and oneness that only the infant at the breast has. All loss has been transcended in this moment of unity.

FEEDING ON BLOOD

The vampire's grotesque parody of the Christian Eucharist needs to be considered in the context of the present age. Blood for us has undergone a metamorphosis of substance. It used to be the very stuff of our selves, defining us as noble or common, for example. As one of the four humors, furthermore, blood had powerful psychological and medical properties, so much so that blood-letting was a necessary practice, as was the practice of "building up one's blood." Now, however, blood is a commodity that is bought and sold: it is a chemical soup capable of being shared among many physiological systems.

The vampire is a blood addict. Blood enables the vampire to maintain its animated corpse in the pink of health. The analogy to stress management is thus palpably evident: stress is for humans what blood is for vampires. There is in effect no surprise in learning that people have become addicted to lives of stress. The energizing effect of undergoing stress has the potential for compulsive activity, especially when it has power as its accompaniment. "I work best under pressure," or as Waino Suojanen, an organizational psychologist, observes: "There is plenty of anecdotal evidence that some executives deliberately seek out the management life because they get a high out of controlling people."[17] Suojanen later observes, some "managers become so proud of their ability to stand up under crises that they are always creating crises to stand up under, or are always starting fires in order to put them out."[18] But not only managers get addicted to stress. It is nearly universal for people when under stress to feed on speed, pressure, and energy. In short, to consume stress pure and simple is to be powerful, superhuman.

The phenomenon of stress-addiction has arisen in recent years in part because addiction has become a catchall term for bad habits and in part because a consumer society pushed to its limits has the addict as its ideal type. The vampire in other words dispenses with trivial commodities, sinking its teeth into the ultimate product. The Jungian psychologist Linda Leonard concurs with this analysis in her claim that "Dracula as Demon Lover is an archetypal symbol of addiction."[19] The figure of the addict so exercises the contemporary imagination that whereas in the past the addict was an Other, now it appears as a figure of the self. Stress addiction, or "how to turn tension into energy," goes to the source of what addiction desires: the high, the vertical thrust that lifts us above the merely human. We stress addicts thus share in the vampire's fate, becoming bestial in our search for the next hit, the next sublime moment, the next crisis.

Stress management produces vampires, then, to the extent that it aids in the loss of the flesh and in an adaptation to a world of relentless change. As "I" lose my flesh, "I" feel more at home in an abstract, formless, noisy space-time. Stress thus managed promises immortality as human limits are transcended; but the ersatz immortality is the deathlessness of the vampire.

> "I've done with grief," she said, her eyes narrowing as she looked up at me. "If you knew how I long to have your power; I'm ready for it, I hunger for it."[20]

So says one vampire to another. By converting the passion of grief into energy, we buy time. The profound conflict that the working through of grief would heal becomes harnessed for work.

COMPLETE FREEDOM FROM STRESS IS DEATH

What alternative is there? The phrase which heads this section comes from Hans Selye,[21] the great physiologist whose investigations of stress established our concern with it, and although Selye did not mean it in quite the way I will take it, he indicates that direction. Where death has a place, stress cannot abide. The vampire narratives give the truth of Selye's statement: only when mortals dig up and face in the light of day what they fear becoming, and only when they dispatch their vampire-like selves in a ritual of burial, can they lay their fears to rest. The ritual slaughter of the vampire is not an act of violence. The vampire craves rest, but its will cannot act on its desire. Its will has capitulated to addiction. Like insomniacs, vampires cannot find peace by themselves: They cannot succumb to passion, cannot be possessed by the elemental force of death that would lift the burden of life from their shoulders.

In the stories, the primary means of vanquishing a vampire is to locate its grave, unearth it, drive a stake through its heart, and bury it again. Then and only then will the Undead find release from "life" and its soul seek its final reward. What heals the vampire thus informs us as to the place and the time of the healing action: The place is the body; the time is the empty time of mourning that begins at the graveside.

THE FLESH OF LOSS AND REMEMBERING

A loss that occasions grief is a wound. This is no mere analogy, but a painful reality that the bereaved feel. Insofar as stress is unresolved grief, it is necessary to recover the felt sense of the wound that is loss in order to mourn. The location of the wound varies, but typically the pain centers in the heart. With stress, however, the sense of being stricken is usually diffuse, less focused, the result of its disembodying nature. Stress can bombard, or we take flak from all sides. At other times, stress has a peculiar precision: "employees feel like we're the anvil and everybody's beating on us with a hammer."[22] But whether the wounds come from the flak of hurry or from the hammer of criticism, the first task is to disengage these moments from the engineering mentality that asks: How much can I take? Is my material adaptable enough? Can I cope? For these moments are not attacks, they are wounds in the heart of the vampire. They embody the potential to bring back to reality an old idea and perception that things that matter have their dwelling in the flesh. The work of grief that this pain facilitates can have the salutary effect of so wounding us that we realize that the flesh is no animated corpse but our very selves. Loss wounds the *heart* (not the *pump*) because love and commitment dwell in the heart. When we feel loss as loss, then we can suffer it. Taking loss to heart makes it impossible to convert the anguish of the wound into energy. Taking it in makes us "dysfunctional." Loss that is felt gives weight to the flesh: the weight of depression, sadness, and helplessness. These are the effects one seeks in order to escape being under stress. It means in the first instance that the animated corpse that stress management constructs is beginning to decay. This decaying corpse is in truth the body becoming flesh again.

The flesh is the body of the familiar. This description is true to the old echoes of "flesh" from Scripture and elsewhere, which bring together the self as somebody and all that belongs as part of somebody: "flesh of my flesh" (children, kin), "one flesh" (husband and wife), "the flesh is weak" (desire, passion, resistance to excesses of the spirit). Like American philosopher William James's notion of the "material me," the flesh is also all that is concretely mine: clothes, dwelling, possessions, land.[23] As Maurice Merleau-Ponty writes in his philosophy of the flesh, the things of the world are enfleshed and reflect my lived-body. To the extent I experience my own flesh, I can perceive the world as flesh of my flesh.[24] Under stress the flesh withers, vanishes, is transcended, so that dwelling in the flesh becomes problematic. The concept of "psychic numbing" that Robert Jay Lifton developed in his studies of survivors of Hiroshima has relevance here,[25] although I do not want to conflate everyday stresses with such a disaster. But the perception of our griefs as stress numbs us to the pain that we might otherwise feel. We are numb, anaesthetized by our hurrying to keep up with the changes, unable to stop and notice our own pain and that of others.

To bring the flesh back into perception, an anti-stress meditation may prove helpful. The *Secretum* of Petrarch contains a meditative exercise from a late Medieval tradition. It is particularly graphic, even grotesque, flying in the face of our sanitized images of the healthy, anatomized body. It evokes the flesh in all its materiality. Petrarch provides a preliminary guide to a meditation on death that is the polar opposite of our command: Relax!

> So here is a test which will never play you false: every time you meditate on death without the least sign of motion, know that you have meditated in vain, as about any ordinary topic. But if in the act of meditation you find yourself suddenly grow stiff, if you tremble, turn pale, and feel as if already you endured its pains . . . [and after meditating on the Four Final Things] then you may be assured you have not meditated in vain.[26]

As to the meditation itself:

> . . . of all tremendous realities Death is the most tremendous. So true is this, that from ever of old its very name is terrible and dreadful to hear. Yet though so it is, it will not do that we hear that name but lightly, or allow the remembrance of it to slip quickly from our mind. No, we must take time to realize it. We must meditate with attention thereon. We must picture to ourselves the effect of death on each several part of our bodily frame, the cold extremities, the breast in the sweat of fever, the side throbbing with pain, the vital spirits running slower and slower as death draws near, the eyes sunken and weeping, every look filled with tears, the forehead pale and drawn, the cheeks hanging and hollow, the teeth staring and discoloured, the nostrils shrunk and sharpened, the lips foaming, the tongue foul and motionless, the palate parched and dry, the languid head and panting breast, the hoarse murmur and sorrowful sigh, the evil smell of the whole body, the horror of seeing the face utterly unlike itself.[27]

The meditative practice comes from a mentality alien to the modern mind, although in one way at least the late medieval period resembles our own. It too was a time of war and plague, when death was ever present. In our own day, when "megadeath" has been coined in the wake of two world wars, when bureaucratically organized genocide and the specter of a nuclear winter or an ecological disaster are everyday news, the practice of meditation on death should not be entirely foreign to our secular mentality. But it should not be foreign to our time for a more profound reason. Writing a generation ago, the French philosopher Gabriel Marcel discerned that the mood of our time is one of a "choking sadness."[28] Martin Heidegger found the same mood implicit in the "turning" of technology into its truth: The restoration of technology into its truth will resemble, he wrote, "what happens when, in the human realm, one gets over grief or pain."[29] The metaphor of stress has been an impediment to the recognition of this mood.[30]

I call the meditation that comes from Petrarch an "anti-stress" exercise because it makes us neither more nor less resilient to stress. Its aim is to pierce the "I" that lives under stress and to expose it to the losses that stress as a construct makes difficult to mourn. It holds up to the imagination an image of the body as bound to loss and to death, an image not of the anatomized body, fixated by embalming fluids, but an image of the body as flesh with its feelings and frailties. This vision of the dying flesh, less experienceable today than in Petrarch's time, may move us from stress to a passion for living. We do not seem able to care passionately about the world or of things unless we are enfleshed, for things reflect our flesh in their own. As historian Philippe Ariès comments:

> "We must leave behind our house, our orchards, and our gardens, dishes and vessels which the artisan engraved," wrote Ronsard, reflecting upon death. Which of us faced with death would weep over a house in Florida or a farm in Virginia? In proto-capitalist eras—in other words, in periods when the capitalist and technological mentality was being developed, the process would not be completed until the eighteenth century—man had an unreasoning, visceral love for *temporalia*, which was a blanket word including things, men, and animals.[31]

People can love things with intensity to the extent they know the impermanence of things and of themselves. Numbed, we cannot attend to the ephemeral nature of things. We need to become materialists again.[32]

THE RITUAL OF EMPTY TIME

To bring the flesh back into perception, we need a time for ritualized mourning. How can that be arranged in a world which leaves no time for anything, much less grieving? By a negative ritual, a content-less ritual that no one authorizes or plans, an unmanaged ritual, a ritual of empty time. In a moment of empty time, one can begin to listen to the story of one's flesh, and begin to reformulate the meaning of one's life. In the hearing of the story, past and future can begin to be reconciled. To what end? No one knows. The future, like empty time, cannot be managed. All we know for sure is that when we stop coping, we can grieve; and when we open our hearts to grief, we can love again. To the extent we thus stop, we step out from under stress. To stop, we must step into empty time, a ritual step for an age of technological management.

Empty time is simplified time. In order to prepare a time for mourning, we "open up" time. Time is "expensive" and vanishes to the extent we maintain ourselves under stress. The pursuit of goods leaves us time-paupers, as economist Steffan Linder has observed.[33] I offer neither a moral nor a rationalistic ground for the critique of the headstrong pursuit of wealth, but affirm that the ground of our days is of necessity psychological and spiritual. We need time for the simple life that comes from unluxurious living in order to have the empty time for grief.

The ideal of simplicity constitutes the horizon of this meditation on stress management and the vampire-like self it fosters. What is simplicity? To be simple is to stay within the bounds of necessity. I do not presume to delimit what is necessary for a human life, except to say that time is necessary. We, under stress, are time-paupers, and simplicity gives us time.[34]

THE RITUAL OF EMPTY PLACE

As empty time is necessary, so is empty place, for just as stress and its management eliminates meaningful time, so it eliminates dwelling. In a profound sense we are no place when under stress. Humans under stress live in no-man's land; like the figure of Octavio Paz's poem they say: "I'm in a hurry to be. . . . Who and what is that which moves me and who and what awaits my arrival to complete itself and to complete me? I don't know. I'm in a hurry."[35] Whatever else *place* means, it means first and foremost where the flesh is and where human dwelling occurs.[36] In an existential sense, dwelling occurs when one is at home. Being-at-home is not only or even primarily being at ease, but it is "a radical and crucial tension that emerges . . . between openness and enclosure."[37] Being at home is thus not primarily relaxation, though that may be part of it, but it is a being bound and contained and simultaneously open to the outside, to others. Among the resonances of at-homeness that are relevant here, I want to single out being at home with oneself, the polar opposite to the figure in the Paz poem cited just above. Being at home in this restricted psychological sense thus refers to the act of being intimate with oneself.[38]

A place, a dwelling, an at-homeness, is necessary for the act of grieving. Because grief enables continuity between the past and the future, it needs a place to be present, to present the persistence of the past into the future. What kind of place? Not the geometric void of stress, the formless white noise where we hurry after the chimera of energy. In conjunction with the kind of time required for transforming stress into grief, the place of grief for our lost worlds will have to be by necessity a minimal place, reached by a *via negativa*. It will be an empty place. Only such a place is appropriate to a time when old cultural forms no longer nurture the soul and the spirit, when the horrors of the age make appeals to old pieties problematic, and when the cultural forms that might exist some day have not been formulated, such that for now continuity with the past is uncertain.

The ritual of establishing an empty place has this form: in the midst of the creature comforts of our age, in the midst of the infinite number of consumer goods and services, in the midst of the techniques for accommodating our anomie to the boundless stimulation of desire, simply to greet the neediness that emerges from the core of our being with "yes." We do naught to ease the pain, but acknowledge and witness it. The "I" of stress stops when it greets with hospitality the hunger that hitherto it has called the need for energy. The hurry of stress masks this poverty, a poverty all the more profound because unrecognized. The alien world, the ambivalence toward loss, the accommodation to change—a stockpile of emptiness builds up, and not being recognized, not lived through in bereavement, feeds the frantic pace. Then, "wiped out," the cycle begins anew. To refuse energy in the name of poverty makes the celebration of grief possible. Mourning thus begins and stress ends when we are exhausted, stressed out, frazzled. At that moment, if we embrace the ideal of simplicity we can occupy the empty place that removes us from the white noise of stress. We then greet our neediness with hospitality and not with infusions of energy. To be thus impoverished is a condition no commodity can enrich; only the gifts which come freely in celebration can answer such poverty.

What constitutes such an empty place? An image of an open grave will suffice for it: an emptiness that waits to be filled, for a human gathering to celebrate by recalling the past through story and public ceremony, by acknowledging the emptiness and sadness of the present, and by hoping for a future in which the wounds of loss will be healed, the loss comprehended by new patterns of living that incorporate the past. As in the vampire stories, hope returns at the gravesite when the vampire, its animated corpse transformed again into flesh, is laid to rest. The flesh, the empty time, the empty place: imaged as an open grave, ready for mourners to begin.

How to make the celebration of loss possible? How to find the empty place that will foster connection between the past and its flesh that we have already lost with our present world of white noise? The precondition for celebration is dwelling or being-at-home. When at home, a person can host others, and the duty of the host is to offer hospitality. The host offers guests gifts, the first of which is time. With the giving of gifts people leave the domain of scarcity and escape the grip of stress. In fact, abundance proliferates to the extent that one gives gifts. Energy is not lost, because energy cannot exist in a dwelling place, where host and guest meet. To greet neediness with hospitality, we need to be at home to greet it.

Gifts are not scarce commodities. They are always essentially plentiful. With arms outstretched, backs turned to the temples of scarcity, we celebrate. "A festival is essentially a phenomenon of wealth; not, to be sure, the wealth of money, but of existential richness. Absence of calculation, in fact lavishness, is one of its elements."[39] A mentality of feasting escapes the instrumental reasoning that manages stress.

Thus enfleshed and impoverished, we celebrate our losses, not nostalgic for the past, not enthralled with the brave new world. The absence of stress is nothing positive. It exists as a negativity, an emptiness in which we are free to bid the past *adieu*. In grieving for our selves and our world, we take up a place. True, our place is filled with modern junk; it is surrounded by white noise with its swirling winds and fast lanes; it is populated by fleshless, energized, calm, stress-managing people, the time-paupers, but it is a place nonetheless in which to bury the dead and hope for the future.

NOTES

1. JoAnn Brown, "The Semantics of Profession: Metaphor and Power in the History of Psychological Testing, 1890–1929," Ph.D. diss. Univ. of Wisconsin at Madison, 1985.

2. Cited in Susan Banham, "Stress in the Workplace—What Can Be Done About It?" *Insurance Review* (May/June 1985), 12.

3. Peter Marris, *Loss and Change* (New York: Anchor Books, 1975), 31–32.

4. Ibid, p. 34.

5. Peter Marris, "The Social Impact of Stress," in *Mental Health and the Economy*, ed. L. A. Ferman and J. P. Gordus (Kalamazoo, MI: W. E. Upjohn Institute for Employment Research, 1979), 311.

6. Gregory D. May and Michael J. Kruger, "The Manager Within," *Personnel Journal* (February 1988), 57.

7. Ibid, p. 65.

8. Ibid, p. 57.

9. Edward Charlesworth and Ronald Nathan, *A Comprehensive Guide to Wellness* (New York: Atheneum, 1984), 60.

10. Ibid., 62–63.

11. James R. Beniger, *The Control Revolution* (Cambridge: Harvard University Press, 1986), 7.

12. Irving Kenneth Zola, in "Healthism and Disabling Medicalization," (in *Disabling Professions* [Boston: Marion Boyars, 1977], 65), summarizes some of the arguments that medicine has replaced religion as the source of authority on the good life and the inequities in this cult of healthism. "Basically my contention is that the increasing use of illness as a lever in the understanding of social problems represents no dramatic shift from a moral view to a neutral one but merely to an alternate strategy. . . . The problem being scrutinized and the person being charged is no less immoral for all the medical rhetoric. It or he is still a 'problem,' though the rhetoric may convince us that he and not the society is responsible, and he not the society should be changed."

13. On the creation of needs, see Ivan Illich, "Disabling Professions," in *Disabling Professions* (Boston: Marion Boyars, 1977), 11–40.

14. Aristotle *De Anima*, III, vii.

15. Anne Rice, *Interview with the Vampire* (New York: Ballantine Books, 1976), 21.

16. Ibid., p. 18.

17. Quoted in Richard Lyons, "Stress Addiction: 'Life in the Fast Lane' May Have Its Benefits," *New York Times*, late edition (21 July 1983).

18. Larry Pace and Waino Suojanen, "Addictive Type A Behavior Undermines Employee Involvement," *Personnel Journal* 67, 6 (June 1988), 40.

19. Linda Leonard, *On the Way to the Wedding* (Boston: Shambhala, 1986), 93.

20. Rice, *Vampire*, 270.

21. Hans Selye, *Stress Without Distress* (Philadelphia: Lippincott, 1974), 32.

22. Curtis Austin, "DART's Problems Shake Staff," *Dallas Times-Herald* (2 April 1989).

23. William James, *The Principles of Psychology*, Vol. I (reprint 1890), (New York: Dover Books, 1950), 292.

24. "My body is made of the same flesh as the world (it is a perceived), and moreover . . . this flesh of my body is shared by the world, the world *reflects* it, encroaches upon it and it encroaches upon the world, . . . they are in a relation of transgression or of overlapping." Maurice Merleau-Ponty, *The Visible and the Invisible*, trans. Alphonso Lingis (Evanston: Northwestern University Press, 1968), 248.

25. Robert Jay Lifton, *Death in Life: Survivors of Hiroshima* (New York: Vintage Books, 1967). Mitchell Young and Cassandra Erickson ("Cultural Impediments to Recovery: PTSD in Contemporary America," *Journal of Traumatic Stress 1*, [1988], 4) write that in this time of cultural transition, "when cultural images and symbols are inadequate, individuals may become devitalized—a sense of meaning and continuity in life becomes difficult to find." Lifton refers to this affective response as "psychic numbing" (*Death in Life*, 436).

26. Francesco Petrarcha, *Petrarch's Secret or The Soul's Conflict with Reason*, trans. W. H. Draper (London: Chatto & Windus, 1911), 34–35.

27. Ibid., 32–33.

28. Gabriel Marcel, quoted in William Luijpen, *Existential Phenomenology*, Rev. ed. (Pittsburgh: Duquesne University Press, 1969), 255.

29. Martin Heidegger, "The Turning," in *The Question Concerning Technology and Other Essays*, trans. W. Lovitt (New York: Harper Colophon, 1977), 39.

30. In *Technology as Symptom and Dream* (New York: Routledge & Kegan Paul, 1989), scholar and psychotherapist Robert Romanyshyn calls for

an "ethic of sadness" as a way to come to terms with the depression that plagues people in a technological society.

31. Philippe Ariès, *Western Attitudes toward Death from the Middle Ages to the Present*, trans. P. Ranum (Baltimore: Johns Hopkins University Press, 1974), 45.

32. For the meaning of materialist in this sense, see Alan Watts, *Does It Matter? Essays on Man's Relation to Materiality* (New York: Vintage Books, 1970): "The commonly accepted notion that Americans are materialists is pure bunk. A materialist is one who loves material, a person devoted to the enjoyment of the physical and immediate present. By this definition, most Americans are abstractionists. They *hate* material, and convert it as swiftly as possible into mountains of junk and clouds of poisonous gas" (p. 29). Watt's book is rich with such comments, though I take issue with his depiction of the body as a swirling dance of energy.

33. Steffan Linder *The Harried Leisure Class* (New York: Columbia University Press, 1970).

34. In a related critique of luxury, Langdom Winner, "Techné and Politeai," in *The Whale and the Reactor: A Search for Limits in an Age of High Technology* (Chicago: University of Chicago Press, 1986), 57, writes: "A crucial failure in modern political thought and political practice has been an inability or unwillingness even to begin . . . the critical evaluation and control of our society's technical constitution. The silence of liberalism on this issue is matched by an equally obvious neglect in Marxist theory. Both persuasions have enthusiastically sought freedom in sheer material plenitude, welcoming whatever technological means (or monstrosities) seemed to produce abundance the fastest. It is, however, a mistake to construct one sociotechnical system after another in the blind faith that each will turn out to be politically benign. Many crucial choices about the forms and limits of our regimes of instrumentality must be enforced at the founding, at the genesis of each new technology." Earlier in the essay, he indicates how the Founding Fathers of the United States, Jefferson in particular, warned against the heedless pursuit of luxuries as a threat to republican virtues.

35. Octavio Paz, *Aguila o Sol?/Eagle or Sun?*, trans. E. Weinberger (New York: New Directions, 1976), 75.

36. For a discussion of "place," see Edward Casey, *Remembering: A Phenomenological Study* (Bloomington: Indiana University Press, 1987).

37. Frank Buckley, "An Approach to a Phenomenology of At-Homeness," in *Duquesne Studies in Phenomenological Psychology: Volume I*, ed. A. Giorgi, W. F. Fischer and R. von Eckartsberg (Pittsburgh: Duquesne University Press, 1971), 207. For further reading on the phenomenology of at-homeness, see Gaston Bachelard, *The Poetics of Space*, trans. C. Gaudin (Boston: Beacon, 1969).

38. An age of stress is thus an age of depression, insofar as depression is a pathology of not being at home, of longing for a lost or even a nonexistent home. After all, under stress we are "exiles." For consideration of the theme of homelessness and depression in the American psyche, see Robert Romanyshyn and Brian Whalen, "Depression and the American Search for Home," in *Psychopathologies of the Modern Self*, ed. M. D. Levin (Albany: SUNY Press, 1988).

39. Joseph Pieper, *In Tune with the World: A Theory of Festivity*, trans. R. and C. Winston (New York: Harcourt, Brace & World, 1965), 15.

7

The Materialization of the
Body: A History of Western
Medicine, A History in
Process

INTRODUCTION

More than once in the course of writing this essay, I have been
intrigued by the image of appearing suddenly in magician's gear
before you, the reader, of doffing my top hat, of tapping it with my
cane, and of drawing a body out of the hat.

Clearly there are two senses in which a materialization of the
body can be understood.

Actually materializing a body out of a hat might nicely epitomize certain changes currently underway in the traditional Western
conception of the body insofar as those changes, like the magician's
sleight of hand, are an unexpected and fascinating turn of events. Of
course the traditional, strictly physicalist, conception of the body

still predominates in Western culture, but this hard-line materialist conception *is* shifting, moving away from a construal of the body as mere material object or dumb show of movement. The coming into being of a new construct of the body has formidable implications. The deeply encrusted Cartesian view that has long characterized Western metaphysical thought, and long informed cultural practice, is being challenged—by new culturally-expansive practices, by new medical research findings, by original and deep questionings of received wisdom about the body. A radically different valorization as well as conceptualization of the body is in the making.

The potential for this new valorization and conceptualization has been there all along; our minds, so to speak, have simply been too busily engaged elsewhere to notice. They have in fact been busily attending to the needs and treatments of an already materialized body—keeping it fit, feeding it oat bran, counting its pulse, monitoring its blood pressure, x-raying its bones, ultra-sounding its tissues, and so on. This strictly material body has been progressively constructed by Western medicine over the past several centuries, particularly the present one, and is still in the process of being built. Indeed, our twentieth-century American materialist conception of bodies has in great measure evolved hand in hand with the development of Western medicine. The relationship is not surprising. A history of medicine—Western, Eastern, aboriginal, or whatever—is a conceptual history of the body. The reverse is also true. The concept of the body in any culture at any time is shaped by medical beliefs and practices, or more precisely by an accepted medical, and in turn, societal, even cosmological, conception of what it is to be a sick and healthy body. Have we been invaded by demons? Are we out of sync with the universe? Are our emotions playing havoc with us? Or is it our liver?

How a sick or diseased body is explained, understood, ministered to, and cured, become culturally engrained habits of thought and practice. At the same time, the very habits themselves engender a certain metaphysical *Zeitgeist*. In our own case, a staggering array of scientific information about the body, and a staggering array of correlative technological devices and pharmaceutical compounds—arrays which together define twentieth-century American (Medical Association) medicine—go hand in hand with a thoroughly physico-chemical conception of what it is to be a human body. Put in historical perspective, this means that our present-day Western concept of disease and illness has not only a complex scientific and technological history behind it, but an ideationally consistent one as well. It is an ideational history subsumed both in the term *materialization* and in that term's collateral dualistic metaphysics.

The materialization of the body—in the literal sense of progressively reducing the body to matter in the consummate way that a bone or a shell is progressively fossilized—of necessity demands certain metaphysical accommodations, since to account for what it is to be human, whether a sick one or a healthy one, requires accounting for something more than a material body. It requires, for example, an explanation of how a pill composed of nothing but sugar can cure ulcer patients,[1] and how it is that what a person designates *reluctance* to get out of bed on a certain morning has a certain bodily feel about it that is altogether different from, say, the bodily feel of anticipation or excitement. The historian–philosopher of Western medical science is thus required to consider the metaphysics entailed in the materialization of the body, putting that metaphysics itself in historical perspective, assessing its truth, and tracing out its implications. My own theses in this historico-philosophical enterprise are first, that materialization is the metaphysical corollary of animism, animism in the simple sense of being imbued with life—animated; and second, that materialization of the body, as epitomized in the prevalent twentieth-century Western view, eventuates in both an eroded sense of self and an eroded sense of responsibility. The two theses combined affirm that, when measured on a scale from metaphysical miser to metaphysical philanthropist, a headstrong materialization of the body registers at the extreme of metaphysical miserliness. Radical materialization, the polar opposite of a spirited animism in which the inanimate is everywhere infused with life, takes the living juice out of animate bodies, leaving only bare bones and pulp.

The combined theses will provide the connecting thread in what follows—an abbreviated chronicling of the history of Western medicine as a metaphysical history of the body. I will highlight the metaphysical construct by juxtaposing Western and Eastern (ancient, Far, and Middle) construals of sickness, and twentieth-century Western and ancient Greek conceptions of certain bodily realities, among which the breath. These juxtapositionings will show certain differences in the way physiognomic aspects of the body are regarded, and that even in our quite recent Western historical past, physiognomic properties of the body were heeded as such. The pulse, for example, was read directly as perceived, in ways comparable to the ways in which it is read in traditional Chinese medicine. Physiognomic properties ascertainable by touch were thus not perceptually and conceptually compromised by materialist notions that either sanctioned their dismissal or transformed them into strictly measurable things.

A GENERAL HIGHLIGHTING OF THE MATERIALIST CONCEPTION

The proportions to which the body is materialized are reflected in the proportions to which it is de-animated and in turn the proportions to which an animating substance, force, or entity is required in order that the livingness of living bodies be explained. We might characterize the ratio in extreme terms by saying that if it is only my liver, then it is nothing to me. It is only a matter of matter—not to say of time since all material things decay. Being only a matter of matter, proper material treatment will take care of it. *Only where sickness is not conceived as something purely material is the medical response to it not strictly material.* Consider, for example, an ancient Egyptian cure for a cold. It is an invocation, a rather lusty one: "Depart, cold, son of a cold, thou who breakest the bones, destroyest the skull, makest ill the seven openings of the head! . . . Go out on the floor, stink, stink, stink!"[2]

Ancient Egyptians clearly did not regard a cold simply as a noxious material state to which the flesh is liable. A cold was itself an animate presence in the body, a presence having powers over the body, but a presence which also could be inveighed against and driven out. Contrast this view with the view of a twentieth-century Western doctor who says, "It's your liver, madam." The doctor relegates sickness to a singular, large, glandular piece of body tissue, an "organ," as it is called, a structure geared to the performance of certain functions, but whose functions I have never been and never will be privy to, indeed, an organ I have never seen nor felt, an organ neither I nor my doctor ever conceive of talking to, or appealing to directly in any way. In all these senses my sick liver is out of my control. What controls sick livers are certain substances compounded by pharmacists and prescribed by doctors. The way to health in present-day Western medicine is not by invocation but by ingestion.

To put the metaphysical point in further perspective, consider a common experience. Suppose you are climbing a hill and begin to feel an ache in your mid-thighs. Are you surprised? Certainly not. You relegate the ache to muscles and the build-up of lactic acid and give no more thought to the matter. Contrast this lack of surprise with the sequences of questions posed in a book called *Problems,* a book found in the works of Aristotle:

"Why is it that in descending a slope we feel the strain most in the thighs, and in ascending in the legs? Is it because in ascending the strain is due to the raising of the body?"[3]

The composite question is related to several earlier sequences of questions:

"Why is it that in ascending a slope our knees feel the strain, and in descending our thighs? Is it because when we ascend we throw the body upwards and the jerk of the body from the knees is considerable, and so we feel the strain in the knees? But in going downhill, because the weight is carried by the legs, we are supported by our thighs, and so they feel the strain."[4]

Or again,

"Why is it that on journeys the middle of the thigh is the part which feels the strain most? Is it because in anything that is prolonged and continuous and fixed the strain falls most upon the centre, and so it is most likely to break at that point?"[5]

Or finally,

"Why is it that the thighs feel fatigue more than the legs? Is it because they are nearer to the part of the body which contains the excrement, so that, when that part overflows with heat owing to the movement, the thighs contract more readily and to a greater extent?"[6]

In the original composite question and first related series of questions, aches and pains are connected with what a person is doing, specifically with the bodily nature of the doing: in going uphill we are "raising" the body; "we throw the body upwards and the jerk of the body from the knees is considerable." In the last two related sequences of questions, explanations of aches are connected with the ways of the physical world: on the one hand, in any motion or activity that goes on for a long time without surcease, the greatest pressure is felt at the center of the thing moving; on the other hand, a body in movement produces heat, in turn can overheat excrement, and in turn can make spatially contiguous body parts like thighs contract more strongly and readily. The last two explanations are material explanations, but non-reductive ones. They hinge on *spatial relationships,* spatial relationships obtaining between centers and peripheries in the case of stresses and strains, and spatial-elemental relationships obtaining between movement and heat, and between excrement and the proximity of thighs in the case of fatigue. In effect, thighs *feel* strain and *feel* fatigue because certain spatial or spatial-elemental relationships obtain with respect to the world generally and to the human body in particular.

The fact that the authorship of *Problems* is in question—it may not have been written by Aristotle—is not important. What matters is (1) that 2,300 years ago, people felt the same aches and pains we feel; (2) that like us they noticed these aches and pains coincident with the doing of certain activities; but (3) that unlike us, they had no notion of muscles and how they work and thus wondered how it is that such aches came to be. In short, what has changed in 2,300 years is not the body and our experience of it, but ways in which we conceive it. What has in consequence changed is how the healthy body is understood and how it is treated when it becomes ill.

That the concept of the body should change is strange. It is not, after all, a matter of ascertaining the nature of something outside of us—is the world not round rather than flat?; is the sum of the angles of a triangle not 200 instead of 180 degrees? It is a question of our very selves, of what all humans experience in some quite fundamental ways three-hundred-and-sixty-five-days-per-year. Why should the fact that present-day Western humans have found out in more and more exacting *material* terms what is inside the body precipitate an astounding change in how humans conceive of themselves as living beings? How, given the fact that in a quite fundamental sense, human bodily experience does not change over time, can there be a wholly different metaphysics of the body—different understandings and explanations of material insides, yes, but how can these different *material* understandings and explanations of insides be so dominant as to lead to a radically material metaphysical construal of the living body? Can metaphysics be relative in this way when it comes to conceiving something so basic as what it is to be a human body, conceiving what in actuality we are and have been for at least the past 40,000 years?

People who have dissected human and/or nonhuman animals sometimes testify to a profound and unsettling experience. When they first cut open a cadaver they are struck not so much by the wonder of what is there but by the wonder that that is *all* that is there. Just this maze of tissue and bone? Just this oozy, pulpy labyrynth of flesh, tubules, ligaments, and no more? Is this *all*? A radical materialization of the body can follow relatively fast on the heels of this experience—but only on the condition one forgets that a corpse, or even an anesthetized person, is not a living body. Celsus, a Roman physician of the second century A.D., expressed just this realization when he affirmed that an examination of a dead body tells us nothing of the living body. His concluding reasons for railing against the cutting open of corpses and dying people in order to learn something about living bodies run as follows:

> For when the body had been laid open, colour, smoothness, softness, hardness and all similars would not be such as they were when the body was untouched; because bodies, even when uninjured, yet often change in appearance . . . from fear, pain, want of food, indigestion, weariness and a thousand other mediocre affections; it is much more likely that the more internal parts, which are far softer, and to which the very light is something novel, should under the most severe of woundings, in fact mangling, undergo changes. Nor is anything more foolish . . . than to suppose that whatever the condition of the part of a man's body in life, it will also be the same when he is dying, nay, when he is already dead. . . . It follows, therefore, that the medical man just plays the cut-throat, not that he learns what our viscera are like when we are alive. . . .

Celsus affirms in conclusion that "an observant practitioner learns . . . whilst striving for health; . . . he learns in the course of a work of mercy, what others would come to know by means of dire cruelty."[7]

MATERIALIZATION, ANATOMY, AND HEALTH: SPECIFICS FROM WESTERN HISTORY

Materialization of the body began in earnest in the sixteenth century when dissection of humans became legal in the Western world. Before this there were attempts at dissection—as just noted, Celsus speaks of them with horror. By the time human dissection was legalized, however, dissection of nonhuman animals had been carried out for centuries, though not of course for medical reasons. For example, in Babylonia, the liver of sacrificial animals, particularly the liver of sheep, was of great portent. It was studied with an eye to divination: "If the gall-bladder were swollen on the right side, it pointed to an increase of strength of the King's army, and was favorable; . . . If the bile duct was long, it pointed to a long life. Gall-stones . . . might be favorable, or unfavorable."[8] "Hepatoscopy," as it is called, was widely practiced from as early as 3,000 B.C. in Babylonia. A clay model of a sheep's liver complete with divination text dated *circa* 2,000 B.C. testifies to the seriousness and complexity of the practice.

Clearly, for Babylonians the liver was not simply a hunk of matter—much less a physiologic organ; it was the center of life. Sir William Osler, a major historian of medicine, states that "Of all the organs inspected in a sacrificial animal the liver, from its size, position and richness in blood, impressed the early observers as the most important of the body. Probably on account of the richness in blood it came to be regarded as the seat of life—indeed, the seat of the soul."[9] He goes on to say that "The liver being the centre of vitality—the seat of the mind, therefore, as well as of the emotions—it becomes in the case of the sacrificial animal, either directly identical with the mind of the god who accepts the animal, or . . . a mirror in which the god's mind is reflected. . . . If, therefore, one can read the liver of the sacrificial animal, one enters, as it were, into the workshop of the divine will."[10] Western humans are a long way from a valorization of the liver as the source of life. Indeed, over the past 5,000 years there has been a dramatic reshuffling of priorities among the organs of the body: from liver to heart to brain— to say nothing of Woody Allen's axiology.

Not only were the nature and significance of organs profoundly reconceptualized with the advent of dissection. Illness and health were profoundly reconceptualized also. The significance of the conceptual shift is best appreciated by contrasting ancient Greek humoral theory and present-day Western systems theory, a theory based upon a belief in the localization of functions.

There were medical theories before ancient Greek humoral theory, but ancient Greek humoral theory is generally agreed to have held sway for 2,000 years after its definitive formulation by the acknowledged father of Western medicine, Hippocrates of Cos, in the fifth century B.C.[11] The enduring centrality of humoral theory to explanations of illness and health is well-documented, for example, in *Regimen Sanitatis of Salernum*, a book that detailed in engaging poetic form popular health procedures, and which issued around 1140 from the acknowledged center of medical learning in the Middle Ages, the famous School of Salernum in the south of Italy. Translated into English in the early 1600s, the book amply documents the sway of humoral theory. We read, for example, that "Foure Humours raigne within our bodies wholly, / And these compared to foure elements."[12] (We also read that "Joy, temperance and repose slam the door on the doctor's nose.")[13] Humoral theory is even now evident in our current English speech; we still speak of being in a good or bad humor, of humoring someone, and the like. Moreover as late as 1921 Sir William remarked that "echoes of [humoral theory] are still to be heard in popular conversations on the nature of disease."[14]

Empedocles, a Greek physician-philosopher and forerunner of Hippocrates, laid the foundation of ancient Greek humoral theory in his theory of the four basic elements of Nature—air, fire, earth, and water—and their attendant basic qualities: heat, cold, dryness, moistness. In relating the four basic macrocosmic elements to the four basic elements of living beings—blood, phlegm, yellow bile, and black bile—Hippocratic medicine affirmed that humans were coterminous with the world. Though variously esteemed in the Hippocratic Corpus with respect to their significance in maintaining health and in treating sickness, heat, cold, moistness, and dryness retained their status as fundamental qualities of both macrocosmic and microcosmic elements.

Hippocratic medical theory was anchored in the concept of the proportionality of the elements—in the concept of their harmony or disharmony. In other words, sickness signalled a disproportionate relationship among the humoral elements and their attendant qualities. A particular disease was the result of an overabundance or deficiency of the sanguine (associated with the heart and with the hot and moist), the phlegmatic (associated with the brain and with the cold and moist), the bilious (associated with the liver and with the hot and dry), and/or the melancholic (associated with the spleen and with the cold and dry). As is apparent, the bodily humors were related to principal bodily organs. The latter were considered the reservoir of the former, that is, humors were fluid substances. As such, one humoral fluid could drain off from one organ and travel to another, at the same time being replaced at the first organ by another humoral fluid. By over-accumulations and depletions, bodily humors caused illness. Supporting evidence for the movement of humoral fluids came from everyday life: just as water on a table will flow to the edge if a wet streak is made in it, but will otherwise remain intact, so bodily humors will flow off to another reservoir if disturbed in some way, but will otherwise remain where they are.[15] Analogical reasoning linked the unseen ways of the body to the perceived ways of the world, and thereby explained them.

Proportionality also anchored the treatment of disease. For Hippocrates and his followers, detailed knowledge of the body was not essential; what was essential was knowledge of the course of a disease and of the means whereby the effects of the disordered humors could be counteracted. To this end, diet was primary. Food was *concocted* in the stomach and intestines, concocted in the now metaphoric sense of "cooking up" something, as in concocting a scheme or a story. The concocting of food affected the internal heat or innate hot matter of the body (the *pneuma*, of which more later), but food also powerfully affected persons in different ways according to their humoral constitution. Second to diet was exercise, which included not only the activities of gymnastics but also reading aloud and singing. As with the humors themselves, proportion was again important. Moreover disease could result from an overabundance or deficiency of exercise in relation to food or food in relation to exercise. The general idea and guiding principle was that disease comes from nature and is cured by nature. In other words, given proper food and exercise, it is of the nature of the body itself to restore itself to health.

Finally, proportionality figured in the various relationships of the sick person to the environment and surrounding people. While humoral theory placed great emphasis on the healing powers of the body itself, the body was not considered something apart from the world about it. On the contrary, a body was in and of the world and as such was affected by other bodies, by the atmosphere, the seasons, the air, the water, the city, and so on. The well-known credo of the Hippocratic doctor points up the importance of these environmental relationships: "Life is brief; art is long; the opportune moment is fleeting. Experiment is risky, and judgment difficult. Hence one must not only oneself do what the situation requires, but the patients also and all who are present. External conditions also must be right."[16]

In sum, ancient Greek medicine was structured on the concept of proportion, which included a harmonic relationship among elements and their qualities, a harmonic relationship among treatment variables, a harmonic relationship between living creatures and the world about them. Thus, as the Hippocratic book, *Breaths*, tells us, "Medicine is substraction [*sic*] and addition, substraction of what is in excess, addition of what is wanting. He who performs these acts best is the best physician; he who is farthest removed therefrom is also farthest removed from the art."[17]

Present-day Western medicine, in its insistence on discrete systems—not only the standard digestive, reproductive, and circulatory systems, but the immunological, neuromuscular, and hormonal systems, the parasympathetic and sympathetic nervous systems, the multiple organ systems, the innumerable chemical systems, and more—is far removed from such harmonies. Perhaps nowhere does the construct of a multi-systematized body become more reified than in the brain where systems as *centers of activity* are localized. Indeed, one could speak of a cerebral mall. There is, for example, a sleep center, a respiratory center, a pleasure center, an emotion center, and a language center. Even a learning center might be designated if frontal lobe functions in their identified role in "higher intelligence" were considered. Each of these centers is minutely defined, the anatomical substrate being given in, for laypersons, body-bogglingly precise terms. To illustrate the astonishing exactness, I will quote a passage from a series of lectures I choreographed and performed some years ago. The passage was on neurophysiology and was taken from an actual, but long-since forgotten text. It went as follows:

> Generally speaking, the respiratory center encompasses the medial and lateral reticular fields overlying the rostral half to two-thirds of the inferior olivary nuclei. In terms of more easily identifiable external landmarks, the center underlies the caudal third of the floor of the fourth ventricle, from the posterior borders of the auditory tubercles, rostrally, to the obex, or slightly below caudally.

Each system or center clearly has a localized place on the body chart. "A place for everything, and everything in its place," an adage found in Samuel Smith's book *Thrift* published in 1875,[18] admirably captures the pith of the conceptual scheme of present-day Western medicine. Though materialization of the body began much earlier than 1875, the concern with place is apparent from the very beginning of those human dissections in the mid-1500s by Vesalius, the father of modern anatomy, which first revealed remarkably organized systems of muscle, bone, and nerve. Physiological specifications followed closely upon the identification and localization of these systems. William Harvey's discovery of the circulation of the blood in 1628 is a landmark instance. For every structure, a function; for every function, a structure. Once human dissections became the medical rule, the body was progressively *organ-ized* into discrete functional systems.

Given this conceptual and practical framework of localization—of *place*—it is not surprising that present-day Western medicine treats illnesses as specialities of the body. (And what else can specialties create but specialists?) Hearts have strokes, colons have cancer, stomachs have acid, brains have lesions, intestines have diverticulosis. A place for everything and everything in its place. In such a scheme, the range of possibilities is limited. If a certain locale is dysfunctional, then it is that locale, and that locale only, that is pinpointed for treatment. Of course the problem of side effects is not infrequent. That there are side effects should say something basic to us about the nature of the body. Basic insights aside, side effects also raise a perplexing question about treatment, a question once voiced by a comedian: How do the pills we take know where to go? The male comedian posed the question generally, then specifically in terms of taking Midol. But how is it that pills know where it hurts— or where the wild things are? It is one thing to regard the body as being made up of distinct parts with distinct functions and distinct possible dysfunctions, but it is quite another to join this notion of localization to mere pills as if mere pills were familiar with the general layout of the body, and when ingested, knew precisely where to go and how to get there. However naive sounding, the question is not unrelated to fundamental questions posed by immunological reactions. How does a thoroughly material body know what is *it* from what is not *it*? How can a strictly material body, which we are told is everywhere made basically of the same molecular stuff, *know itself as a unique individual*? More pointedly in terms of localization of function, how can a strictly material body, which we are told is everywhere made basically of the same discrete systems, *know itself as a single individual*? Where precisely in a strictly material body does specialization end and wholeness begin?

The passage from a humorally organ-ized body to a functionally organ-ized one marks an incisive step in the passage to radical materialization. Only in our folk anatomy and physiology— the epithet *folk* being for many present-day philosophers an opprobrious qualifier for anything falling below the level of twentieth-century Western science—do vestiges of animism surface, as when we feel or do something halfheartedly or with a full heart or with no heart at all, or when we have no stomach for something, give a gut response, or turn a deaf ear. By the same vestigial tokens, only in our folk linguistics do we organ-ize things and the world, including our own faculties, in the image of our own bodily organs—as when we conceive the liver the seat of cowardice and the heart the seat of love, or when we speak of the brow of a hill, the mouth of a river, the bowels of the earth, or the limbs of a tree.[19] In such folk moments a strictly material body composed of localized functions and dysfunctions is far from view. We might justly say that in its place is the original *Organon* body—the original animate "instrument" in whose image we first think, reason, and symbolize the world.[20]

FURTHER CONCRETIZATIONS AND THEIR IMPLICATIONS

We can concretize the passage to materialization further by considering extremes in the way the relationship between illness and ill person is conceived: on the one hand, there is a medical science in which persons are intimately connected with their illnesses; on the other hand, there is a medical science in which persons and their illnesses are only functionally, perhaps even only contingently, related. A medicine such as one in which bodily humors hold sway is one in which the body disposes a person tempermentally—toward the sanguine, for example, or toward the choleric—as well as constitutionally, that is, toward a certain state of health or illness. Accordingly, if there is any disequilibrium in the distribution of the humors—any illness—basic changes are required in the afflicted person's daily regimen: more fluid is needed, certain exercises are to be undertaken, and so on. The harmony of the body must be reestablished, and it can be reestablished only by specific efforts of the person him/herself. In this sense, the person redresses his or her own ills. Just such personal involvement is apparent not only in accounts of ancient Greek humoral theory, but in the practice of certain present-day non-Western medical sciences. In Tibetan medicine, for example, wind—or air—bile, and phlegm are the three natural humors of the body, and they can accumulate or dissipate to ill effect. In *Health Through Balance*, Dr. Yeshi Donden, personal physician to the Dalai Lama, writes that "[you] should avoid the two conditions giving rise to illness; unsuitable eating habits and unsuitable behavior."[21] Such habits and behavior adversely affect the humors, and not just in themselves, but in conjunction with the seasons, for example, and with one's age. Here too, then, a person redresses his/her own ills by attending to the body, which means changing baneful ways of living to life-enhancing ones, and in turn reestablishing the proper ratio among the humors and their qualities.

If we contrast this notion of sickness and treatment with one at the other extreme, one in which illness and treatment are both localized, in which diet and exercise are quite secondary to fast-acting pills and even surgery, and in which a person is actively involved in the cure of his/her illness only to such proverbial extents as taking two aspirin and calling the doctor in the morning, then it becomes clear why sickness as a life-encroaching reality seems commonly conceived, by American Westerners at least, mainly in terms of temporary withdrawal, that is, as a purely provisional cessation of usual everyday living habits. As soon as the sickness is over, the person springs back into action, resuming the life that was left in abeyance by the intrusive sickness. There is little or no thought of the body, not to say of oneself, being out of harmony in some way. There is commonly only the thought of the body being for some reason vulnerable, at this particular time, manifesting these particular symptoms, and so on. Indeed, "Why me? No one else caught a cold or got sick." On this view it appears that our body has betrayed us. On the former view, in which illness is conceived as a disharmony—whether a humorally based disharmony or not—it appears more likely that we have betrayed our bodies. At a metaphysical level, the contrast in views raises the question "Which comes first: me or my body?" or more basically still, "What am I?"

There is another historically and philosophically interesting, and indeed, chilling, dimension of a personally detached attitude toward illness. It is well exemplified by current interpretations of what is designated "the serotonin system." Serotonin is a neurotransmitter that stimulates nerve cells in the brain. It has been artificially manufactured and used to treat depression, anxiety, overeating, and schizophrenia. But it is also *causally* implicated in the production of migraine headaches.[22] How it works is obviously far from fully understood. As a matter of fact, a recent issue of *Science News* was devoted to "Serotonin's Tantalizing Tangles," and though a reporter wrote that "Nothing is black-and-white when it comes to the gray matter of the brain," in this same issue, one of the articles stated that "behavioral studies now appear to link flaws in the serotonin system to violent suicide attempts and aggression."[23]

What exactly does the serotonin system control? Apparently murder, among other things. Convicted male murderers who killed without premeditation—in other words, impulsively—have been found to have chronically low levels of 5-HIAA, a "breakdown product" of serotonin. Furthermore, men who had murdered more than once had lower levels than those who had murdered only once. In addition, men who had committed "violent offenses"—of an unspecified nature in the article—likewise had abnormally low levels of 5-HIAA, while those who, after prison release, went on to commit more violent offenses were reported to have the "lowest levels" of all. The male-murderer researchers concluded that "a deficiency in serotonin metabolism may cause an inability to control impulses, leading to violent behavior." *"An inability to control impulses."* Powerful, absolving words reminiscent of the person who murdered a San Francisco mayor and councilman several years back and who was given a light sentence on the grounds that he had eaten too much sugar-rich junk food.

Some years ago it was popular to blame one's parents for one's ills and actions. It is quite another thing to blame one's own body chemicals. A reasonable case can be made for maintaining responsibility for one's actions and one's life even in the face of overwhelmingly negative parental odds. A case can hardly be made against overwhelmingly negative chemical odds. At this strictly material level, one is unequivocally captive of one's body; one does whatever it commands. In this current twentieth-century American scenario, illness of whatever sort—including the metaphorical 'sickness' of murder—is simply an event played out by the body of the helpless person it belongs to. In a very short time we will likely find the slogan "guns don't kill, people do," amended to proclaim "people don't kill, body chemicals do." Such is actually already the explanation given of poet Sylvia Plath's suicide. As her doctor avers, if "brain chemistry" was responsible for her final act, "then nothing and no one could have saved her and nobody bears any blame."[24]

Given the ethical implications of the reigning scenario, materialization, far from being the impeccably rational scientific doctrine it is reputed to be, is suffused by irrationalism: the irrationalism of a subject whose behavior is out of control; the irrationalism of a subject who has nothing to answer for; the irrationalism of a subject who in fact is not there. In a critical respect, the scenario brings us close to Celsus's views about a medical science based on corpses and dying people: How much does Western medicine know about *living* bodies? How much does Western medicine treat *living* bodies? Studies of placebos, for example, show that humans respond to something not just *more*, but to something *other*, than chemicals. They respond to the color of pills, the size of pills, and to the credibility of their physicians, for example, and their response is furthermore very much tied, too, to their beliefs about whether the pills they are going to take are going to work.[25] There is no lack of subjects in the literature on placebos; they are incontestably there in every study. Only lack of acknowledgment of the patient as person (and more generally, of such things as placebos and placebo effects) prevents their recognition.[26] Given the typical American doctor's predominant concern with strictly material bodies, we should in truth more aptly refer today not to our personal physician but to our impersonal one.

There is a deep irony in the fact that those non-Western and early Western medical doctrines which take the patient as person seriously are presently regarded naive and unscientific. Consider just a few of the aspects of the patient that were attended to by an ancient Greek physician in order to make a diagnosis: the talk, the manner, and the silence of the patient, his or her thoughts, sleep, dreams, urine, vomit, belchings, silent and audible flatulence, breathing, coughs, sputa, mode of life, customs, and more, including his or her memory, attitude in standing, behaviors such as plucking at the bed-clothes, and temperament.[27] Historian of Greek science, William Heidel, states that the object of diagnosis for the Hippocratic physician "was to obtain a total unified picture of the patient's condition . . . because the whole body was felt to be involved in any ill that befell it."[28] It is clear from the foregoing list of aspects attended to that the whole body to which Heidel refers is the whole *living* body—the patient as person. Perhaps precisely because the whole living body was taken into account in pre-twentieth-century Western medicine—perhaps precisely because the suffering person was taken seriously—we are left with a historical record at all. In other words, notwithstanding all the gaps in anatomical/ physiological knowledge, and notwithstanding the lack of insights derivable from the germ theory of medicine, *something* was right about ancient Greek and earlier forms of Western medicine, as it is uncontrovertably right about non-Western medicines whose anatomical and physiological anchorage is by Western standards wanting. Moreover in admittedly hyperbolic, but not on that account wholly fanciful terms, something must have been right about all those earlier forms of medicine or we ourselves would not be here today. We are certainly not the result of exclusively healthy persons' surviving, all the sick ones having died off, since we ourselves suffer from many of the same ills as those earlier peoples did: tonsillitis, dysentery, edema, diseases of the intestinal tract, scurvy, inflammation of the lungs, tetanus, and epilepsy.

It is of particular interest to point out something concerning the power of belief in the context of treating the patient as person. If early Greek physicians believed in the curative powers of the body itself, as the Hippocratic Corpus shows, then that belief must have played a central role in a person's regaining his/her health, and this for at least two reasons. First, if early Greek physicians believed in the curative powers of the body itself, then it is absurd not to think that their patients did also. Whether verbally expressed or a tacit element of the culture, the physicians' belief must have in some way been communicated to their patients. This means that patients themselves would likely have believed that their health was in their own hands, that whatever their illness, it was literally in their power to restore themselves to health. Second, belief in the curative powers of the body may be likened to belief in the curative powers of a pill. As noted above, studies of placebos have shown that if a person believes in the efficacy of the pill he or she is taking, then that person is likely to be helped by the pill. The same must be true if one believes in the efficacy—the restorative powers—of one's own body. Thus, rather than being considered a quaint, naive, and unscientific idea today, a belief in the healing powers of the body itself is in actuality a formidable medical variable, a variable to be reckoned with in the treatment of illness.[29]

Pre-twentieth-century Western medicine clearly took the environment as well as the suffering person seriously. A further deep irony thus lies in the fact that twentieth-century Westerners become sick from an inattention to those very aspects of life earlier Western medical practices recognized, and many non-Western medical practices recognize, as central: the air, the water, the soil, the seasons, differences in the character and quality of life as determined by the place one lives, and so on. Jean-Baptiste Lamarck's intriguingly perspicacious remark—that we die when we have ingested too much of the environment—appropriately and unsettlingly puts the irony in sharp relief: the twentieth-century environment Westerners (or at least Americans) create and ingest, all the way from incessant violence in popular movie fare and television, to acid rain, polluted waters, industrial waste, and more, ultimately sickens and destroys life. We are learning in arrears the truth of the observation that "external conditions must also be right," that what we create and ingest may be out of harmony with healthy living bodies and a life-enhancing world, and that in a very real sense, the environment is us. Medicine, from this extended vantage point, is far from being a matter of prescribing pills or recommending surgery. Medicine is rather something close to what Aristotle had in mind when he remarked, at the conclusion of his discussion and explanation of respiration, that: "As to health and disease, not only the physician but also the natural scientist must, up to a point, give an account of their causes. The extent to which these two differ and investigate diverse provinces must not escape us, since facts show that their inquiries are, to a certain extent, at least co-terminous. For those physicians who are cultivated and learned make some mention of natural science, and claim to derive their principles from it, while the most accomplished investigators into nature generally push their studies so far as to conclude with an account of medical principles."[30] Natural science in Aristotle's time was, of course, the province of such persons as Aristotle himself, persons concerned to understand all aspects of nature, from the motion of heavenly bodies to the motion of human ones. In this natural science, living creatures were part of the natural world; and the natural world was not something separate from living creatures. While it is true that Western medicine today is co-terminous with the natural sciences, it is co-terminous in a completely different sense.

MATERIALIZATION AND ITS PROSPECTS

Three final but brief considerations will be adduced to sum up the materialization of the body—a history in process—and to point toward a possible future. The considerations center on the pulse, on the breath, and on organs and functions. Together they will highlight what was once present, what has since been lost, and what may yet resurface, though in different conceptual guise, in Western medical practice.

It is fairly common knowledge that an acupuncturist is concerned with physiognomic aspects of the pulse and that what is felt is read as an expression of the health of certain bodily organs, organs not in our present-day structural/functional Western sense, but in the sense of dynamic interrelated orbs of energy. Thus, a "systematic correspondence" exists between what the acupuncturist feels with a certain degree of pressure on a particular wrist and the character of a certain organ or energy sphere.[31]

Though not tranplanted as such from China, a physiognomically-readable and -read pulse was until relatively recently of central diagnostic importance in the history of Western medicine. The pulse was felt and read physiognomically at the time of Galen in the second century; it was still felt and read physiognomically in the eighteenth century,[32] and even in the early twentieth century. Physician W. H. Broadbent's highly esteemed book, *The Pulse*, published in 1896, attests to a thoroughgoing physiognomic attention to the pulse. Earlier, in the late 1600s and early 1700s, Sir John Floyer, an English physician, studied the pulse and in 1707 published a two-volume work called *The Physician's Pulse-Watch*. Influenced by

Galen's humoral theory and by Galen's discovery that both heart and arteries contained blood, and influenced as well by the central role of the pulse in Chinese medical practice, Floyer attempted to correlate experienced variations in pulse rate with humoral theory. To this end he designed a pulse-watch by which he could keep accurate count of the pulse. He wrote, for example, that at 65–70 beats per minute, the pulse is "cold" in the first degree. "It is associated with the PHLEGMATIC disposition, and caused by cold air, idleness, sadness, fear, cool meats, and water drinking." At 75–80 beats per minute, the pulse is "hot" in the first degree: It is "associated with the CHOLERIC disposition; it is caused by hot seasons, hot air, exercise, passions, cards, study, hot medicines, hot baths, hot diet, and retained excrements."[33]

By the time Broadbent was practicing medicine some two hundred years later, the significance of the pulse was no longer tied to humoral theory, but the physiognomic features of the pulse still figured quite prominently. In his book, Broadbent discusses the frequency, rhythm, and force of the pulse, and then correlates specific variations in pulse features with specific illnesses such as high tension, fevers, pneumonia, migraine, and so on. In the process, he gives attention to the size of the artery as it is felt *by rolling it under the finger*, at the same time distinguishing between congenital and pathological influences on size; he gives attention to the degree of fullness between beats, assessing intra-arterial pressure or "pulse tension" as it was called, as that fullness or tension was felt *through the sense of touch*.

Not quite one hundred years later, the pulse is no longer so read, and in American medical practice at least, it is not even anymore so *felt*. What was once touched—one living body by another—what was once listened to by feel, has been transposed to sight and to an artificial intelligence, reified into a visually identifiable entity, a number on a mechanical pulse-taking device. As suggested at the beginning of this essay, concern with the (tactile) physiognomic character of the body runs counter to the radically materializing march of Western medicine over the past one hundred years, a march whose aim is to reduce the body ultimately to lumps of tissue and chains of molecules that can be therapeutically manipulated either surgically with tools or orally with pills. To that end, whatever its presenting physiognomy, the body is anatomized and quantified. The sickness of the body in turn is not palpably read or heard but computed. As a matter of fact, though controversy exists with respect to the practice, the body is often computerized for diagnostic purposes.[34] With such practices, it is not surprising that materialization has all but effaced empathic dimensions of medicine. Materialization takes away the living body of the other person and replaces it with a material object. As French philosopher Maurice Merleau-Ponty once wrote, "Science manipulates things and gives up living in them."[35]

This same discounting of living physiognomic aspects of the body is apparent in Western medicine's disregard of the breath except as a mechanism for oxidization. To bring the physiognomic aspects of the breath to life, one need only put aside notions of oxygen, carbon dioxide, respiratory centers, and so on, and pay attention to the sheer experience of breathing itself. What is found remarkable in this experience? Surely the two-phased rhythm of breath; surely its seemingly unsuppressible persistence; surely its extraordinary warmth. When twentieth-century scientific conceptions and assumptions are put aside and one simply notices breathing itself, the warmth of the breath in particular appears quite incredible. The air breathed in can be as cold as you please, but lo and behold, when breathed out, it is all warm and toasty. Perceived in this way, perceived physiognomically, one can readily understand why, chemical understandings aside, the breath is regarded in many non-Western traditions, and was regarded in the early history of Western thought itself, as something other than a mechanism for oxidizing tissues. The ancient Greek concept of *pneuma*—the connate heat—is powerful and striking in this regard. After noting that *pneuma* cannot be adequately translated, classics scholar Arthur Peck characterizes it as follows: "*Pneuma* is certainly corporeal; it is, as we should say, a kind of matter; and it is connate, congenital, present in an animal from the moment of conception and so long as the animal remains alive. It is, in fact, the primary vehicle of life and of the processes peculiar to living organisms, and occupies a key position in Aristotle's interpretation of these processes."[36] While Peck goes on to emphasize that *pneuma* is not the breath—not the air the animal inhales—yet since respiration, warmth, and life are connected, and non-respiration, coldness, and death are connected, *pneuma* is intimately related to breath. Indeed, as Aristotle explains it, breath is what cools *pneuma:* "The source of life is lost to its possessors when the heat with which it is bound up is no longer tempered by cooling."[37]

Pneuma has a corollary of sorts in the concept of coenesthesia, a concept that dropped out of medical and popular circulation around the 1930s, possibly even before.[38] Coenesthesia means literally common sensation or perception. Its *Oxford English Diction-ary* definition reads: "The general sense or feeling of existence aris-ing from the sum of bodily impressions, as distinct from the definite sensations of the special senses; the vital sense." Coenesthesia is in fact the opposite of anesthesia. When someone is anesthetized, no specific sense organ is shut off; the body as a whole is shut off, rendered insensible. To paraphrase Epicurus (on life and death), when coenesthesia is there anesthesia is not; and when anesthesia is there, coenesthesia is not. To judge from the *Oxford English Dic-tionary*, the word coenesthesia entered the English vocabulary in the 1800s, precisely the time when anesthetic agents were being devel-oped. Chloroform, for example, was introduced in 1847. Unlike anesthesia, however, coenesthesia had a short-lived Western medical existence. What has no organ—no identifiable structure—has no reality in Western medicine. Unlike Chinese medicine, which rec-ognizes functions without structures, Western medical science lacks the conceptual framework for recognizing coenesthesia. Ac-cordingly, it does not deal with "the vital sense," the feeling of aliveness, anymore than it deals with *pneuma*, which might well be conceived the metaphysical basis of coenesthesia.

As suggested earlier, in Chinese medicine, organs are not func-tional parts but dynamic energic orbs. This is why Manfred Porkert, German dean of studies of Chinese medicine, characterizes Chinese understandings of the body as orbisiconography. Concern is not with physical properties as such but with the vital energy spheres that constitute the person and that are ultimately related to the cosmos. It is in this sense that traditional Chinese medicine can be said to be concerned with functions, but functions without structures in the Western sense of anatomy. Now this notion of functions as dynamic processes that *together*, that is, through intricate and multiple inter-relationships, contribute to health or disease, to equilibrium or dis-equilibrium, is coming to the fore in new developments in tradition-al Western medicine, or more exactly in not-so-traditional Western medicine. Some medical researchers are moving away from "a place for everything and everything in its place" to the notion that "every-thing is connected to everything else"—a rather sensible notion to arrive at and cultivate, it would seem, in view of the basic self-evident fact that everything bodily is housed under one roof and moves all of a piece. The new conception of the body centers on connections discovered among three heretofore separately con-ceived systems, in practice, of course, on connections discovered among three separately conceived specialties: the hormonal system, the immunological system, the nervous system. Interestingly enough, the connection is spoken of in terms of "tear[ing] down barricades" that "separate nothing less than the mind and the body." Science writer Stephen S. Hall states that Aristotle, Charles Darwin, and Sir William Osler were all three convinced of the "apparent connection between mind and body, emotions and health. Yet . . . [they] were essentially powerless to sketch out that connection in anything but the broadest and fuzziest of strokes. The tools they brought to the task—dissection, microscopes, x rays and the like—simply were not powerful enough to discern the links."[39]

What the nontraditional scientists are discovering as they seek to tear down the barricades is simply that "our anatomical systems, separated by nineteenth-century tradition, routinely communicate with one another."[40] (Why does that statement seem like such a homely truth? Or perhaps better, why, given the integrity of bodily life, would one not start with that premise rather than with the reverse? As it is, one can hardly keep from responding, "Communicate! No! Not really!") Anatomy, the science of *situ*, the bedrock of twentieth-century Western medicine, is giving way to something akin to orbisiconography. Not that energy conduits or channels are envisioned, of course, only that the body is beginning to be conceived as a dynamic interlocking whole in which everything influences everything else. In brief, a body of separate and distinct parts is giving way to a networking body, a body with some sense of life to it, a body that is, well, *animated*. It is of interest to note that the clue to this new conception of the body lay in the discovery that everything was not in its place. Certain molecules turned up in places where they were not supposed to be, a hormonal researcher having found what amounts to a neurological fly in his ointment.

The new conception promises much in the way of braking a runaway materialization in which nothing but matter matters, in which the integrity of the body is compromised, and in which such living body realities as emotions and motivations have no place. Moreover the simple thought that everything influences everything else is close to the heart of what might be called the "new-age Western body" or the "new-age Western metaphysics" that sees human life on a continuum with the cosmos, and health and illness in far more personally involved terms than present-day Western medicine. Make no mistake, however. The new conception is still within the framework of a materialist doctrine, and to this extent is a thoroughly reductive enterprise. But a new dimension is breaking through, perhaps sufficiently so that towards the close of the twenty-

154 Giving the Body Its Due

first century, medical researchers will say that, like their century earlier predecessors, they too are "tearing down barricades" and that just as their predecessors discovered the errors of nineteenth-century conceptualizations of the body, so they are discovering the errors of twentieth-century conceptualizations of the body, and with those errors, also discovering the truths of an earlier Western medicine in recognizing the patient as person, in appreciating the manifold wonders of the living body—all the way from its warm breath to its powers of self-healing—and in acknowledging the fact that no rigid, divisionary lines can be drawn around living bodies any more than inside living bodies.

If this new paradigm of health and illness is truly in the making, we might best hope that it ends by abjuring the errors of fanaticism on either side, the errors of a rampant animism, or of a radical materialization. Given the fact that we humans are here today, and in particular not just we Western humans, the truth of health and illness clearly lies neither in a blindered animating of the material nor in a blindered materializing of the animate. The truth likely lies in a balanced wholism. Indeed, given the fact that the organic grew out of the inorganic, why would we not carry our origin with us, even as the star-stuff of which astronomer Carl Sagan has spoken? At the same time, given that same fact, why would we not carry our evolution with us, even as the potentiality of form of which Aristotle wrote? From the viewpoint of a balanced wholism, the first steps necessary to achieving a true metaphysics of sickness and health would lie in the realization and acceptance of the fact that there are living harmonies—dissonant ones and consonant ones—to be fathomed, and that understanding these harmonies, in the sufferings of illness as in the flowerings of health, will lead us both to the insights we seek concerning our own well-being and to a metaphysics true to the human bodies we are.

NOTES

1. Daniel Moerman, "Minding the Body: The Placebo Effect Unmasked," this volume, pp. 70, 72–3.

2. Will and Ariel Durant, The Story of Civilization, Vol. 1 Our Oriental Heritage, (New York: Simon and Schuster, 1935), 182. Cited originally in Adolf Erman, Life in Ancient Egypt (London: Macmillan, 1894), 353.

3. Problems, in The Complete Works of Aristotle, ed. Jonathan Barnes, Vol. 2 (Princeton: Princeton University Press, 1984), 883ª 29–30 (#24).

4. Ibid., 882^{b}1, 25–30 (#19).

5. Ibid., 882^{b}1, 37–39 (#20).

6. Ibid., 883^{b}1, 14–17 (#26).

7. Celsus, *De Medicina*, trans. W. G. Spencer, Vol. 1 (Cambridge: Harvard University Press, 1948), 41–44.

8. Sir William Osler, *The Evolution of Modern Medicine* (New Haven: Yale University Press, 1921), 19.

9. Ibid., 18.

10. Ibid., 19.

11. For a brief overview of the role of Hippocrates in Greek medicine see, for example, Henry Osborn Taylor, *Greek Biology and Medicine*, (Boston: Marshall Jones Company, 1922). See also the original works themselves (Loeb edition) with W. H. S. Jones's introductions: *Hippocrates*, trans. W. H. S. Jones, vols. 1–4 (London: William Heinemann, 1923–1931).

12. Quoted in Osler, *Evolution*, p. 67. (From *The Englishman's Doctor, or the Schoole of Salerne*, trans. Sir John Harington [1608], ed. Francis R. Packard, [New York, 1920], 132. Harington's book was originally dated: London, 1607.) Osler describes the book as "the popular family hand-book of the Middle Ages."

13. Ibid., 89. (A full account of the original *Regimen* appears in Sir Alexander Croke's *Regimen Sanitatis Salernitanum; a Poem on the Preservation of Health in Rhyming Latin Verse*. Oxford: D. A. Talboys, 1830.)

14. Ibid., 118.

15. William Arthur Heidel, *Hippocratic Medicine* (New York: Columbia University Press, 1941), 94.

16. Ibid., 124. The Loeb edition translation of this aphorism reads: "Life is short, the Art long, opportunity fleeting, experience treacherous [or, as noted in a footnote, 'deceptive'], judgment difficult. The physician must be ready, not only to do his duty himself, but also to secure the co-operation of the patient, of the attendants and of externals." *Aphorisms*, in *Hippocrates*, vol. 4, 99.

17. *Hippocrates*, vol. 2, 229.

18. Samuel Smiles, *Thrift* (New York: William L. Allison, 1875).

19. Cf. George Lakoff's general theory of metaphor: metaphors are not a linguistic play upon properties of objects, something equivalent to a *façon de parler*. They are conceptualizing systems, *façons de penser*. Though not elaborated in the direction of a somatology, Lakoff's analyses of

156   *Giving the Body Its Due*

many metaphors demonstrate the unmistakably central role of the body in thinking. See his *Women, Fire, and Dangerous Things* (Chicago: University of Chicago Press, 1987).

. Cf. Aristotle: *Organon*, the general title of Aristotle's logical treatises, is taken here in the sense in which Aristotle describes living bodies: "All natural bodies are organs of the soul." *De Anima*, trans. J. A. Smith, in *The Basic Works of Aristotle*, ed. Richard McKeon (New York: Random House, 1968), 415[b] 18.

21. Yeshi Donden, *Health Through Balance: An Introduction to Tibetan Medicine*, ed. and trans. Jeffrey Hopkins (Ithaca, N. Y.: Snow Lions Publications, 1986), 137.

22. "Serotonin causes arteries in the brain to constrict and dilate—a sequence that seems to produce migraine symptoms." K. A. Fackelmann, "Low Dose of Aspirin Keeps Migraine Away, *Science News* 137/7 (February 17, 1990): 103. It might be noted in the context of contradictory effects—a particular drug or chemical being at the same time "good for this" and "bad for that"—that the "black or white" approach of much medical research is perplexingly naive in that it attempts to identify in a wholly linear manner whether and how something—be it a chemical or a full-grown vegetable—is *either* beneficial or harmful. When the research filters down to a popular level, it is not infrequently offered in the form of advice as to what people should or should not eat. For example, broccoli is good, hamburgers are bad. Further research, however, can challenge the original research-derived advice. A recent newspaper article titled "Myths in the Market" (*The Register-Guard*, Eugene, Oregon, 7 November 1989, section B), for instance, indicated that broccoli was bad and hamburgers were good: original values were reversed. The article began as follows: "Could candy bars and hamburgers be deemed health foods in the not-too-distant future? Not exactly, but recent research has shown that many foods considered bad or unhealthful also have redeeming qualities." The food editor went on to point out as well that "everything natural isn't necessarily benevolent: Some vegetables such as broccoli and alfalfa sprouts contain harmful carcinogens and toxins." Since the text of the article did nothing to suggest that ingested substances can have multiple effects precisely because bodies are integrated wholes, *and differentially responsive ones at that,* the article could only make the skeptical wary, the naive assured, and leave the insecure in a quandary.

23. Ron Cowen, "Sociopaths, Suicide and Serotonin," *Science News* 136/16 (14 October 1989): 250.

24. A. Alvarez, "A Poet and Her Myths," *New York Review of Books*, August 17, 1989, 35.

25. Moerman, "Minding the Body."

26. Another highly interesting dimension of the patient as person was emphasized in the writings of Paracelsus in the late 1500s. Paracelsus, an itinerant physician, and a highly vociferous critic of Galen and of humoral theory, emphasized the importance of the will—and the imagination—in sickness. He wrote that "the effect of the will is of major importance in medicine. For one who does not mean well with himself, and is hateful to himself, it is possible that such a person may be afflicted by the very curse he utters against himself. For cursing derives from the obfuscation of the spirit. And it is also possible that the representations are by curses converted into sicknesses, into fevers, convulsive seizures, apoplexies, and such like so that they are brought about as indicated above. . . . And let this not be a jest for you, you physicians: you know not in the least part the power of the will; for the will is the genetrix of such spirits as the prudent will have no dealings with." Quoted in Iago Galdston, "The Psychiatry of Paracelsus," in *Science Medicine and History*, ed. E. Ashworth Underwood, vol. 1 (London: Oxford University Press, 1953), 413.

27. See particularly *Prognostic*, in *Hippocrates*, vol. II; and *Humours*, ibid., vol. IV.

28. Heidel, *Hippocratic Medicine*, 128–129. The detailed diagnostic observations of the physician certainly appear to substantiate Heidel's earlier claim that "Nothing is more characteristic of Hippocratic medicine than its insistence on the closest attention to the individual" (p. 63).

29. O. Carl Simonton's work using relaxation techniques, exercise, and mental imagery has, of course, been well-known since the late 1970s when his book *Getting Well Again* (New York: Bantam Books, 1978) was published. The restorative powers of the body have been more recently discussed by an endocrinologist in his study of healing. See Deepak Chopra, *Quantum Healing: Exploring the Frontiers of Mind/Body Medicine* (New York: Bantam Books, 1989).

30. Aristotle, *De Respiratione*, trans. G. R. T. Ross, in *The Works of Aristotle*, ed. W. D. Ross, Vol. 3 (Oxford: Clarendon Press, 1908), 480^{b}1 22–30.

31. Manfred Porkert, *Theoretical Foundations of Chinese Medicine* (Cambridge: M. I. T. Press, 1974).

32. Stanley Joel Reiser, *Medicine and the Reign of Technology* (Cambridge: Cambridge University Press, 1978).

33. Quoted in Gary L. Townsend, "Sir John Floyer (1649–1734) and His Study of Pulse and Respiration," *Journal of the History of Medicine* 22 (1967): 286–316, p. 299.

34. See Reiser, *Medicine*, chapter 10.

35. Maurice Merleau-Ponty, "Eye and Mind," trans. Carleton Dallery, in *The Primacy of Perception*, ed. James M. Edie (Chicago: Northwestern University Press, 1964), 159.

36. Arthur Peck, "The Connate *Pneuma*," in *Science Medicine and History*, ed. E. Ashworth Underwood, Vol. 1 (London: Oxford University Press, 1953), 111.

37. *On Length and Shortness of Life*, trans. G. R. T. Ross, in *The Complete Works of Aristotle*, ed. Jonathan Barnes, Vol. 1 (Princeton: Princeton University Press, 1984), 740–763; see specifically 479^{a}1 8–9.

38. While not specified as such, coenesthesis has figured in a recent essay on Heidegger and Schwarznegger, the experience in weightlifting called "the pump" being connected with the rapture of being. See Jerry Sandau, "Heidegger and Schwarzenegger, Being and Training," *Philosophy Today* 32/4 (Winter 1988): 156–164. For a brief but fuller discussion of the meaning and history of *coenesthesis*, see Jean Starobinski, "The Natural and Literary History of Bodily Sensation," in *Fragments for a History of the Human Body*, ed. Michel Feher, Part Two (New York: Zone, 1989), 351–373.

39. Stephen S. Hall, "A Molecular Code Links Emotions, Mind and Health," *Smithsonian* 20/3 (June 1989), 64, 66 respectively.

40. Ibid., 64.

ROBERT D. ROMANYSHYN

8

The Human Body as Historical Matter and Cultural Symptom

INTRODUCTION

In the mid-nineteenth century, a new moment in the cultural-psychological history of Western humanity began. First in Paris at Jean-Martin Charcot's clinic, Salpetriere, and then, somewhat later, in the Vienna consulting room of Sigmund Freud, the hysteric walked onto the stage of history. With her bodily symptoms she challenged the reigning scientific-medical paradigm of the day, a paradigm whose roots were well anchored in Cartesian metaphysics. Unable to account for those strange paralyses, aphonias, disturbances in vision or in gait in terms of the dualism of physical body and "*une chose qui pense,*"[1] Freud, unlike Charcot, set a new stage upon which these symptoms could tell their tale. If, today, there are criticisms to be made of his theories, as many feminist writers correctly do, we should not for that reason forget what Freud's consulting room allowed. In the space of that room the dream of Cartesian metaphysics, which ironically began with a series of three dreams that Descartes had one night in November 1619 in a stove heated room in Ulm, Germany, came to an end. Or perhaps, anticipating the theme of this paper, it is better to say that from those dreams of Descartes, which have provided the epistemological ground for the anatomical body of modern thought, the hysteric was born. The body of the hysteric, cut by time, memorial in its presence, its organs a network of social relations, and symbolic in its powers to create and to transform meaning, was the shadow of Descartes' dream, the shadow of that other body created within the space of that dream, the body of the corpse cut by the anatomist's knife, an interior space stuffed with organs, displayed in the moment, and fixed within a network of inscribed forces.

Addressed by this body, called to attend to its symptoms, Freud discovered that symptoms are primarily neither a physical nor a mental matter but rather a matter of history. In this paper, I want to reverse that discovery to suggest that history is a matter of symptoms. Specifically I want to show that Cartesian metaphysics is a specific and particular cultural, historical, psychological space within which we have created the corpse and the hysteric, or in more extended terms what I call the "abandoned body and its shadows." To do so, however, I have to take leave of Descartes in order to indicate that the ground of Cartesian metaphysics is already prepared within the space opened up by linear perspective vision. Descartes' seventeenth-century vision presumes that space invented and created in fifteenth-century Florence. And it is within that space that the human body as a corpse with an official and a shadow history appears.[2]

LINEAR PERSPECTIVE VISION

If there is a link between the cities of Ulm, Germany in 1619, and Paris and Vienna of the nineteenth century, then the first chain in that link might very well be the Italian Renaissance city of Florence in 1425. In that year and in that place, Filippo Brunelleschi performed an experiment in painting, which ten years later became codified as the rules of linear perspective drawing in Leon Battista Alberti's treatise *De Pictura*. As an artistic invention, linear perspective drawing prescribes the geometrical rules for representing the illusion of three-dimensional space on the two-dimensional flat surface of the canvas. Were this invention limited to the realm of art, its significance would still be considerable. But this technique, which began as an artistic invention, was destined to become "the innate geometry of our eyes,"[3] a cultural convention, a habit of mind and heart if you will, which has shaped the foundations of the scientific-technological world. Its significance was nothing less than a radical shift in Western humanity's existence, a transformation in its cultural, historical, and psychological life. It played its part in bringing to an end the closed cosmos of Medieval consciousness and initiating the open, infinite universe of modern life. It played its part in negotiating the shift from the sacred, symbolic, vertically layered world to the secular, empirical, horizontally explained one. It played its part in transforming a consciousness that as religious was essentially a matter of faith into a consciousness that as scientific has become primarily a matter of fact. That we are not claiming too much for this fifteenth-century invention is attested to by the art historian Helen Gardner. She writes, for example, that linear perspective drawing "'made possible scale drawings, maps, charts, graphs, and diagrams—those means of exact representation without which modern science and technology would be impossible.'" In addition, the cultural historian William Ivins notes that "'Many reasons are assigned for the mechanization of life and industry during the nineteenth century, but the mathematical development of perspective was absolutely prerequisite to it.'" And, as if to secure the point beyond any shadow of reasonable doubt, the art historian Samuel Edgerton states: "'Space capsules built for zero gravity, astronomical equipment for demarcating so-called black holes, atom smashers which prove the existence of anti-matter—these are the end products of the discovered vanishing point.'"[4] The vanishing point, one of the two procedures required to construct a linear perspective drawing, was and is that place where the world of medieval consciousness and space ended, and where the world of the modern subjective self of Cartesian consciousness, of the self as spectator, of nature as an objective spectacle for observation, and of the body as an anatomical specimen, began.

A WINDOW ON THE WORLD

Linear perspective drawing is a prescription for vision which invites the viewer to look upon the world as if he or she were fixed and immobile on this side of a window. It prescribes for the onlooker on this side of the window a single, overall vantage point, and it displays on that side of the window an homogeneous, geometric field in which all objects lie on the same horizon-tal plane and recede toward the horizon of infinity.

All of these features of linear vision are contained in the procedure for constructing the vanishing point, which along with the procedure prescribed for the distance point constitute a linear perspective field. To begin his drawing Alberti says that he regards the surface on which he is going to paint ". . . as an open window through which the subject to be painted is seen . . . ,"[5] and he makes it quite clear that this window is in fact a grid composed of parallel square sections and interposed between the eye of the artist and the object to be represented. Alberti's window on the world is, therefore, a prescription for geometric vision, the grid being in fact a mathematical veil of evenly spaced coordinates projected upon the world.

This condition of the window for the construction of the vanishing point already contains three significant implications for the genesis of modern consciousness and its relation to body and world. First, the window as a mathematical veil places a boundary and establishes a separation between an onlooker, a subject as spectator, and the world which as a spectacle becomes an object of vision. Second, the window as a condition for vision is an invitation not only to keep an eye upon the world but also to lose touch with it. Seen through a window, the world is primarily a matter for the eye and in being so there is a consequent de-emphasis of the other senses as legitimate ways of knowing the world. The sound, touch, taste, and smell of the world are destined to become secondary qualities as increasing emphasis is placed upon what is visible, observable, measurable, and quantifiable. Galileo's distinction between the primary and secondary qualities of the things of the world are already being imagined behind Abberti's window, and the Cartesian distrust of embodied life, as we shall see, is already being dreamed. Within the space opened up by linear perspective vision, the body as a carnal knowledge of the world is destined to be increasingly less important as a way of making sense of a world itself destined to become increasingly insensible except as a matter of light. For, indeed, the third implication of the window condition is that as an object of vision the world is on its way to becoming a matter of light, a "light matter" both in the sense of becoming a matter of information, a bit of data, and in the sense that as a space to be explored, explained and exploited it becomes a place which we no longer take so seriously as home, as our place of dwelling.

The window is only one of two conditions attached to the construction of the vanishing point, and in the implications attached to the second condition, the anticipation of Cartesian attitudes toward consciousness and the body are further revealed. This second condition has to do with the location of the vanishing point.

THE SPACE OF EX-PLANATION AND THE ABANDONMENT OF THE BODY

Imagine the surface of a flat table and within that surface choose one side as a base line and set opposite it a point called the "vanishing point" through which another line, to be called the "horizon line," is drawn. Establish in principle that no object within that space between the base and horizon lines is to be higher than the horizon line. Then from each corner of the base line draw orthogonal lines converging toward the vanishing point, and imagine parallel to the base and horizon lines transverse lines across these orthogonals. At this point you will have constructed a space of receding parallels which would roughly resemble the grid pattern of an airport runway. Finally, imagine yourself within that space to be fixed opposite the vanishing point staring straight ahead at the horizon line. Imagine, too, that in principle the distance between you and the vanishing point can be infinite. Under this condition you will have established a potentially infinite space in which you and all objects appear to be upon the same horizontal plane, and in which objects in receding parallels become smaller and appear to decrease in size from the bottom up as their tops or heads remain aligned with the horizon line.[6] Figure 8.1 illustrates these points.

Of the several implications of this condition, there are two which most concern us. First, insofar as this way of placing the vanishing point allows the viewer and all the objects within his or her field of vision to appear to be on the same level or plane, it opens up the space of explanation. Within this space, things, which belong to different levels of reality, like angels or demons, are eclipsed in favor of an equalzing vision which establishes, so to speak, a democracy among things. Linear perspective vision, anticipating the space of modern scientific consciousness, opens that space within which things are flattened or leveled or reduced to the same plane. Within that space, already having become a habit of mind for Galileo, all bodies, regardless of their difference, will fall at the same rate. Within that space the motion of all bodies will be leveled or reduced to the same laws. Within that space they will be ex-plained.

Second, insofar as this way of placing the vanishing point means that all objects within this space shrink from the bottom up

Figure 8.1.

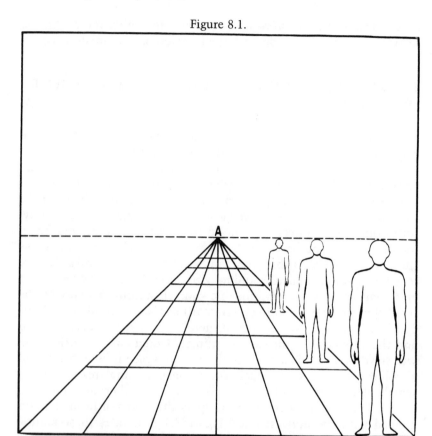

Source: Adapted by Liota Odom from Samuel Y. Edgerton Jr., *The Renaissance Rediscovery of Linear Perspective.*

while their tops or their heads remain in touch with the horizon line, it establishes a space within which the body becomes increasingly eclipsed in the face of a world now opened as an infinite horizon. At the level of the head we remain in touch with the infinite horizon, and in this respect the very geometry of linear perspective space anticipates the space of the Cartesian *cogito.* As we approach the vanishing point within that infinite space of linear perspective vision, the human body progressively shrinks into the head. As we approach the vanishing point, the body is progressively taken up into the heady eye of mind. When Descartes says he is *"une chose qui pense,"* a thing, a mind which thinks, he simply articulates in philosophical language that transformation in consciousness already mapped out in the field of linear perspective vision. "In that head space of Cartesian consciousness which is prepared . . . in this space of linear perspective, in this move toward the infinite, in our vision of infinity, we shall lose our senses." Within that infinite space opened up by linear perspective vision, "our senses will make increasingly less sense of the world as the body matters increasingly less than thought."[7] Indeed, within that space of explanation the human body, leveled and reduced to the anatomical corpse, is destined to be abandoned.

THE CORPSE: ITS HISTORY AND ITS SHADOWS

Linear perspective vision as a window on the world, as an invitation to keep an eye upon the world as we increasingly lose touch with it, is a style of consciousness, a cultural habit of mind, a psychological disposition, which requires that we take leave of our senses. Within that infinite space opened up by this vision the self becomes a spectator of a world that has become a spectacle. Moreover, within that infinite space and for a spectator self behind its window, the body is not only no longer necessary but it is also a positive obstacle to the spectator self's projected dreams of infinity. Within the space of linear perspective vision, then, there is reason and motive to abandon the body. And that body no longer needed by a self which has withdrawn itself from the world, that body now abandoned, becomes a specimen, an object for observation and study, a thing. Stated in terms which more accurately reflect the cultural-historical context, the corpse is the body abandoned and invented for the space of explanation. In the mid-fifteenth century, the spectator self with its eye fixed upon the world is born. By the middle of the next century the body that is increasingly abandoned in this retreat from the world is ready to be fully realized in the image of the corpse lying upon Vesalius' dissecting table.

In a famous woodcut by the fifteenth-century German artist Albrecht Dürer, illustrated in figure 8.2, we see a draftsman looking through a gridded screen at a reclining nude on the opposite side of that screen. That screen, which came to be called "Leonardo's window," is the prescription for spectator vision made visible, and in looking through it the draftsman is, following Alberti's description, transferring those parts of the nude body, which appear in specific square sections of the screen, to their corresponding square sections on a piece of paper. In offering this illustration, Dürer was in fact indicating his conception of the ideal nude, a body "'. . . to be con-

Figure 8.2.

Albrecht Dürer, *Artist Drawing a Nude through a Gridded Screen.*

structed by taking the face of one body, the breasts of another, the legs of a third, the shoulders of a fourth, the hands of a fifth—and so on.'"8

Notwithstanding Dürer's intention, what we also have here is a prescription for the anatomical gaze. The gridded screen through which the body is seen fragments and dismembers that spectacle.

Anatomy literally means dismemberment and the gaze which generates the fragmented, dismembered body of linear perspective vision also generates the anatomical body, the corpse. It is true, of course, that the purpose of each of these gazes differs. Nevertheless both of them share the same attitude of distance and both of them share the same space of separation between spectator and specimen. The nude on the other side of Dürer's screen is a body cut to pieces and an object of observation. The corpse lying upon the dissecting table is also a body cut to pieces and opened for inspection.

Of all that could be said about the corpse and the cultural-historical context of its invention, what matters most to our discussion here are two of its major characteristics, the history of its development, and the shadows which have haunted this invention.

THE CORPSE

The corpse, the body as anatomical object, the body as specimen for a spectator, is a body *in* space and a body of *interior spaces* mapped with organs. As such, this body differs in radical ways from the body of living flesh. To appreciate these differences consider the question of where your muscles are. From the viewpoint of the abandoned body, the corpse, the muscles are inside the body, underneath the skin. This reply to the question of location also determines what muscles are. Located within that interior space, they are already defined in terms of their anatomical functions. Such muscles, both with respect to their location and definition, are muscles about which we know. They are *not*, however, the muscles with which we live in the world.

From the viewpoint of the body as living flesh, one's muscles are within the world. These muscles are in fact even more specific than that last statement would suggest, since these muscles, the muscles that we live with, are one's situation. As such, they are not anatomical functions but human activities. In this respect one knows one's muscles and not about them. One knows one's muscles in and through the heavy boxes of books, which one moves from office to home, in and through the embrace one gives to one's friend, in and through the ball that one throws to one's child. These muscles, unlike those of the corpse, are not neutral or detached from one's living situation. On the contrary, they *are* one's situation, just as my mind at this moment is not an interiorized phantom more or less locatable in the brain, but my activity of thinking and writing these words.

In much the same fashion, the body of living flesh is not in space, like the corpse is in that neutral, homogeneous space apart from any specific situation. Again, on the contrary, the body that one is, is the genesis or generation of space, more akin to the things in Albert Einstein's universe which shape and curve space than those in Sir Isaac Newton's universe where space is a container for things. The woman who is in love walks through the world in such a way that her movements carve space into so many places of proxminity to and distance from the one whom she loves, into areas of warmth and intimacy, into zones of quiet whispers and shared conversations. The body of living flesh which one is, unlike the body as anatomical object which one *can* have, shapes space into a place. And I say *can* here with respect to the anatomical body, because the corpse is an invention in relation to the adoption of a specific attitude or point of view, that attitude whose historical origins lie in the development of linear perspective vision. The corpse, the body as anatomical object, the body abandoned by the spectator behind the window of consciousness, is *not* so much a natural fact as it is a cultural-historical matter. If we forget it, it is only because we have forgotten its origins, just as in daily life we uncritically grant the anatomical body the index of reality, because we forget the special attitude one needs to adopt to transform the activities of living flesh into the functions of a thing. I can lend my body to the physician for his treatment, thereby making it into a body that I have, only because first and always I am a body, and as such I am that power to transform and to make my situation.

In saying that the corpse is an invention that belongs to a specific moment in history, and that is realized in daily life only under special attitudes and conditions, I have also said that the human body is a historical matter, that the matter of flesh is a matter of history. Within the space opened up by linear perspective vision, the history of the flesh has taken two distinct but related paths. There is the history of the corpse, of the abandoned body, which is a kind of official history, of that body which we uncritically index with the notion of reality. And there is an unofficial history, a kind of shadow history, which remembers the body of living flesh disguised, forgotten, or otherwise ignored in that official history. This latter history is a history of the repressed living flesh. It is, if you will, the unconscious of the corpse, and this history, as we shall see, is rediscovered in the context of psychoanalysis. It is, moreover, a history which indicates that human flesh is not only a historical matter but also a cultural symptom.

HISTORY AND SHADOWS

Table 8.1 summarizes the major moments in the history of the abandoned body and its shadows.[9] Limitations of space in this essay permit me to consider only one moment in this dual history. Before doing so, however, it is important to highlight a few features illustrated in this table.

In the upper half of the table, that part which plots the history of the abandoned body, the relation among the images is rather linear. Between the corpse and the astronaut, there is, so to speak, a line of development which is as it should be since this official history is made by a consciousness which exists within a linear field. Indeed, when we consider that the work by Vesalius which announces the corpse appears in the same year—1543—as the work by Copernicus which announces the moving earth, the connection between corpse and astronaut becomes quite clear. The corpse, the body as anatomical object, is invented by a spectator who has withdrawn to a distance behind a window. Within that same attitude of distance, the earth becomes a moving ball in space. The Copernican achievement, however, makes the measure of that distance quite explicit. Copernicus stands upon the sun to move the earth. He adopts an astrophysical point of view. He makes it quite clear that the distance of spectator consciousness, a distance which ideally is infinite, is a distance that is apart from the earth. In this regard, we might say that Copernicus was the first astronaut, and that the attitude of distance from the body, which is so necessary for inventing the corpse, has become the event of departure with the astronaut. In addition, we should add that the astronautic body that goes into space is the supreme realization of the body as technical function which begins with the corpse. The body of the astronaut suited for space is, like the corpse, a chiasm of physics and physiology. It is the anatomical body readied for departure. We should understand

Table 8.1.

The abandoned body and the shadows of the abandoned body.

CORPSE—resurrected as—MACHINE—reanimated via—REFLEX—to become—WORKER (INDUSTRIAL)—as ROBOT—earth as—ASTRONAUT
(1425–1543)   (1628)   (1641)   (1700s–1848)   (1928)   ready to depart   (1945)

THRESHOLD OF REMEMBRANCE AND BARRIER OF REPRESSION: BODY AS SYMPTOM

BURNED WITCH	IMPRISONED MADMAN/MADWOMAN	MESMERIZED AND HYPNOTIZED BODY	MAN-MADE MONSTER	DIAGNOSED HYSTERIC	TREATED ANOREXIC
(15th–18th c.)	(1656)	(1778–1784)	(1816)	(1888)	(1689–TODAY)

Source: From Technology as Symptom and Dream, Robert D. Romanyshyn, © 1989, reprinted by permission of Routledge.

that we are all astronauts insofar as we participate in this attitude of distance which creates the body as technical function. And we do participate in this attitude daily, in small and large measures when, for example, with fast foods we treat eating as a matter of digestion and thereby lose its sense of communion; or when we give over our bodies to the medico-pharmaceutical complex and thereby disown our own abilities to respond to the sense and significance of our suffering. I do not mean to suggest a blanket critique of medical interventions. I mean only to indicate the attitude we so readily and unknowingly adopt that allows us to reduce illness and well being to the level of the medical body.

So different from the upper portion of Table 8.1, the lower half, which traces the history of the abandoned body's shadows, presents images which belong more to the space of a dream. There are no linear connections among them. On the contrary, they haunt respectively each and all of the images of the official history, and collectively they orchestrate a continuing theme. In the final section of this essay I will illustrate this relation of haunting between the abandoned body and its shadows by focusing on one moment in this history. For the moment, I want to indicate two features of this continuing theme.

One feature which is predominant throughout this shadow history of the living flesh is the treatment accorded to the cultural-historical epiphanies of this body. These shadows of the abandoned body, these reminders of the living flesh we would forget in distancing ourselves as spectators behind a window from a body that *matters*, are either burned as witches, imprisoned as madness, mesmerized and hypnotized into sleep, abandoned by their creators, diagnosed and treated by the scientific-medical complex, or otherwised silenced, ignored, and relegated to the margins of history and society. That such has been their fate is not, however, surprising, since these shadows, in their activity of remembering what would otherwise be forgotten, are symptoms. As the return of the repressed, these symptomatic disguises of the living flesh require spectator consciousness to remember that the body matters, and that as such spectator consciousness' heady retreat from the world is a cultural-historical invention, a perspective, and a motivated dream. The marginalizing of these shadows of remembrance, often brutal, is in this regard only an expression on the cultural-historical level of what individually is done to the symptom. Individually and collectively at the level of culture and history, we have tended to ignore the symptom as a vocation, as a calling to attend to what has been neglected, and we have tended to negate the symptom and to treat it away. Consequently, each age in the span of this history has missed how its shadow body is the other side of the body it invented. To cite just one example, the body of imprisoned madness is the caricature of the body as machine, indicating in its excesses of passion and animal fury the limits of the body regulated as a machine. The madman and madwoman imprisoned in their cells are also the shadow of the machine body reanimated via reflex to become the industrial worker. As I have written elsewhere, "'Perceived and judged from the perspective of a body whose reflexes have been honed for work, a body which does not fit the mold of productive, useful, efficient labor, a body which in its idleness as well as in its animal fury cannot work, be prudent, sober, industrious, and controlled, must be mad.'" Diagnosing this body of madness we affirmed "'. . . the efficient, productive body of the industrial worker.'" Imprisoning this animal body which was out of control, we took another step on the line of the body's mechanization and industrialization. Shutting madness away, we missed how the "'Madman and madwoman in their cells are the shadows of the workers in their factories, and [how] the factories . . . are the social counterpart of the asylum.'"[10]

The second feature of this shadow history is the predominant feminine character of the symptomatic figures. From witch to hysteric and anorexic, it has been primarily the body of the woman which has carried the shadow. That this has been the case should perhaps also not be too surprising. Susan Bordo has described Cartesian metaphysics as a psycho-cultural story, and in doing so she has made a persuasive case for regarding this achievement as a "flight from the feminine."[11] My own investigation into the genesis of linear perspective vision as the space for the appearance of Descartes supports her thesis. Linear perspective consciousness as a psychological, cultural, and historical context for the genesis of our scientific-technological world can persuasively be read as a split between a masculine spectator consciousness behind its window and a feminine shadow body. Dürer's woodcut of the draftsman drawing the reclining nude mentioned earlier is an iconographic display of this theme. The draftsman with his vision mediated by a gridded screen is staring at a nude woman. If linear perspective vision is an eye upon a world now stretched to infinity; if it is a flight into the infinite, then, as the evidence of the body's history suggests, it has also been a flight from the feminine. By its creation of the abandoned body, linear perspective vision has also denied, subjugated, and destroyed the feminine. The final section of this essay, in taking up one moment in this history of the abandoned body and its shadows, illustrates this theme.[12]

THE ASTRONAUT AND THE ANOREXIC

The astronaut and the anorexic are one of our modern fairy tales, a way in which we both remember and continue to forget the split between a body invented out of a masculine spirit in flight from matter and a body essentially feminine and discarded as the shadow. Indeed, it might even be appropriate to say that the anorexic is the psychological sister of the astronaut, and to regard this tale in the context of the awesome technological powers which linear perspective vision has unleashed. In this respect, the astronaut is masculine spirit taking leave of a despoiled earth, while the anorexic is the dying, starving body, the discarded feminine, left behind. Of course, in speaking of the astronaut as masculine spirit, I am speaking psychologically about gender and not biologically about sex. That some astronauts are women is not, therefore, the issue. The issue is the attitude, the cultural, historical, psychological disposition which defines the astronautic figure in departing earth. And that attitude, whose genesis lies in the development of perspective vision, has been essentially masculine with its dreams of order, clarity, regulation, domination, control, and exploitation, its consciousness as primarily an exercise of the will to power, and its nightmares of destruction. Whether or not we are destined to finish the tale along the lines so far developed remains an open question. But that the astronautic body as a body of technical function finds its shadow and symptom in the body of the anorexic there is little doubt.

As shadow and symptom, the anorexic is a caricature of the regulated body, of the body perfected as machine. In numerous ways she mimics the transformation of the body as human activity into the body of technical function, and in doing so she shows the shadow of death which haunts this transformation. Consider, for example, the anorexic's relation to food. In her obsessive counting of calories, weighing of portions, and dividing of servings, she mockingly imitates how our objectfication of food has transformed the ritual of eating into the functions of ingestion, digestion, elimination. For the astronautic body, suited for space flight, eating is a matter of physiological processes, and for that context our knowledge of the body as technical function is appropriate and correct. It is not the actual astronaut in space which is at issue here. It is rather the attitude that is required for that achievement and its uncritical transference to the context of daily life which is the issue. The plethora of fast food establishments and the mania for the quick meal divorce eating from its significance as a gathering, and the anorexic, in her attitudes and behavior toward food, displays the other dark side of this convenience. She starves in the midst of plenty, and her symptoms dramatically indicate how non-nourishing this shift to eating as technical function has been. The anorexic's symptomatic presence is not, therefore, primarily at the launchpad. It is, on the contrary, in the fast food drive-ins, and in the eclipse of the family meal around the shared table that her presence appears. Indeed, through another of her symptoms we are called to remember how the increased tempo and pace of contemporary life, with its requirements of speed and efficiency, have eclipsed the ritual dimensions of eating.

The ritualizations that often accompany her purchase, preparation, and eating of food symptomatically recall the significance of eating as a ritual of gathering and remembrance, a communion in which the offering and the eating of food bonds us together into a community and installs us within the circle of life and its seasons. " 'The anorexic's rituals display in symptomatic form the forgotten value that food matters, that it is not just a consumable thing but a vital potency, that it is alive, not of course with calories but with a power to sustain life *and* to bring death.' "[13] Ignore this psychological dimension of food and the human activity of eating, ignore its soulful dimension, the anorexic is saying, and surely you must die. In her dress of skin and bones, then, she stands as mute witness to the fact that *how* we eat can and is killing us. And yet in our deafness to her symptoms we continue to believe that *what* we eat is at fault. We continue, then, in the attitude of objectification and we worry about the calories and the cholesterol, the sugar and the starches, the fats and the oils. I am not saying that we should abandon this knowledge, for certainly it is of value. I am saying only that these items of information are not the real issue and that in isolating our focus upon them we relieve ourselves of the responsibility to recognize that in our objectification of food and eating we are revealing that attitude of distance which separates us from each other, from our bodies, and from the material world of nature. In the anorexic's symptomatic behavior toward food, there is remembered for us our terror of intimacy, and that destructive exploitation of animals and nature that allows us to separate ourselves from the world and to treat it as a consumable thing. The anorexic would bring us into this circle of awareness. She would remind us that her sufferings are a mirror through which we can imagine our astronautic selves. In diagnosing and treating her, however, we isolate her suffering and we remain oblivious to the connection between who she is and what we are. The astronaut remains a figure of accomplishment and the anorexic a condition to be cured, and in the separation between them we remain unaware that we are all astronauts whose shadow is the starving living flesh which she bears.

There is another way in which the anorexic as a cultural-psychological symptom shadows the astronaut. In her pursuit of airy thinness, the anorexic compliments her attitude toward food with a manic zeal for exercise. " 'She diets and she runs, seeking, as it were, the image of a perfect body' " and in all of this she caricatures "'an image of the body as machine and reminds us that the dark side of this pursuit of perfection is the shadow of death.' "

Again, however, it is not so much in relation to the actual astronautic body prepared for space flight, a body designed and tailored as technical function, that the anorexic serves as a symptom. Rather it is in relation to the ways in which we exercise our astronautic attitude in daily life that her symptomatic value appears. For example, " '. . . in her manic zeal to exercise the body to the point of perfection, the anorexic appropriately casts her shadow upon the exercised, properly toned, well muscled bodies so visible in our health spas and our television advertisements.' " Imaginatively introduce the anorexic into that space and look at those bodies from her perspective, and you get the sense of how those bodies "'. . . whose muscles protrude from the inside, like the bones of the anorexic, are bodies which fit everywhere and anywhere and hence belong nowhere.' " Such unsituated and anonymous bodies are precisely bodies defined in terms of technical functions and not human activities which relate the muscles of one's body to the situation one lives. Something of the full range of her symptomatic commentary on this issue is captured in the following words:

> In her dramatic ritualization of exercise, then, the anorexic becomes a stark commentary on the corpse, on those bodies which, in exercising for exercise's sake, pursue a perfection which has become detached from the specificity of any living situation. She becomes, in her haunting presence, with her haggard features and tired eyes, the other, exhausted side of the

anatomized corpse resurrected as machine and exercised to death. Imaginatively installed within this space of the perfected body, the anorexic shows us how our health spas, like our attitudes toward food, can be inimical to life, gymnasiums of death. In that space, she shows us the curious, ironic, but terrifying fact that our manic pursuit of health may actually be a loss of life.[14]

Adrienne Rich, writing about the effects of technological society, has said:

I am a feminist because I feel endangered, psychically and physically, by this society, and because I believe that the women's movement is saying that we have come to an edge of history when men—insofar as they are embodiments of the patriarchal idea—have become dangerous to children and other living things, themselves included.[15]

The astronautic figure might very well be the most illustrative embodiment of the patriarchal idea about which Rich speaks, and the anorexic the embodiment of our collective endangerment. Each in their manner of incarnation might very well reflect the soul of technological society, ". . . its psyche split into the departing masculine self and the abandoned feminine. As we take leave of the earth, then, in a body newly created and designed for space, we might pause, turn back, and catch a glimpse of who and what of ourselves we leave behind. There on the departed and perhaps fully deadened earth stands the anorexic, starving skeleton who mocks our 'ideal of mind over body'."[16]

CONCLUSION

The astronautic and the anorexic bodies belong to the same space of perspective vision, and if out of that space the former has been generated as the body as it really is, then the latter has been generated as a cultural symptomatic reminder of what this assumption of the real body leaves behind. The body as living flesh lends itself to definition as technical function, as the continuing presence of the images in the top half of Table 8.1 indicate. But it lends itself in this fashion because the human body of living flesh is also a historical matter and not only a matter of nature, because the nature of human flesh is to be a history. Furthermore, in lending itself in this fashion, to be shaped and designed as technical function, the human body of living flesh is also a cultural symptom. I have tried to demonstrate these two points in order to indicate how they are related to the origins of perspective vision, and to suggest that the dualism of Cartesian metaphysics is a cultural-historical development from these origins.

The figures of the astronaut and the anorexic are one moment in the psychological-cultural history of the human body within the space of linear perspective vision. Within that space which has seeded and nourished the scientific-technological world, we have redesigned the human body for a consciousness which as spectator of the world has increasingly learned to distance itself from what we might call the "shock of our incarnation." That much benefit has come from this achievement there is no doubt. From the body as anatomical object to astronaut we have perfected our knowledge about the body as technical function. The birth and development of the modern sciences of anatomy and physiology and the concomitant development of medicine bear testimony to the power of this knowledge.

The achievement, however, has not been a benefit without a price. In its heady success of redesigning the body as technical function, and in its increasing withdrawal from the body as human activity, spectator consciousness has forgotten that the body we have refashioned is an invention, the incarnation of a shared cultural-historical dream motivated as much by the desires of soul as the reasons of mind. The figure of the astronaut is in this respect as much the incarnation of a wish as it is the realization of an idea and in forgetting all this we have made the body of technical function the index of a reality all too reasonable and all too purified of its cultural, historical, psychological dimensions. We have, within the space opened up by linear perspective vision, come to believe in an uncritical way that the body we know about is the body that we have, and in so doing we have lost sight of the fact that the body we have is grounded upon the body we are, the body as that power to lend itself to our cultural-historical dreams.

The figure of the anorexic is one moment in a long history of painful reminders that as creatures of human flesh we belong both to nature and to history. In this respect, the figure of the anorexic has been a cultural symptom, indicating that human flesh as a matter of nature and of history is also a matter of soul, a psychological matter, the embodiment of collective cultural-historical dreams.

It has been the intention of this essay to recover these notions of the human body as historical matter and cultural symptom. By indicating how the body as technical function, the anatomical body of modern medicine and culture, originates within the well-defined historical-cultural moment of linear perspective vision, I have tried to demonstrate that the body, which we assume to be a natural fact, is both a cultural-historical matter and a collective psychological dream. Such a demonstration, of course, neither invalidates our scientific-technological knowledge of the body nor detracts from its importance. Rather, it sets this achievement within the wider contexts of human history and psychology, allowing us to recognize that the body as technical function from corpse to astronaut is a particular vision of the body, a perspective. Acknowledging that this body is a perspective invites us to remember what we would otherwise forget: that the human body is a power that lends itself to the dreams of human history and of the soul. In the last analysis, such a work of remembrance can be culturally, historically, and psychologically therapeutic, permitting us to integrate those shadows of the body which the cultural-psychological history of the abandoned body has created. So integrated, perhaps, the split between the astronautic figure and the anorexic can be healed. Then, perhaps, the astronautic figure can hear from the figure of the anorexic something of the limits of its infinite vision, and the anorexic figure can be drawn back into the fullness of the world by the soulful wonder of that vision.

NOTES

1. René Descartes, *Meditations on First Philosophy*, Trans. Lawrence J. LaFleur (Indianapolis: The Library of Liberal Arts, 1960), 27.

2. Before taking leave of Descartes, however, I wish to draw the reader's attention to an instructive book by Susan Bordo, *The Flight to Objectivity* (Albany: State University of New York Press, 1987). Her analysis of the cultural, historical and psychological contexts of Descartes' thought supplement this essay as well as some of the themes of my recent book (see note 4) from which this essay is drawn.

3. S. Y. Edgerton, Jr., *The Renaissance Rediscovery of Linear Perspective* (New York: Harper and Row, 1976), 4.

4. All quotes are taken from Robert Romanyshyn, *Technology as Symptom and Dream* (London, New York: Routledge, 1989), 33. For a more detailed treatment of the issues raised here readers are referred especially to chapters two, four, and five of that work.

5. Ibid., 39.

6. In order to simplify my description I have left out of it the role which the distance point plays in the construction of a linear perspective space. Suffice it to say that the distance point, which is the viewpoint of the viewer set opposite the vanishing point, determines the degree of depth as spatial distance between the viewer and the horizon. In principle that degree can be infinite. For a detailed treatment of the issue see Romanyshyn, *Technology as Symptom*, 48–57.

7. Ibid., 48.

8. These words are not Dürer's but those of John Berger in his *Ways of Seeing* (New York: Penguin Books, 1977), where they are used to summarize Dürer's conception. Berger sees in Dürer's illustration and conception "a remarkable indifference to who any one person really was" and in consequence of that indifference a prescription for the murder of the body in pornographic vision. I am not willing to charge Dürer in the same way, since for him this vision was one which would glorify humanity. Moreover, linear perspective vision in its origins offers a possibility, and if this kind of vision can and does lead to indifference, then it is those who have followed Dürer who have largely made it so. For a more detailed discussion of this point, see Romanyshyn, *Technology as Symptom*, 115–117.

9. Ibid., 134. See especially chapter five for the relevance of the dates attached to each figure.

10. Ibid., 153.

11. Bordo, *The Flight*.

12. For a detailed discussion of these issues of the feminine character of the shadow body and the psychological splitting of masculine and feminine in perspective vision, see Romanyshyn, *Technology as Symptom*, especially the discussions of the man made monster and the anorexic in chapter five. For an excellent consideration of the anorexic see also Angelyn Spignesi, *Starving Women* (Dallas: Spring Publications, 1983). Her work is a sensitive reading of the anorexic's symptoms on their own terms and in this respect her book helps one to recover the cultural symptomatic aspect of anorexia.

13. Romanyshyn, *Technology as Symptom*, 171.

14. This quote and the four preceding ones are all from *Technology as Symptom*, pp. 171–72.

15. Adrienne Rich, *On Lies, Secrets and Silence* (New York: W. W. Norton and Company, 1979), 83–84.

16. Romanyshyn, *Technology as Symptom*, 173.

9

Making the Unknown Known:
Art as the Speech of the Body

Making your unknown known is the important
thing—and keeping the unknown always beyond you. Catching, crystallizing your simpler
clearer vision of life—only to see it turn stale
compared to what you vaguely feel ahead—that
you must always keep working to grasp.
                                        Georgia O'Keeffe

My aim in this paper is to explore the relationship between felt
bodily experience and the creative process—specifically in regard to
visual art. Such an exploration holds implications for creativity in
all areas of human endeavor. It has enabled me to intertwine two
significant threads of my life, psychotherapy and painting, into a
deeply meaningful process of discovery. Much has been written
about the process of art, about its creation and its creators. However,
even the notes and journals of artists give few glimpses into the
creative process as it is lived and felt: into the actual, particular,
sensed experience of bringing a work of art into being.

In my nearly ten years of work as a psychotherapist, I have
rooted my practice in the focusing process, as developed by Eugene
Gendlin.[1] I have found that meaningful, lasting change necessarily
means change that is felt in the body. Even when a problem is addressed cognitively, the only way one ultimately knows whether or
not a particular insight or solution will be helpful is whether or not

it makes a difference in how one actually feels about the issue at hand. Thus, one can tell oneself that "everything will be fine now," but still feel constricted in one's life because the feeling inside is "not fine." We are not used to relating to our bodily experience in such a manner, although what we call "intuition" can provide a window into this rich inner ground. Our usual way of dealing with feelings is either to limit the extent to which we "let them in" or to find ourselves "over-whelmed" by them. So we say "I am mad" when feeling anger, or "I am exhausted" when feeling tired, thus identifying ourselves with our feelings so completely that it is as if they are all we are. This point will be particularly important later, as I speak about the artist's experience of feeling blocked. Focusing and the psychotherapeutic stance it embodies has as its intention to enable us to accept felt experience fully and regard it with respect and compassion, while inviting it, as a kind of inner voice, to speak. This invitation often enables a freeing up of what is distressed or unclear inside. Focusing is a process of paying attention to our bodily sense of things and thus of inviting the unknown to make itself known; it helps us to move forward in life by opening to exactly where we happen to be right now.

The seed for this paper was planted in November of 1989, when I heard Gendlin speak about creativity. He said:

> But when an artist creates a new design, it's just like that. S/he has a bunch of lines up there and the design is starting to work and it's sort of exciting but it needs something, and s/he stands back . . . and looks at it and says . . . it needs something, and the body knows it needs something and the body has a sense of this something that it needs. And that line that it needs has never existed before because the whole design has never existed before, and this time it's not a matter of just balance, although the words we use will still be like that . . . this body senses that . . . it's not words you want, it's not something from the past, it's a new line.[2]

I was surprised to recognize, in these words, my own experience as an artist and began to reflect upon my felt experience while painting, while searching for that color or line that is "needed." In my years of using focusing, I had never fully considered its implications for my work as an artist nor had I thought that a description of my inner experience of painting might epitomize listening to the body in the way that focusing fosters. I began to think about the implications of focusing to help both understand and facilitate the creative process. I felt as if an inner door were opening, flooding me with ideas and questions. My curiosity was also aroused about what other artists, unfamiliar with focusing, would say when asked to describe their felt experience of creating. And finally, I wondered about the implications of using focusing as an effective way to deal clinically with the experience of frustration and creative paralysis commonly known as "artist's block."

A short time later, I had a firsthand opportunity to look, experientially, at just this last area. In the process of starting a painting I had contemplated doing for a long time, I encountered just such a period of frustration. After struggling with the feeling without being able either to understand it or to "un-block" myself, I decided to use focusing as a way to relate to it. Thus, rather than regarding the feeling literally as an obstacle and fighting it, I opened up to it. Eventually, I had the sense of the "blocked-ness" itself opening up inside . . . allowing me to emerge on the "other side," and find myself in a new relationship with my painting. After realizing what this different way of being with my feelings had enabled, and recognizing it as exactly the kind of experience Gendlin's example had inspired me to explore, I decided to write a detailed account of what I had gone through, and use it as a foundation for my exploration with other artists. A condensation of this account will follow later. First I would like to articulate the phenomenon of artistic creation as a process rooted in bodily experience.

In Georgia O'Keeffe's words, creating art is a process of "making your unknown known." Indeed, this phrase speaks to the intrinsically felt quality of the creative process quite precisely. What is known has already been brought into being: it exists. Thus, we think of what is unknown as having no existence at all. Yet, our sense of what is as-yet-not-known is certainly a sense of "something" that, while not fully manifested, is also not simply the absence of something. It is unknown in that it is not an identifiable presence within the realm of our awareness, and yet there is a bodily feeling, though the sensation is often subtle, of that something that is possible or beginning-to-be. This points back to "this body which is better informed than we are about the world."[3]

The felt quality of the unknown serves as a kind of beacon. When we pay attention to it, the unknown is born into being and develops, and our felt sense of what we are seeking to create changes. We experience such a change most graphically when, somehow, we arrive at a point where what we've created resonates with our sense of what we intended: when we find our work saying what we have set out to say. The unknown, *our* unknown, constitutes itself into what is knowable as we give it shape. In so doing, we co-constitute ourselves and that which is becoming. We are both birth mother and midwife to our own creative process.

Edvard Munch wrote in his diary, as he reflected upon his sense of a new movement arising in art, "It will find expression for what now is so refined as to be recognized only in vague inclinations, in experiments of thought. There is an entire mass of things that cannot be explained rationally. There are newborn thoughts that have not yet found form."[4] Even though he speaks of "thoughts," there is clearly a felt quality, a call to move beyond the bounds of the rational, into the realm of "vague inclinations," sensed but as yet unknown. Artists live on the threshold between the unknown and the known where things begin to become manifest. Having an inner, bodily sense of what they want to say through their work, their effort goes into bringing into being a creation that will speak precisely in the voice of that inner sense. Paul Cézanne said that "The man of letters expresses himself in abstractions whereas the painter, by means of drawing and color, gives concrete form to his sensations and perceptions,"[5]

As part of this study, I interviewed three artists in the Seattle community—Pat DeCaro, Kevin Harvey, and Ed Praczukowski—and read in particular the writings and comments of artists such as Cézanne and Munch. I stumbled upon the rich quote by Georgia O'Keeffe that begins this paper. Descriptions surfaced of the experience of creating art in relationship to felt experience: emotion, intuition and the larger, fuzzier arena of body sense which includes both emotion and intuition and more. As Cézanne said in conversation with his friend Joachim Gasquet, "An art which isn't based on feeling isn't an art at all. . . . Feeling is the principle, the beginning and end; craft, objective, technique—all these are in the middle."[6]

I was somewhat taken aback initially when many of my questions to the artists I interviewed were answered with comments such as "I never thought of this before," or "You're asking me to look at how I feel while I'm working in a way that I never do." In the first interview, Pat could think of nothing to say in response to the question: "How do you feel in your body when you paint?" Yet later, as she told the story of her early years in art, she described how tight and constricted she had felt, especially in her shoulders and neck, when her paintings were all very detailed, realistic still lifes that were, in her words, "tedious to paint." She contrasted this with a description of how she paints now, moving with great energy and freedom, creating large, colorful, intensely expressionistic canvasses. I was struck by the fact that, while Pat could not initially provide me with a description of her felt experience of painting, such a description emerged spontaneously later in the interview. In this and other interviews it became clear that although each artist could, with pause for reflection, speak of and describe the bodily experience of her or his creative process, it was not necessarily true that any one of them was aware that it was this felt experience that had been attended to while working. Thus, the felt sense guiding the bringing-into-being of a particular work of art was a touchstone for the artist outside of explicit awareness. None of the artists interviewed specifically identified, located, or dialogued with this inner feeling in a direct manner. In fact, as their initial comments to me suggested, none of them had really thought about the relationship between their inner felt sense of wanting to create a painting and the creative process itself until my questions pointed to it. What emerged were descriptions of an attunement to an inner sense of something wanting to be created, and of an attention to this sense as an essential feature of the process of creating a work of art.

An articulation of Kevin's intention emerged in the context of his story about a painting:

> the [painting] of the universe over the telephone wires and the trees . . . that's from Carl's front porch. . . . [I was] standing on his front porch one day, looking up and just seeing these weird angles of trees and these weird telephone wires . . . and originally seeing that at night and being able to see all that stuff in the darkness, and then coming into the studio and trying to restructure that image . . . because I just liked that image for some reason, and in the process . . . going back to his house, looking at it again in the daylight, not to get so much an exact replica of it, but just to capture the feeling that I first had when I saw it . . . and also knowing that whatever it was that I saw there was important and it was important to me to get that same feeling across to somebody else, . . . to know that [the painting] had the feeling that I originally saw when I looked out. . . . I moved those telephone wires around a lot, just to make them have some sense of purpose. They had to have direction and purpose, otherwise they just seemed like a bunch of lines crossing a page . . . otherwise they wouldn't have been convincing. They would have read as telephone wires, but they

wouldn't have read the same way . . . not fitting the internal
image.

Kevin's guiding aim is clearly to recreate an explicit felt experience
for the viewer, with success measured by the extent to which he can
do this.

This kind of intention is echoed by the other artists interviewed. For all of them, creating art is more than making a pretty, or
even a beautiful picture. Artists work from an inner sense, an "internal image" of what they want to make happen and this includes,
implicitly, seeking to evoke a certain response from the viewer. It
may also include wanting to draw the viewer to look more deeply
into the piece, or to think about certain issues as well as to experience certain feelings. Marc Chagall said that,

> For me, a picture is a surface covered with representations of
> things (objects, animals, human shapes) in a particular order, in
> which logic and illustration have no importance at all. Perhaps
> there's a mysterious fourth or fifth dimension—perhaps not
> just for the eye—which intuitively sets up a balance of plastic
> and psychological contrasts, forcing the onlooker to take in
> new and unusual ideas.[7]

Of the three artists I interviewed, Ed's paintings in particular
bear out this desire to involve the viewer intensely. His paintings of
human beings moving in and through a "cosmic soup" of
impressionistic-like strokes of color call for the viewer to work at
really seeing what is there. They are subtle, yet powerful pieces in
which the human forms nearly merge into the moving, swirling
threads of paint. The longer one looks, the more figures become
discernible, and the more the painting's complexity emerges. Ed
wants the viewer to have to spend some extra time and effort in
order to see what is fully there. His aim is vital to the creation of
each piece: wanting people to confront and contemplate the inter-
relatedness of all that exists in the cosmos, and to experience the
permeability of boundaries we consider absolute and unsurmount-
able. This aim has fueled his painting for decades.

With each artist, there is a strong sense of how intention enters
into his or her creative process, although the content of each artist's
intentions varies. What is known is not how a particular piece will
finally turn out, but the felt experience from which the painting
springs. To be successful, the painting must ultimately evoke this

experience in the viewer. Thus, the specific coming-into-being of the painting is a revelatory process. Even if one has an idea of what image and colors one is going to use, it is only in putting paint to canvas that the work of art comes into being. In Cézanne's words, "To make a picture is to compose. . . ."[8] Form, color, and composition enter into the creative process as the servants of the artist's felt intention. In a similar vein, Chagall says:

> I find it very hard to talk about my painting. There's only one thing that guides my hand, and that's the urge to paint, and to offer love with my dreams and colors and shapes, and maybe with that something I was born with and don't really understand.[9]

The artist, guided by this inner sense, this "urge to paint," this internal image of what is seeking expression, tries this color or shape or shift in perspective to bring forth on canvas the painting within. Kevin captured this process succinctly in saying,

> You start with knowing what it's supposed to be and then you go through all these stages where it isn't what it's supposed to be, and then it ends up being what it's supposed to be, even if it's not what it was (in appearance) when you started.

Intention and the felt experience of artistic creation are difficult to separate. At one point Pat said:

> . . . sometimes it's not even an image, but it's a feeling of it, . . . Sometimes there is an image of it, but a lot of times you may not even know what it might look like. But [you have] a sense of just what it's going to be . . . [and] you do find it, and it is part by part . . . You're working over here, and suddenly it tells you what to do over here, and then that tells you what to do in another part, and so . . . I wouldn't say the work's speaking to you, I think your self is speaking to you as you're working . . . but it's not articulated in words.

When artistic creation flows, it might well be described as both preverbal and precognitive. As Cézanne said, "The artist does not perceive every relation directly: he senses them."[10] Artists speak of the experience of "losing oneself," of disappearing into the process, into the free flow of creative movement involving body, arm, hand, brush, paint and canvas. The felt sense is, paradoxically, often described as the experience of having no body or of losing one's sense of one's body. There is no "thinking about," no self-consciousness, only painting, only—as Pat put it—"the pure responsiveness" of the painter to the painting and the painting to the painter, without any sense of hesitation or awkwardness. This fluidity of process cannot be had on demand, but it seems possible to cultivate certain conditions that make such a smooth flow of expression more likely to occur.

Artists' reports of being in the state of pure responsiveness sound very much like descriptions of a state of grace. Paul Klee at one time wrote,

> I now abandon work. It penetrates so deeply and so gently into me, I feel it and it gives me confidence in myself without effort. Color possesses me. I don't have to pursue it. It will possess me always, I know it. That is the meaning of this happy hour. Color and I are one. I am a painter.[11]

It is only as one emerges from this state that one even knows she or he has been there. Words like "joy" and "energized" and "lightness" recur in descriptions. Again, a quote from Pat,

> I was doing this new painting . . . and I did something that was just a little different. I always do a painting study, and I didn't. I just did the drawing, and I said, "Gee I don't know how this color's going to be, well I'm just going to try it like this," and I just went for it. I had no idea what the rest of it was going to look like . . . but it just led me by the nose. The next day I went back into it, and I went back the day afterwards, and I thought, *oh, this is love . . . this must be love* and afterwards I thought, *that's the way it should always be,* but it's not always like that.

Two important experiences are described here: not knowing what a painting-in-progress will finally look like (even while having a distinct felt sense of it), and recognizing that the "loving" nature of this process is not always apparent. Often the creative process doesn't flow quite so freely.

Artist's block is a perennial problem. The felt experience is, loudly and clearly, "this isn't working." Paul Klee writes eloquently of this in his diary:

> In my eyes, the engravings lie before me as completed Opus One, or more exactly behind me. For they already seem curious

to me like some chronicle taken from my life. I ought to prove this to others, not to myself, by doing something. I have very definite feelings, but have not yet transformed them into art.

So now I have to struggle again, and chiefly against the inhibitions that prevent me from exploiting my original talent. . . . I still struggle much too impetuously; if I were to pursue this matter rationally, I should not even think of the word "struggle." Thus furious surges and fits of depression alternate in a frightful way. For the time being, a spectator's interest in this process keeps me alive and awake. An autobiographical interest. Dreadful, if this were to become an end in itself.[12]

An earlier diary entry emphatically concludes, "As if I were pregnant with things needing form, and dead sure of a miscarriage!"[13] Speaking of artist's block during our interview, Kevin laughed as he stated, "It's so obvious . . . it isn't intellectual . . . you can just tell right away . . . no, this isn't what I want . . . and you feel like grabbing your paintbrush and scrubbing it out." The felt sense of what is wanted is there, but the manifestation is not. The unknown has not yet become known.

My own experience as an artist provided me with additional insight and a deeper understanding of artist's block. I had started a large painting I'd been planning for months of a group of giant rocks off the coast of Washington; they have great significance for me. After doing the underpainting, I diligently blocked in the composition but could not recreate the very powerful felt sense that was the impetus for the painting in the first place, and this even though I felt deeply the exact experience I wanted to express, and the image I wanted to use as a vehicle. After several long and frustrating studio sessions, I felt a great tension and a sense of being thwarted. I began to feel blocked, and feared I'd never move forward. I had concretized my inner sense of something into a belief of what was really so. My husband suggested that I put into use what I knew about focusing. He urged me to look at this felt sense of being blocked as part of the experience of creating the painting, rather than as a concrete obstacle.

Once I began to approach the *block* as a feeling and not as a fact, I could make room for it and ask it to help me find a solution to my painting dilemma. Weeks later, as I sat in a workshop, I felt a rush of excitement in my middle. The image of the rocks of Stonehenge loomed suddenly in my mind's eye. The awe and reverence I had felt when I visited the great circle of stones years ago was with me in that moment. I knew that *this* was the felt sense of my painting, struggling to find its way onto the canvas and I saw that my adherence to a literal realism was exactly what was standing in the way of my ability to express my felt experience. Returning to the studio, I worked for hours on the painting, grouping the great stones off the coast as the monoliths stand on the Salisbury Plain. Clearly, this was what was needed! By making room for the blocked feeling and accepting it as a natural part of the process of creating the painting, I allowed the unknown to be made known. I made a connection within that provided me with a bridge between what I was feeling and a way to express it.

How did the artists I interviewed describe their experiences of feeling blocked, and their ways of coping? To my delight, they had each found ways to accept and work with such frustrations, regarding them at worst as something to be tolerated. For Ed, they were actually described as something to revel in as a most wonderful part of the creative process. "Being an artist is not knowing where you are going", he insisted. Ed recalled a time in his life when each morning he would take some house paint, some kind of nontraditional painting tool and a stack of pieces of paper, and make a series of quick paintings, often just a single stroke or two. By bringing to mind a word (e.g., "love," "cat," "tree") and trying to complete the stroke before a thought about the subject interjected itself into his awareness, he felt he could sometimes access a preverbal level of experience that produced something fresh, exciting, and authentic. His aim was not to create a finished work of art, nor even a lasting image, but to keep himself supple and open. It is this kind of freshness and authenticity he still tries to bring to each painting, saying, "One should leave a painting in a place of beginning."

The other artists, while less enamored of being in a state of "not-knowing" in their work, have each found ways to make allowance for this experience when it comes, while continuing their artistic exploration in other ways. In Pat's words, "I'd say blocked or detoured—like going on the road, and you come to this fork, and it's "Oh, oh, which one do I take?" and it's kind of not-knowing, or walking halfway down one and then turning around and realizing "this isn't the way . . . and going back." Pat scrapes off a painting when it's not working, and starts again, having learned to trust that she will continue to paint. Kevin usually puts a painting aside when it's not working. He says, "I just tack it up at the end of the wall so that it's there, and I'm looking at it and I'm thinking about it, but

I'm not actually painting on it until something inside suggests what to do next."

There is an acceptance of the ebb and flow of a natural process in the above descriptions. The blocked feeling is seen as an integral part of the process of the unfolding of the unknown. It is in a quite real sense the very source of artistic creation. Creating art is, literally, a bodily process of making space (in the studio, on the canvas) for the unknown to emerge and become manifest. The experience of being paralyzed by an artist's block is a result of constriction of the source of our creative energy, a closing off of the stream that needs to be open if we are to express effectively our felt experience. By closing off to the unknown out of fear, we also close off to the wellspring of our creativity and, thus, our art. We cut ourselves off from the very energy with which we seek to reconnect. In the focusing process, what is essential is that we make room for, and respect our inner experience, whatever it may be, even as we seek to understand it and bring change into our life. I have been reminded of this truth in important ways in my own struggle. And the veracity of it echoed in the words of the artists who have shared their stories with me. The implications of their experiences for helping others to relate more easily to "not being able to paint" (or sculpt, or draw . . .) have renewed and deepened my appreciation for the focusing process. My respect has deepened equally for artists who pay such close attention to their inner experience in order that they may share something meaningful with others.

NOTES

1. Eugene T. Gendlin, *Focusing* (New York: Bantam Books, 1981), *Let Your Body Interpret Your Dreams* (Chicago: Chiron 1985), "The Wider Role of Bodily Sense", paper presented at "Giving the Body Its Due: An Interdisciplinary Conference," University of Oregon, Eugene, Oregon, November 1989.

2. Gendlin, "The Wider Role of Bodily Sense."

3. Maurice Merleau-Ponty, *Phenomenology of Perception* (New York: The Humanities Press, 1982), 238.

4. Reinhold Heller, *Munch: His Life and Work* (Chicago: University of Chicago Press, 1984), 62.

5. Richard Kendall, *Cézanne by Himself* (Boston: Little, Brown and Company, 1988), 237.

6. Kendall, *Cézanne*, 310.

7. André Verdet, *Chagall's World* (Garden City: Doubleday and Company, Inc., 1983), 19.

8. Kendall, *Cézanne*, 298.

9. Verdet, *Chagall's World*, 24.

10. Kendall, *Cézanne*, 298.

11. Felix Klee, *The Diaries of Paul Klee: 1898–1918* (Berkeley: University of California Press, 1984), 297.

12. Klee, *Diaries*, 1987.

13. Ibid., 141.

10

The Wider Role of Bodily
Sense in Thought and
Language

INTRODUCTION

This paper will attempt a way of thinking with, and about, that which exceeds logical forms and distinctions. Today it is widely held that any form (rule, pattern, concept, distinction, category . . . . .)[1] always involves an inseparable so-called excess. It is furthermore held that that *excess* is chaotic, a limbo. I will show on the contrary that excess is a vital part of thinking, and that it is not chaos but a greater *order*.

It is widely assumed that language is inherently just a conceptual system. If language is more than that, we seem unable to *say* what exceeds concepts (rules, distinctions, ...) because we can only speak by means of concepts (rules, distinctions, ...). It is assumed that if anything did exceed concepts (rules, distinctions, ...), it would only work to *dis*-organize what we say. In contrast, I will show that language has an *order* greater than its conceptual system, its distinctions, rules. . . . . .

The body functions vitally in that thinking and saying which exceeds forms. It is in that excess mode of thinking and saying that I will talk about how the body functions in thinking and saying.

Let me give an example: You are walking on the street and you meet someone who says hello. You say hello back. You don't remember who it is. But your body knows who it is. Any moment *who it is* will pop into your head. Then it doesn't. You scour the world, work, home, neighbors, stores, colleagues. Perhaps suddenly you know, perhaps not. But you have a felt sense—a bodily felt quality—in which that person is *implied*. At that point you may think, "Gee, isn't that interesting. I know that I don't like this person, but I don't know who it is yet." And when at last it comes to you who that is, you may be surprised. You say, "Gee, I didn't know I didn't like this person in this funny way." But while as yet you didn't, this bodily *implying* knew who it is.

So the body *implies* a next step of speech or action or knowledge or feeling. The word "implies" is important to me. Suppose though that I didn't say the body *implies* the next step. Suppose I said the body is *pregnant* with the next step. You would say, "Yes, I understand." Suppose I said that the body *loves* the next step. You would say, "All right, you can say that." Suppose I say the body *cooks* the next step; *bakes* the next step; *lacks* the next step, or *holds its breath longing for* the next step. By this time you would know what I am saying, even if I use no word at all but just write that the body . . . . .s the next step. In that blank, my word "implying" says *and is* the intricacy which is greater than the schemes that any one of the possible words brings with it. In whatever way I might actually say it, you would let the word work newly and freshly when it comes into a spot like that. All the words can in this way acquire a new meaning, provided of course they're part of the situation, part of a context, part of an interaction. It is right to say that language is inherent in experience, but we have to understand by language this way in which words can work newly in a given spot.

Language is implicit in the body. The body knows language. But language is not a closed system. The body can always give the words more feedback than can possibly be derived just from concepts or forms or distinctions. I mean the familiar body, the one that is sitting in the chair or standing by the stove, knows language in this way. In other words, it is the physical body that you enter to get to the *intricacy* that I am talking about.

The physical body is continuous with the universe, but to enter it you start not with microscopes. You start with quite ordinary experience; you start in just the same place where you are hungry or scared. Starting with this ordinary body you get a wider, at first confusing, murky (. . . . .) sense that we're taught to consider as nothing. But a felt sense comes. And when we have a point to make, words come. You know how words come? We open our mouths and expect. Really, and if they don't come, there is not much we can do except try again.

This *coming* is characteristic of the body. What else comes like that? Sleep comes like that, and appetites. If they don't come, you just have to wait. We all know that. Tears come like that, and orgasm. Emotions come like that, and so also this felt sense, which is wider and at first not clear, comes like that. Then steps come from that felt sense, and they can be quite new steps, and often more intricate than any common concept or distinction.

A SKETCH OF THE BACKGROUND AND THE OPENING TO THE GREATER ORDER

Forms (categories, concepts . . . . .) are always already functioning in anything human. It is true that what exceeds them cannot be separated from them, or they from it. My issue is only whether what exceeds them is chaos, or rather, another order.

It seems that all words bring distinctions, that language works by distinctions. Even the statement that there is *another* order seems itself to be a distinction. So it is often said that there is "no other of language."[2] Sometimes this is also said in Friedrich Nietzsche's way: There are only interpretations, there is nothing to interpret. He means that there is nothing that first *is*, and is then later interpreted. And indeed, insofar as forms and distinctions are always implicit in any human experience, they would seem to bear out the claim. But the question is: Are forms and distinctions the only order? I will show and say another order.

When the philosopher Edmund Husserl developed phenomenology as a method for uncovering the structures of experience, he discovered another order.[3] Phenomenology finds something more than theories and concepts in experience. Husserl denied the old theory that, for example, a tree is seen as bits of color. We see a tree, he said. Even if we think that perception can only be of color and light, still—it's a tree we see. Similarly, we hear a door slamming, and motorcycles going by. Husserl found that our ordinary experience of situations is utterly different and more complex than our theories and concepts render it. For instance, in every event there is always something definite and something vague; time relations are different and much more intricate than our usual use of clocks would have us believe. Moreover taken phenomenologically, every concept or distinction opens out into an experiential field, an intricacy that is compellingly there for us in quite another way than the concepts and distinctions are there for us. In all this, Husserl thought he discovered a realm of eternal essences, finer distinctions far exceeding any extant concepts, theories, or philosophies. But he went in like Adam, naming all the animals. For example, he began by dividing everything into three sections: perceiving, feeling, and willing. It didn't occur to him to question that old, three-way distinction. He thought he found it in the phenomena and went on to render much more into finer and finer distinctions.

Husserl did not realize that intricacy cannot be caught within distinctions. With different distinctions, a somewhat different intricacy opens. But that doesn't mean intricacy depends wholly on the distinctions. Rather, after any distinctions, the intricacy is always again *more*, and can overthrow the very distinctions that first brought it. The finest distinctions open into a further intricacy that is not consistent with them.

The task is to think with this fact! To think how intricacy functions is the task I am setting up here.

Since phenomena do not have that simple independence Husserl assumed, it can seem as if phenomenologically speaking, experience has no order of its own at all, as if it depended *entirely* on the distinctions that one reads out or into it. Martin Heidegger, who followed Husserl, wrote early on that all concepts and distinctions depend upon a more basic kind of understanding that already exists in all human living and practice. It is that felt, "moody" kind of understanding with which we create our situations, the implicit understanding with which we go about acting, trying, going-for, and avoiding. It is an understanding which, he said, "reaches much farther than cognition."[4] That would seem to set up the task, in philosophy at least, of changing our approach so that we would think with this felt, moody understanding which reaches further than ordinary cognition. But Heidegger did not go on to do this. Instead, he proceeded along Kantian lines[5] to look for antecedents which determine the making of all experience. Where Husserl had given the intricacy of experience too much independence from concepts, Heidegger credited all of the intricacy to a general metaphysics. He assumed that the more-than-cognitive, felt, "pre-understanding" (as he called it) is always entirely determined by a philosophical approach. He believed that every age has a certain philosophical understanding of being, and that it is exemplified by everything that happens in that age. He believed this basic understanding to be the crux of a period's dominant philosophy. While he denied that the basic understanding consists of concepts, he affirmed nevertheless that a dominant philosophy has the power of determining everything under it, just as concepts would, or perhaps even more thoroughly than concepts would. Heidegger argued that no change can move *from* practice *to* philosophy, only from philosophy to practice, only in one direction.

The relativism that is current today in Western culture stems from this one-way direction, from *interpretive* approaches to cultural practice, to people, to bodies. A belief in relativism (and nihilism) is so widely held today because it is assumed that all experience is derivative from forms, that these forms are given by history, and that they are therefore utterly relative. A lot of interpretations but nothing to interpret. Thus the view, for example, that there is no nature, no human nature, no truth, and no rightness, other than whatever variant happens to have been programmed into us by culture. There is also new programming, of course, but as relativist thinkers see it, it is always from the top down, from the outside in, never *from experience.* For instance, Michel Foucault's understanding of California is that you can, with Gestalt psychologist Fritz Perls, get into your body more, or you can, with death counselor Elizabeth Kubler-Ross, learn something called "leaving your body." Equally, with psychoanalysis, you can make yourself more controlled, or with assertiveness training, less so. Such thinkers think that nothing new can ever come from within the body. Animals might have instincts, but the human body, says Foucault, "was utterly destroyed by history."[6] One might say that on this view, you make yourself as one is said to make a work of art: you build into yourself certain values and concepts that are determined in advance. Foucault thinks it can only be an illusion that you find anything coming from deep within yourself. Everything is assumed to be a product of some arbitrarily imposed order of one sort or another.

In sum, relativists assume that the intricacy of experience is entirely derivative from forms (social rules, distinctions . . . . .) which always already determine any individual's experience in advance. They think that cultural practice consists only of derivatives of an implicitly functioning program of historically imposed forms and rules—ones which can of course break down, but then leave us only in limbo. But experience is neither independent of concepts nor just dependent on them. We will find that we can enter into the intricacy between the poles of the distinction: dependent or independent. In so doing, we will miss neither the greater intricacy of experience and practice, nor the patterned forms which are, indeed, always already at work. But we must see how forms work in and after the intricacy. (Notice, by the way, the distinction here between a "we" and an "it"—we who will see how intricacy works.) I will show that all distinctions, when broken into, do not break down into meaninglessness. Rather, they work and at the same time open into a more exacting intricacy.

Since intricacy is not separable from distinctions, and since it is somewhat different with different distinctions, you might wonder what independence from them it can have. You will see that intricacy has an order of its own because it always responds with an unavoidable exactitude that vastly exceeds what could possibly follow from the distinctions. So it is wrong to say that they—the distinctions—made (found, lifted out, synthesized, differentiated . . . . .) what comes. That attributes the intricacy to *them*. While it is true that what comes is always orderly and exact, yet much more comes than could have followed from the order and exactness alone.

For example, my ideas about another person (or myself) can lead to finding something in direct experience. But what comes in direct experience is always much more intricate than my original ideas. Moreover what comes can also overthrow the very idea that helped to bring it up. For example, I wrote this down after a therapy hour: "After following my client very closely, I give a well-considered interpretation. I say: "Oh—isn't that about your father?" My client is silent a bit, and then says something like: "Oh, it really helped me when you asked me that—it, uh, I can hardly touch it inside—it's my mother."

Yes, I get a lot of credit for interpretations like that. They help to bring to the fore the experience which proves them wrong. But even if it had been her father, what comes is always ten thousand not-yet-separated-stands, never simply just what we said or thought.

All the same, one might object: "Sure, any experience has a more intricate order than the concepts you bring to it, but doesn't any experience implicitly contain many old distinctions and concepts, and aren't these really the intricacy of which we speak here?" We will answer first that those concepts that *are* implicit in experience do not work in the same way as if they were explicit. They do not work in that clean, determinative way to constrain everything that follows to be consistent with them, as concepts and distinctions were long said to do. Nor do they just contradict or make disorder. We will go on to say that, "Yes, there is a welter of implicit concepts in any experience; but no, the intricacy vastly exceeds them as well." How can we know that? We can know it from how the intricacy functions; it does not function like concepts, whether implicit or explicit.

The issue depends not on mere assertions; it depends on whether we can examine, think with, show, and say, how the order greater than distinctions *functions*, and how distinctions function after, in, and with it.

THE FUNCTION OF THE BODY IN THOUGHT AND LANGUAGE

Let us now think with stories, with incidents from practice, to show how one can move *from* practice *to* philosophy.

Suppose again, for instance, that someone says hello to you as you walk down the street, and that you don't know who it is but you certainly know the person. It is uhm, ah, ... Now you feel how you don't particularly like the person, something odd, yes, sort of uhm . . . . . . You rotate your hand. The dislike has no words either; it is your uniquely felt sense of knowing that person. But if you now go into this sense of dislike, a vast intricacy opens—all your situations with that person and your own quirks are implicit in making that dislike.

Take another example. The others are talking and you are waiting for a break to get in, to make a point which came to you as you listened to them. You can feel that it's a good point and you are eager to make it. Now your chance comes, you announce that you wish to say something. They turn to you, and—someone walks in and interrupts. When the interruption is over, everyone turns to you again, but you have forgotten the point! Again, as in the first example, you do have something left; you have the implicit feel of that point. It was so good; just right. And again, in this instance, it is something forgotten, but something which a . . . . . somehow implicitly knows. But this time you never had the point in words as you once had the person's name in words. It was a new point.

Yes, something new can come in this way, but in my examples

so far, what you forgot did exist before you forgot it. In the next example we will see that such a blank can also imply something that has never existed in an explicit way.

When one stands before a painting that hangs crookedly, one feels a certain unease. One can straighten it, then stand back and sense very exactly if it needs finer adjusting. Symmetry, you say. Learned, of course. But by now a *bodily* demand.

An unfinished design also makes one feel what it needs. The artist adds a line and then stands back, and feels very exactly whether the line is what it needs or whether that new line was wrong and must be taken out again. The artist might stand before such a design for a long time—even years, sensing but not finding the needed line. The design needs something, but what? It's not just unbalanced, as if adding most anything to the left side would do. No, it needs—uhm, ah, hmmm, ... That blank seems to know what the design needs. Certainly it knows to reject the line the artist just tried. And also to reject many more lines that come and are never even drawn. That . . . . . knows what and where a right new line goes, and yet that line has never existed before—in the history of the world.

Certainly old forms and patterns might function to help bring such a new step, but not by constraining the new to be consistent with the old. Rather, the old forms change as they work implicitly. That shows that they do not work alone to bring a next step.

Here is a story from psychotherapy. Notice how the new next step comes after the silent, stuck blank between.

The client has a felt sense, something about not wanting to live, being pulled to die, something very sore. She says that she badly needs rest, but resting is impossible because *this*, in her, will not rest.

(silence) . . . . . This needs to rest, and it can't. If it lets down and rests it will die.

I keep her quiet company. I only repeat: "Maybe it could let down and rest if you could trust something." As therapist, I think, "If only I knew what to do!" No, wrong. As therapist, if the client is already feeling and sensing that stuck blank, keep quiet. The step comes from that bodily-felt sense:

(silence) . . . . .

After a minute, she says:

Now, suddenly, it feels like a house on stilts that go into the earth. All of me on top . . . that's a house and it's on stilts. It is lifted off of this sore place. Now the sore place is like a layer, and it can breathe. Do you know those steel posts they put into the ground, to hold up a building? These stilts are like that.

(silence) . . . . . Yea (breath), now there's time for that sore place to breathe.

Later she says:

When I was little I played a lot with stilts. I used to go between the power wires on them. It was dangerous, but it was play! I used to make taller and taller ones, and go on them there. Stilts! I haven't thought of those for years. And play, and danger. How does this process do that? It uses all these things to make something that wasn't there before.

Like every experience, this one includes much from the past. The play in the danger zone and the stilts are from the past. But this step is not a deeper experiencing of the past. This client had experienced the past more deeply many times before. *Here something new came instead,* a new physical way of being, a new internal arrangement that never existed before.

This kind of step can be more intricate and novel than any that we could design on purpose. In retrospect we say it is just what we wished. But we could not have designed, in advance, just this intricate arrangement of stilts supporting her, lifting the pressure off, so that something underneath can breathe.

After all of these stories I can state to you directly what they were meant to show. Had I done that without them, you might have only understood my words in one of their old uses. All words, after all, bring old schemes. Even now, if I say that the blank *implies* the next line, someone might object that the word "imply" implies that the line was there, folded under, hidden in the blank. I deny that the word "implicit" says that here. It says rather how a (. . . . .) functions to let such a line come. The next objection might be: "OK, so the line was not there." I deny that, too. "Aha," the person will then say, "so the line was there and also not there. You see! A contradiction. Rupture. Breaking of all distinctions. Limbo."

I want to show that behind a distinction opens an intricacy that is a much greater order. Here, someone might patronize me by saying, "Yes, yes, but it can't be said. All words bring distinctions."

To be sure, words do, I would answer, but their saying is beyond distinctions. If you think the stories with me, you won't need me to tell you that some of these words work in a new way here, and also, that the stories say how it is possible for words to say something new. *Any situation, any bit of practice, implies much more than has ever been said.* That is how poets and artists are possible. It is also why we know in clinical practice to be careful not to limit people to our ideas of them. Much more than that can come from them.

When I said earlier that the blank *implies* the next line, I did not need to tell you that the word doesn't say the line is there, only hidden, folded under. Why didn't I need to tell you that? In that instance and that phrasing, the word has already broken out of its old distinction. It is not in limbo. It is saying something new and more intricate, more orderly than either *was* or *wasn't* there before. This will happen with any word that works in the blank. It might require some degree of genius to let it make sense, but if it does, it will say this blank.

What is this . . . . . ? Language, certainly. Grammar insofar as the words around it hold the blank open. Yes, it is language. But the blank is also our situation. And the . . . . . is also a felt sense in our bodies; for example, it is a felt sense in the artist's body. So it is in ours as we try to say this . . . . . . The felt sense is an odd quality, an unease, a hunger, a wanting that knows in a very exacting way what it wants, ... So the blank is the body (language, the situation . . . . .).

In the (. . . . .), body and situation are not two different things in two different places. In thus opening the old distinction between body and situation, you can see that there is a far more intricate order than just the demise of a spatial division. Now I do not need to tell you that body, language, and situation are not three different things, nor the same thing. After all, three words have worked to say what the blank is, and each word now has the others implicit in it. Yet each still says something different after what the others say.

There are many quite fine ways in which we can say that body and situation are different. Such fine ways also let the word "difference" say a different kind of difference, no longer a difference between two things. Rather, the body can imply what has never yet happened in a situation, and a situation can exceed what the body feels. For instance, when one first learns to fly an airplane, high-up is scary and one relaxes near the ground where everything looks familiar. Later, one's body has learned that it's safe up there, and one feels in peril and most alert near the ground where crashes most easily occur. So, the situation has a bodily implying in it too, and it may be beyond my individual body's implying.

You see how intricacy opens as soon as we think with it. Surely new distinctions do arise, but thinking in intricacy allows them to open into still further steps, which are again very exact but not equivalent to them. Some implied further steps also simplify into a new understanding of a whole. The steps do not always bring finer distinctions. The finer the new distinctions, the better, but there cannot be one consistent system comprising all of them. There is not one eternal or absolute system in which the body is first distinguished from the universe, so that finer distinctions then all fall on one side or the other. We let distinctions work to open an intricacy that is always more exact, and that can always be different.

Let us open another old distinction: it is not a question of trusting or not trusting the body. We cannot trust the result of any one step; we *can*, however, trust the kind of process of steps I am describing. It is also possible to discover a more exacting intricacy about the process itself: how to trust, think, and act with this bodily implying.

FUNCTIONS OF THE BODY IN LANGUAGE

(a) The body is (has, feels, lives . . . . .) an implying of further events.
(b) The body has intentionality, that is to say, it has (feels, knows, is, implies . . . . .) situations.
(c) The body has language implicit in it. (Situation and language are furthermore implicit in each other.)
(d) Words to speak *come* to us in a bodily way, sometimes smoothly, sometimes after a . . . . . . If the words to speak don't come, we are stuck, and must wait for them.

Let me remind you that this coming is characteristic of the body. I mentioned how appetite comes, also orgasm, tears, sleep. You recognize the bodily nature of such comings. Emotions also come in this way. You can feign joy or anger but to *have* them, they must come. So also does the muse come, when she is willing and not otherwise. And new ideas, the lines of a new design, and steps of therapy come in this way.

(e) The body can imply something quite new which has never as yet actually occurred.

It is a mistake to think of the body as a fixed machine, and thought-forms as creating novelty. Just the reverse: logic only rearranges already cut units. In contrast, the body, particularly a more bodily thinking, creates novelty.

When you hold your breath, your body wants and pre-figures the familiar exhaling. But not just exhaling is implied, rather any way to get oxygen, and not just oxygen but anything that would fulfill the function oxygen fulfills, and perhaps not just that function but some other function that would serve to keep the body alive. Implying is always like that, very demandingly exact, but more than a fixed form-in-advance. Evolution *implies* this. The evolution of species is not wholly explained by selection among untold trillions of useless variants. Living bodies imply their continuation more precisely than by just one form. It is for this reason that something new and more intricate *can* always happen.

(f) Bodily implying is a value-direction.

Bodily implying implies steps in the right direction. It helps to expect a step in the right direction, without defining the right direction. Then you are whole in your wanting. You get beyond the patterned forms and every either/or. Instead of either/or, or in between, the little steps bring something else. The intricacy of bodily implying has an other-than-formed direction.

It may seem that every step of such a process changes its direction. For example, suppose you were at a party and felt you were bored and needed to go home. But suppose that instead of going home, you opened up the boredom and found anger. And suppose that in finding the anger you found also that you needed to stay and say something directly about the anger to someone. In a similar way, as we pursue a goal, the goal seems to change. But later we say that our new goal is the one we really wanted all along but we didn't know it. It may seem that "direction" is the wrong word for this more intricate continuity-discontinuity of implying. The word "direction" seems to be taken from geometry. But the kind of direction I am talking about already exists even in plants; it long precedes the geometric kind of direction and geometric kind of form-continuity.

(g) The felt sense used to be little known.

Until recently, there was no established word or phrase for this bodily sensed implying. It was often called "kinaesthetic" but *kinae* means motion, and I need not tell you that you can have it also while sitting still. It was also called "proprioceptive." Etymologically that means sensing oneself. It does not well name "sensing oneself living in interaction in situations." Also, "proprioceptive" is mostly used for sensing one's muscles. Until recently, did most people really sense their bodies only as the five external sense, plus motion and muscles? Of course, some people knew this felt sense, but efforts to describe it show that most people did not. Even today, judging from my own clinical experience, roughly half of the readers probably do not know it.

(h) A felt sense is not an emotion.

A felt sense differs from an emotion. It is wider, and at first unclear, murky—the sort of feeling which we might describe by saying: "This is nothing." Or: "Just confusion." At first it can be very slight, just a whiff of some bodily quality; for instance, a slight unease, a tightness, or a jumpy feeling. Quite soon it may then turn out that very strong emotions were implicit in it, along with much else.

For example, the word "angry" describes an emotion which, in some respects, is always the same regardless of whom or what you are angry at. "Sure, I'm angry," you say, and your heart pounds and your body would be ready to fight if you would so choose. But in another way, if you wait for a few moments, you can find that the anger is only part of something wider—a felt sense. The quality of that felt sense is unique to just this situation. At first it is only a murky bodily quality. For instance, along with your anger, you might find a kind of rush-rush, a sense of hurry. If you focus on that felt sense, you find, perhaps, that you want to *stay* mad. Now, going into it further, there is that most unwelcome sense that you yourself acted stupidly, not only the other person. And in that chagrin is much more, of course. Now it opens into how you never handle this kind of situation well, and that, in turn, is because you feel ashamed of this other thing, which would not make you ashamed except for your lack of self-confidence, which involves a certain other way you are, which is because of still other things and so on. And that was all with you in some implicit way when you got mad.

Because there is always such an *intricacy*, it cannot be said that we just impose meaning. It is incorrect to say that, from the top down, we "attach meaning" to experience, organize or reframe it. We cannot just tell ourselves a story that we like better than all the intricacy that is us. Those who say that our past is a "narrative" understand that situations are not fixed facts. But we must not miss that they are an implying that can be carried forward. And, yes, all meanings, concepts, and distinctions can help toward a genuine new step in which the sense of a situation changes. But if we try a reframing, and then it does not bring a physically-felt step actually from the body, then we better try another reframing. Or, we wait, and let the felt sense give new steps.

The felt sense has all this intricacy, but at first it is a murky bodily quality, quite different from an emotion.

(*i*) A felt sense is found in our located body.

A felt sense comes from the ordinary physical body. In order to find a felt sense, one must first let one's attention go inside this body. My attention must attend here, to this body located, for example, here behind this desk. Your attention must attend to your body seated in the chair or on the couch as you read these words. One first finds a felt sense by attending in the middle of one's ordinary, located body.

(*j*) A felt sense is not automatically there; it must come.

It is erroneous to assume that the felt sense is ever present, that it's just not always noticed. Sometimes a bodily implying moves smoothly into occurring. But when we are stuck, we may just be at a loss. An implying of the next step may not come. To learn how to let a felt sense come opens a great many new possibilities for further steps at any juncture.

We have devised a procedure called "focusing" to make this letting-come teachable.[7] The procedure is now taught in relation to therapy, writing, business, problem solving, healing, and in other situations and fields of endeavor. The instructions are more than I could present here. For each common difficulty one encounters, there are specific ways of working through the difficulty. It takes longer than a few minutes to learn the technique, but over a period of days nearly everyone can learn it.

THE WIDER SENSE

There is an ancient tradition according to which, if we were directly in contact with God, we would burn up. If you think of the body as insulation, then it makes sense that the cosmos comes to us *through* our bodies. It might otherwise be puzzling, given the history of mechanical concepts of the body, why we need to pay attention *through* the body. We must indeed attend through the body to think about a situation or any topic further than the obvious. We need to attend further than the obvious in order to develop as people—and I would argue that we need to develop as people. It is not enough that there is an infinite cosmos. We need to develop ourselves, however discouraging we may sometimes seem to ourselves.

Your own inner phenomenological sense of your own body is not only your sense of your muscles, your legs, the back of your head. It's not only a sensing of things like the floor, the chair, or whatever you see or touch. The bodily sense is also your sense of your situations, your life. For example, I am now part of your situation. You have been permitting my words to have an effect on how your body feels to you right now.

Our bodies carry our situations. We carry our life with us. Our bodies can total up years of all kinds of experience and at any moment give us something new, a new more intricate step.

NOTES

1. I often use a string of words instead of just one in a given slot. For example, I might say you *feel* your life, you *are, have, live* . . . . . your life. The five dots leave room for other possible words. After the string and the sequence of dots once appear, any one of the words can later say what is meant. But furthermore, when we let each of the words work, then each says the (. . . . .) that includes the others so that the (. . . . .) is more than any single scheme. In this way we are not limited by any one formulation.

2. Jacques Derrida, *Disseminations, Outwork* (Chicago: University of Chicago Press, 1981), 3–43.

3. Edmund Husserl, *Ideas Pertaining to a Pure Phenomenology and to a Phomentological Philosophy*, Book I, trans. F. Kersten (The Hague: Martinus Nijhoff, 1983).

4. Martin Heidegger, *Being and Time*, trans. J. Macquarrie and E. Robinson (New York: Harper and Row, 1962), 172–173.

5. Martin Heidegger, *Gesamtausgabe* (*Collected Works*), Vol. 26, *The Metaphysical Foundations of Logic* (*Following Leibnitz*), trans. Michael Heim (Bloomington, Indiana University Press, 1984), 199.

6. Michel Foucault, "Nietzsche, Genealogy, History," in *Language, Counter-Memory, Practice*, ed. and trans. D. Bouchard (Ithaca: Cornell University Press, 1977), 148.

7. Eugene T. Gendlin, *Experience and the Creation of Meaning*, 2nd ed. (New York: Free Press, 1970); "Experiential Phenomenology," in *Phenomenology and the Social Sciences*, ed. M. Natanson (Evanston: Northwestern University Press, 1973); "Two Phenomenologists Do Not Disagree," in *Phenomenology, Dialogues and Bridges*, ed. R. Bruzina and B. Wilshire (New York: State University of New York Press, 1982); "A Philosophical Critique of the Concept of Narcissism," in *Pathologies of the Modern Self: Postmodern Studies*, ed. D. M. Levin (New York: New York University Press, 1987); "Thinking Beyond Patterns: Body, Language, and Situations," in *The Presence of Feeling in Thought*, eds. B. den Ouden and M. Moen (New York: Peter Lang, 1991).

MARY LeCRON FOSTER

11

Body Process in the Evolution
of Language

PRIMORDIAL LANGUAGE

Our language seems almost as inevitable to us as natural events, such as breathing, eating, making love, or childbirth. Speaking, like those activities, is a bodily process, but it does not come naturally, as an inevitable part of living. It is a *learned* activity, determined by culture rather than by physical rules. As such, its beginnings lie far in the prehistoric past.

Language was devised by our hominid ancestors, probably, like tool-making, very gradually over many millenia. By the time that our immediate ancestor, *Homo sapiens sapiens*, appeared, perhaps 35,000 years ago, or even earlier, language had probably reached a considerable degree of complexity, as had tool-making and art. This complexity suggests a high degree of symbolic sophistication, based on the ability to represent one thing by something of a quite different kind, and to use representation as a means of thinking and communicating about the past, the future, and the unknown, as well as reflecting and commenting on the present. Delivery of these complex messages involves nothing more than interaction between surfaces in the mouth and throat. We are so accustomed to producing and understanding human speech that it usually does not occur to us to wonder at it, or to consider either the subtlety of these movements or the complexity of coordination of gesture, sound, and sense that is involved. Nor does it usually occur to us to wonder how it came into being.

I present here a hypothesis, based on a wide variety of comparative evidence, that referential language began with a well-developed capacity for mimicry that included bodily imitation of spatial relationships. Although this imitation was gestural, the hypothesis discussed here differs materially from the gestural theory of language origins in giving primacy to the role of bodily analogy in language evolution.

The gestural theory in its recent form is primarily the result of the work of Gordon Hewes, who assumes priority of hand gesture as signal, beginning "with a few gestures, perhaps with simple deixis or ostension."[1] Although Hewes embraces my term of "phememe," as the Paleolithic precursor of the historically attested "phoneme," for articulatorily differentiated units of speech, he fails to see the implications of the phememic theory, which derives phememes analogically, not as a substitute for hand gesture, but as oral mouth movements made in imitation of spatial relationships in nature.

My contention is that not only language but also the whole of culture derived from an emergent human capacity to build systems of categorization through steadily increasing exploitation of analogical relationships. Although these began with bodily mimicry of spatial relationships, over time they became increasingly abstract, giving human beings an overwhelming adaptational advantage.[2] Far from a specific "language-acquisition device," which provides a child with a biologically innate language template, as Noam Chomsky has argued,[3] it is the uniquely human ability to recognize and utilize analogy in the construction of cultural systems that separates human from nonhuman species. From this evolutionary perspective, it is not rationality that distinguishes human beings, but the ability to use analogy to enhance rationality. Some degree of both analogical and logical thinking is common to all sentient species. Mind and body are biologically inseparable, and the Cartesian dichotomy must be rejected, as well as the Chomskyan separation of language from other bodily systems.

THINKING OURSELVES BACK TO THE BEGINNING

To think ourselves back to what might have been the beginning of language we need to ask ourselves what language actually *is*.

One thing that, in the beginning, it was *not* was writing. All over the world people with no knowledge of writing or reading are using language. Writing was invented much later than language. The earliest known writing system was that of the ancient Sumerians of Mesopotamia, first attested from 4,100 B.C. Both speech and writing require the use of body parts—for speech the various parts of the mouth and the vocal cords, for writing the hand. For reception, speech needs ear and/or eye, and writing the eye alone.

Since the other primates, and in particular the great apes, are the mammals closest to human beings in their physical and mental structure, in trying to see how language could have come about, it is useful to investigate what it is that lower primates can do that both differs from the activities of other mammals and has a greater similarity to what human beings are capable of. We probably think that apes are more intelligent than other animals—which really comes down to *what* and *how* they are capable of learning.

Learning depends upon the ability to watch, to listen, to remember—and, especially, to imitate or to represent in some way, at the moment or later, what has been heard or seen. All mammals have the first three abilities, and to some extent the fourth, but only the primates are capable of more than rudimentary bodily mimicry. Monkeys and apes can mimic gestures and are capable of delayed gestural mimicry. What they do not do naturally (spontaneously) is mimic *representational* gesture, and this is the entire basis of speech. They can also learn and respond appropriately to a sizable repertoire of single spoken words or short phrases. Dog owners are aware that dogs also can learn such a repertory and also respond appropriately to other gestural signs, so *response* to purposeful activity is seen to be common to other mammals than primates. But we need to consider the nature of the response. Mouth movements and sounds of nonhuman mammals are always signals or indications of emotion. They signal such direct survival-promoting awareness as the presence of danger, the presence of food, the presence of other members of the group, or the use of the body to make signs indicating an emotional state—anger, fear, desire, pleasure. Symbols are different in kind. Not only do symbols *represent* something other—and often quite unlike themselves—but they are also members of interlocking systems of *classification*. They do not *mean* by thcmselves; they only *mean* because they operate within networks of symbols and classes of symbols. While lower mammals can classify to some extent (the word "ball" doesn't mean a particular ball to a dog but *any* ball—it is refcrable to an abstract class of ball-ness) such classification is not systematic but idiosyncratic and isolated.

THE BODY IN COMMUNICATION

All meaning interchange, whether linguistic or not, depends upon bodily movements or the result of those movements. Humans, like other mammals, also use bodily movement as signal or sign of emotion. We point to show where; smile, laugh, or nod to show approval or pleasure; grimace or cry to show distaste, anger or sorrow; shrug our shoulders to show lack of concern; turn our heads toward or away to show interest or its lack; hold out our hands to plead; turn thumbs down to show disapproval, and so forth.

Where bodily movements expressed emotional states and warning signals for early hominids, as they do still today for other mammals, the new and unique hominid ability which became language was specifically directed toward expression of reference. Coupled with controlled intake and expiration of air, speech makes use of movable oral muscles and surfaces for its production. Speech accompanies sign gesture but does not replace it. It has often been said that the advent of language in the evolution of a mammalian species built a new system on systems that were originally developed and still are used for other purposes: eating and breathing. A complex evolutionary process was involved which enabled hominids to produce a varied differential repertoire of interconnected vocal sounds without choking. There had been no use for such a differentiated sound repertoire until the social need to interchange differentiated meanings increased. It seems likely that signal and sign by facial movement had become progressively complex before speech began, and that its very complexity led into the new, referential, usage.

LANGUAGE AS GESTURAL SYSTEM

Language as referential gesture is extremely complex as well as thoroughly systematic. That is to say it involves a series of interlocking systems of classification, with each class based on an analogical relationship between members of that class. In grammar, these classes are called phonology, morphology, and syntax. All of them are based on analogy of *positioning:* the place of elements in an utterance. Where identical privileges of position are involved— that is, where one element can be substituted for another within a given utterance—the substitutable elements belong to a class. A syntactic example might be: "The dog bit the boy." "A" could be substituted for "the." These are members of a syntactic class called "article." "Bear" could be substituted for "dog." These are members of a class called "noun." They are not only nouns but they are animate, or sentient nouns because of the verb "bit," positioned where we might equally well find "saw," both being activities of sentient beings. For words, meaning enters into class membership as well as into positioning, that is, "sentient" has a specific meaning, "noun" a very abstract meaning not referable to any physical characteristics.

Because in language the position of elements in an utterance governs its intelligibility, we cannot meaningfully say, for example, "the bit boy dog the." The sounds of language are also conventionally positioned. We say "boy" and not *yob* or *byo.* Most languages operate with only twenty to thirty essential sounds, called "phonemes." Limitation of elements does not mean changelessness. Phonemes, like words, can be added, subtracted, or otherwise changed, but their numbers at any given time or for any given group are limited either by what the users can easily process and/or by the direction that change has taken toward reduction or expansion of the phoneme inventory. Phonemes are classed by two kinds of positioning: sequential positioning within the utterance, and systematic positioning of like phonemes within the mouth or throat. One reason phonemes are easily distinguishable from one another is that similar sounds are organized to be articulated in similar ways, as can be seen in a hypothetical phonemic chart, Table 11.1.[4] I will discuss the chart according to the phonological characteristics of the individual members, that is, as articulatory, "phones" rather than as conventionalized "phonemes." (Phones are traditionally enclosed within square brackets and phonemes within slanted brackets.) The reader is invited to follow the discussion experientially by actually articulating the phones.

Phonologically, the consonantal vocal tract is spatially organized from outer to inner surfaces—read from left to right on the chart. Lip movements of several kinds are shown in the left hand column. The second column shows movements of tongue tip

Table 11.1. Chart of a hypothetical phonemic organization

	Consonants					
	Labial	*Dental*	*Alveolar*	*Palatal*	*Velar*	*Laryngeal*
Stops						
Voiceless	p	t	c	č	k	ʔ
Voiced	b	d	ӡ	ǰ	g	
Spirants						
Voiceless	f	θ	s	š	x	h
Voiced	v	đ	z	ž		ʻ
Sonorants	m	n	l	r	ŋ	
Semivowels	w			y		

	Vowels		
	Front	*Central*	*Back*
High	i	ɨ	u
Medium	e	ə	o
Low		a	

against the teeth or alveolar ridge ([θ] is pronounced as *th* in English *think*, [đ] as in English *this*). The third column shows contact of slightly flattened tongue tip against the alveolar ridge ([c] is pronounced as English *ts*, [ӡ] as English *dz*). The fourth column indicates contact of the central tongue surface with the hard palate ([č] as English *ch*, [ǰ] as English *j*, [š] as English *sh*, [ž] as *s* in English *vision*). The fifth column shows contact between the back of the tongue and the velum (with [ŋ] as in English word-final *ng*), and the sixth column shows glottal or laryngeal closure [ʔ] is glottal closure, often used as the onset of initial vowels in English, and [ʻ] is a voiced laryngeal constriction, foreign to English but common to Semitic languages).

Thus, extending the horizontal readings vertically, we find the same points of contact, in the first line with total closure, the second line with total closure plus vibration of the vocal cords, the third line with partial closure allowing some emission of air, the fourth line with partial closure plus vibration of the vocal cords, and the fifth line with vibration of the vocal cords and emission of air with different kinds of total or partial contoural contact. For sonorants, vocal cords are vibrated and air passage is not stopped. Nasals [m], [n] and [ŋ] are identical with [b], [d] and [g] respectively except that the velum is closed so that air is released through the nose. Liquids [l] and [r] allow air to escape around the sides of the raised tongue. Semivowels [w] and [y] round or stretch lips respectively, with raised tongue but without air blockage. Phonemes with total closure are called "stops." Sounds without complete closure are called "continuants," which are either spirants (fricatives) or sonorants (resonants).

Vowels can also be read according to their front to back articulation and represented as left to right. Because frontal tongue height is highest for [i] and lowest for [u], the vowel chart shows [i] on the left (front) and [u] on the right (back). Central vowels are [ɨ], [ə] (the first more or less as English *u* in the word *just* when it is unstressed, the second when stressed) and [a] as in English *far*. Vowels result from vocal cord vibration with varying tongue height and varying lip positioning short of full closure, thus allowing free expelling of air through a more open passage. Reading vertically, the tongue is successively lowered to produce each sound.

While all languages do not have all of these sounds, and other sounds that some languages do have have not been included in the chart, all languages have orally articulated sounds that contrast with one another, such that if one is substituted for another within a given word, meaning change occurs. It is this contrastiveness and articulatory systematization that distinguishes phonemes from randomly articulated phones—phonetically similar sounds that together constitute a phonological class: a phoneme. Phones of the same phoneme do not change meanings. Most languages have somewhere between twenty and thirty distinguishable phonemes. When a language is written, phonemes (not phones) are ideally distinguished by alphabetical symbols. Sometimes alphabets, like that used for English, reflect earlier stages of the language. For example, *k* in the words *know* and *knit* are no longer pronounced. Our present writing system does not completely represent the current phonemic state of our language, for example, the letter *c* overlaps with both *k* and *s*. Our present working system has been modified to some extent by past history.

LANGUAGE INTERRELATIONSHIPS

Before proceeding to examine how oral gestures became language, I will first describe briefly something of the history of linguistics and how the comparative method in linguistics arose, and in turn how we can know the nature of earlier language stages and their relationships.

Until the nineteenth century, there was little understanding of the interrelationships between languages. In Europe, the ancient and no longer spoken languages, Latin and Greek, were known because they were preserved through writing systems, and were seen to bear some resemblance to one another. Because Greek was the more ancient of the two, Latin was generally supposed to be some form of corrupt or degenerate Greek. Toward the end of the eighteenth century, the British philologist, Sir William Jones, returned from India, where he had become acquainted with Sanskrit. In a talk to fellow philologists, he said that in relation to Greek and Latin,

> Sanskrit bears a stronger affinity, both in the roots of verbs and in the forms of grammar, than could possibly have been produced by accident; so strong, indeed, that no philologer could examine them all three without believing them to have sprung from some common source, which, perhaps, no longer exists; there is a similar reason, though not quite so forcible for supposing that both the Gothick and the Celtick, though blended with a very different idiom, had the same origin with the Sanskrit.[5]

A dawning appreciation of Sanskrit revolutionized European philology, as scholars set about exploring the similarities suggested by Jones. The idea of common ancestry of a group of languages led to the search for ways of discovering the prototype, and the field of comparative linguistics was born.

During the nineteenth century, great progress in language history was made, and "the comparative method," which became the scientific bulwark of language reconstruction, was devised and perfected, with Indo-European as the model. The basic tenet of this approach to the discovery of earlier stages of language became the safeguard against error upon which all subsequent linguistic reconstructive effort has rested. This tenet is that the phonological changes that have occurred over time in any given language are not random but regular. Thus, a genetic relationship can be established only if, when more than a single meaningful form is compared in two or more languages, the phoneme equivalences are kept constant, or if they differ, can be otherwise explained.

For example, (disregarding vowel correspondences which require much more complex explanation), we find English *three* and Latin *tres*, showing a root with a spirantal dental [θ] onset (written th) in English, and a stopped dental onset [t] in Latin, while root

final [r] remains [r] in both languages. Comparing English *father*
with Latin *pater* we find the same correspondences of [θ] to [t],[6] and
[r] to [r], but this time medially and finally; the initial English labial
spirant, [f], corresponds with Latin [p], a labial stop. In phonological
terms, [p] and [t] are both stops, pronounced with total constriction
of the vocal tract, as against spirants [f] and [θ], also pronounced
with lip and tongue constriction respectively but called "spirants"
(or "fricatives") rather than "stops" because the constriction is partial, allowing some air to pass through, rather than total. *–ter[7]
(inherited from Proto-Indo-European as English–*ther*) is a suffix, occurring in other kinship terms, such as *mother*, and *brother*. Roots
with initial *m* for "mother" and initial *p* for "father" are found in
many of the world's languages. They were probably among the very
earliest referential symbols that arose during the Pleistocene. In
Greek, the reflex (the language-specific inheritance from an ancestral form) is pate:r (a colon indicates lengthening of the preceding
phoneme), and in Sanskrit the expanded reflex is pitár. The prototype is hypothesized as *pǝtér because of differential correspondences of vowels and stress patterns.

Because sound change is not only regular, but also tends to be
systematic in such a way that like sounds change in similar ways,
we would expect the velar stop [k] in Latin (written as c) to correspond to a velar spirant [x] (similar to German *ch*) in English, just as
[p] became [f] and [t] became [θ]. English has no velar spirant but does
have the laryngeal spirant [h] where other Germanic languages,
closely related to English, do have a velar spirant [x] as a reflex of *k.
Thus we find, for example, English *horn* corresponding to Latin
cornu. Because the Germanic languages are unique in showing a
spirantal correspondence to any voiceless stop in most other related
languages (e.g. Latin, Greek, Sanskrit), the original phonemes are
postulated as voiceless stops, which evolved in a predictable (i.e.
regular) way to become the corresponding spirants in the Germanic
languages, including English. In these instances, the correspondence
is in the *point* of articulation (placement of the most movable parts
against the most stable parts) in the oral tract, and *manner* of articulation: here voicelessness, or lack of vibration of the vocal cords—
while the *systematic regularity of sound change* is from stopped to
spirantal (or fricative) articulation in Germanic. This can be shown
as a vertical shift (see Table 11.1) from stopped to spirantal articulation in the Germanic languages, with voicelessness retained.

This necessarily brief introduction to comparative linguistics,
with illustration of reconstruction to an earlier prototype from

which a group of modern, or historically attested, languages developed, illustrates the systematic nature of sound change. For it is *system* that is the hallmark of language and must be relied on in language analysis, whether synchronic or diachronic. At the same time the discussion illustrates how body movement is to a very great extent learned and standardized within a given population. Human babies, in contrast to the newborns of many other species, move their body parts randomly at first, but rapidly learn to control them in conventionalized mimicry of their caregivers.

THE INVENTION OF LANGUAGE

We can return now to the question of why, or how, for humans, oral communicative gesture became referential symbol rather than remaining only as signal, as it did for other mammals. The pioneering Swiss linguist, Ferdinand de Saussure,[8] said that words were *signs* rather than *symbols* because they were arbitrary. The point that he was making was that the meaning of words was not dependent upon the nature of the sounds of which they were composed. The sequence [si], for example, in English means either a body of water, *sea*, or visual perception, *see*. In Spanish the same sound sequence means either *if*, or *yes*. Thus, in Saussure's terms, the sounds of language are arbitrary in terms of meaning. But if the building blocks of language are arbitrary, and always were arbitrary, how did oral bodily gesture become a system for conveying infinite nuances of referential meaning? In fact, how did oral bodily gesture make the leap from use as a tool for conveying signal-meaning, or non-reference, to conveying symbol-meaning as reference in propositional language? This is especially problematic when we remember that, as an accompaniment to symbolic language, human beings not only have retained body (including oral) gesture for emotive sign and indicative signal but have given oral gesture a completely new function.

To solve this enigma we need to consider a skill that distinguishes primate behavior from that of other animals: *the enhanced ability to mimic*. Mimicry is the faculty of recognizing the self and the other as similar and acting upon that recognition. Classification, which is the foundation of language, is, like mimicry, based on recognition of likeness and acting upon that recognition. Use of classification, or learning of classification, depends first upon mimicry of gesture and of the gestural sequences produced by others. It is of interest that recent experiments with infants under six months of age demonstrate that from birth they are able to discriminate (by ear, not by speech) all of the phonological contrasts found in the world's languages. At the same time, their motor systems are becoming engaged so that by twelve weeks, with exposure to particular vowel sounds, they are able to produce sounds similar to those that they have heard.[9]

It is this human faculty for oral mimicry that makes human language possible and must be the clue to its phylogenetic emergence. Language, at its inception, must have been based not on the production and learning of *arbitrary* sounds, but on the reproduction of sounds as mimicry—beginning with mimicry of the movements of other like beings, and moving to a more abstract and finely tuned oral mimicry of any observed movements and spatial relationships. A small child opening and closing a small box with a hinged lid, while opening and closing her mouth in unison, is making the kind of analogical gesture that comparative reconstruction shows to have motivated primordial language.

ORAL GESTURE AS REFERENCE

The oral gestures that led to language had referential meanings that were generalized rather than specific. That is, each vocalized oral movement represented some sort of movement and relationship in space. Analogous spatial relationships were produced through interaction between lips, tongue, teeth, surfaces of the mouth, and laryngeal contraction. Because these movements are spatial, and essentially consonantal rather than vocalic, they have a visual as well as an audible dimension that seems to have been of primary importance, at least at the outset. It is of interest that human infants pay great attention to mouths, and early learn to imitate their movements. We can assume that lip movements were the first referential gestures.

Because sequences containing the same sound-meaning units can be reconstructed from global comparison of the world's languages, it is my contention that this new capacity for referential expression began at one time and in one place, probably in Africa, since that is now considered by prehistorians to be the cradle of hominid emergence and evolution into the more highly developed species called *Homo erectus*.[10] In its earliest beginnings—perhaps a million years ago—language development during the Middle

Pleistocene must have been slow at first, limited to a few representational facial—and perhaps also manual—gestures. Just as toolmaking techniques evolved gradually over time, so, we must assume, did the earliest speech efforts. The first representational sounds may have mimicked the body movements involved in making and using the first tools.

The sounds that were made with the most visually salient parts of the mouth were probably the first to be invented: first those produced with the lips alone, then, over time, moving backward through the mouth, involving various tongue movements in relation to other oral surfaces, and, finally, involving laryngeal movements as well. Roots with [mV] (V stands for any vowel) "mother," and [pV] "father" are paralleled by equally widespread roots [nV] "mother," and [tV] "father."

Roman Jakobson considered these consonants with their associated meanings to be evolutionarily primary on the grounds that the slight nasal murmer accompanying suckling activity became identified with the mother and later referentially transferred to her, while the contrastive orality and voicelessness of the consonants at the same points of articulation constituted a transition from the affect associated with the moral (nasal utterances used to express desire or satisfaction) to oral utterances identified with reference to the father as he is observed to leave or return.[11] My similar conclusions as to the primacy of labial consonants are based chiefly on their visual accessibility. All the same, [m] meanings, as will be discussed below, relate to mouth movement, perhaps in the first instance to meanings derived from suckling.

Language as we know it today is composed of linked sounds rather than sounds produced individually. Originally the discrete sounds must have been produced slowly, with pauses separating them. Their meanings, learned one by one in childhood, must then have been clearly understandable. Over time the meaning of the sounds themselves became obscured because as the system developed the sounds came to be pronounced in rapid succession, often causing fusion between what had originally been separate sounds. Concatenations of sounds then became conventionalized with particular rather than generalized meanings, a change which also contributed to the loss of original analogical meanings. As these meanings were obscured, the sounds gradually became phonemes, meaningless but conventionalized units of sound, which achieved meaning only through their combination with other sounds as they evolved into words, roots, or affixes.

GLOBAL COMPARISON

I did not discover the *analogical* origin of language from the logical process of evolutionary deduction that I have described. Instead I discovered it quite accidentally from global comparison across language families. My early attempts at reconstruction were motivated by the observation that similar meaningful phonological combinations were more widespread than the traditional separation of language families, established through conventional application of the comparative method, indicates. For example, the sequence of [mw-V] as [mu-C] ([u] is the phonological counterpart of [w] when it occurs before a consonant (C) rather than a vowel (V)), or [m] plus a central vowel plus [u] or [w], [maw] or [mau], with meanings either of "mouth," "face," "mouth or facial activity" or of "bodily or polluted excretion," or both, is not limited to a single family, but is virtually universal.

To give a range of examples: PIE (Proto-Indo-European) *mu-, *mu: (a semicolon indicates lengthening of the preceding vowel) "mouth, muzzle" (with a variety of suffixed consonants, as in English *mouth, muzzle, mute*), and *mew-, *mu-, *mu:- "damp, unclean flow,"; Ancient Sumerian *mu* "to speak," *mus* "facial feature"; Akkadian (Ancient Semitic) *muu* "water"; Ancient Egyptian (vowels were not written in Egyptian hieroglyphic script) *mw* "water, essence, liquid, seed, sap," *mwy* "essence, seed, urine, to flow"; Nyanja of Africa *mutu* "head," *ku mwa* "to drink," *mwe-* "smile," *mwazi* "blood," *mwa* "water"; Tarascan of Mexico *-mu* "mouth, lip, shore," *-ma* "water"; Maidu of California *mussu* "cheek"; Maori of New Zealand *mowai* "to water," to become "moist"; Japanese *mukau* "face," *mumi* "tasteless," *muzen* "beardless"; Finnish *mauton* "tasteless," *mauste* "spice." These random examples show analogical development from a prototype *mw with meanings of "mouth," or "mouthing with liquid," and, by extension, "opening with liquid," resulting in "pouring out of liquid."

Such examples proliferate and provide a preliminary basis for the reconstruction of Primordial Language (PL). Global comparative analysis of roots of words and meaningful segments of words from languages hitherto supposed to be unrelated reveals similarities of sound and meaning of the kind that could not be due to chance convergence.

Unexpectedly, then, in the course of reconstruction, I discovered that the *individual sounds themselves had originally been meaning-bearers.*[12] For example, the two consonantal sounds, reconstructed as *m and *w (articulatory shapes retained in most languages) originally had the respective meanings of "interrelationship," as between two surfaces, represented by *m as the interaction between the lips, or by extension, "mouth," or "mouthing," and "circularity" (as either "circumference," or "bulk") as represented by lip rounding, or [w]. The meaning "mouth" for *mw combines the interrelationship found in the lip interaction of taking or having something in between, as in sucking or drinking, with the circularity of the open mouth. A similar sequence with a mouth meaning for *w resulted in such reflexes as, for example, English *word*, or Latin *vox* "voice" (Latin /v/ from PIE *w), or Tarascan *wa-* "vocalization," which combines with a second mouth meaning in the verbal sequence *wamu-* "to call."

Shifts in both sound and meaning over time as concatenation with other sounds or sound sequences occurred obscured the original meanings of the sounds. These could only be recovered through careful reconstruction and comparison of reconstructed items. The comparison of languages from many different stocks, combined with reconstruction of common sound-meaning fundamentals— what became root elements in historically attested and modern languages all over the world—makes it possible to hypothesize the nature of the earliest phono-semantic elements. I have termed these *phememes:*[13] the smallest meaningful units of oral sound.

Phememes do not represent particular units or actions, but instead describe spatial interrelationships and movements abstracted from whatever is so-shaped or so-moved. It is this faculty for abstraction that is the striking aspect of early language. *The original impulse toward mimicry of body movements of other similar creatures had been extended to mimicry of interactions found in inanimate nature.* This capacity to see and imitate abstract spatial movements and relationships by means of oral gestures was the beginning of an expanding intellectual process of abstract classification that is the hallmark of language as we know it.

The shift to what is called "duality of patterning"[14]—the duality of arbitrary phonemes and nonarbitrary, or meaningful, phoneme groupings that is now a major characteristic of all languages took place gradually and probably was not finalized until the Neolithic. We know that by the Bronze Age modern language systems were in place, because by that time several languages were being written.[15] Slight but progressive changes in meaning over time, coupled with similarly progressive joining together of separate units into words, brought about the loss of phememic meaning and

instead invested meaning in words formed of sequences of phonemes in roots and affixes.[16]

To establish genetic relationships that pertained before the
date at which language groupings have been firmly established by
the comparative method, we must look for similarities in the reconstructed words and meaningful parts of words in already reconstructed language families. It turns out that this does not get us very
far because PIE is the only linguistic stock that has had the kind of
thorough reconstructive attention necessary to the task. Other reconstructions are quite rudimentary in comparison to Indo-
European, which had the advantage of building upon evidence from
a series of ancient texts. Reconstructed PIE is a uniquely valuable
resource in the attempt to go still farther back in linguistic history.
When globally applied to the comparison of roots rather than whole
words of languages that have no obvious lexical resemblances to one
another, techniques for establishing genetic prototypes, perfected
through the comparative method of recovering prehistoric stages of
language development, yield prototypical segments with definable
meanings for individual sounds. Further toward the evolutionary
present, analysis of shared innovations, including longer segments
and phonological changes, also suggests progressive stages in phylogenetic language development.

As globally distributed selection of languages with no obvious
similarities one to the other were compared, common meaningful
segments were reconstructed. The only criteria for inclusion of languages in the study has been the availability of good dictionaries.
Ancient written languages, such as Sumerian, Egyptian, and Hittite,
are especially important for evidence of early evolutionary stages. Of
reconstructed groupings, PIE is the most useful because most of its
roots and affixes have been established. Other reconstructions are
taken into consideration when available. It is especially helpful to
work with languages with extensive phoneme inventories because
these often indicate retention of phonemes or phonological features
that have disappeared from other languages.

Without complete reconstructions, then, but with evidence of
widespread occurrence of phonetically similar phono-semantic sequences, whether known roots or word-initial root segments, I
found it initially productive to hypothesize a single origin and, after
accumulating such segments, to attempt to establish sound regularities between recorded languages on a global basis. Since languages not only change, but change in systematic ways, discovery of
system within change reinforces the reliability of posited sound
regularities.

Systematic change is both phonological and semantic. It depends upon similar changes of like phonemes within particular languages and language families (such as the stop to spirant shift within the Germanic family discussed above), similar changes between groups of languages, and traceable systematic changes in meaning based on analogies that are found to obtain not just in single languages but widely distributed. These systematic changes in phonology and meaning constitute the isoglosses (shared innovations) that determine genetic branching from the common prototype. To date, I have found no evidence of languages that cannot be demonstrated to derive from this common ancestor, strongly suggesting that all modern languages share a common heritage.

THE PRIMORDIAL MIMETIC SYSTEM

The model for reconstruction described here departs from the traditional comparative model only in that it starts from the top down, that is, from globally distributed phono-semantic root similarities, rather than from the bottom up, that is, from an attempt to match reconstruction to reconstruction of known linguistic groupings, focusing on whole words and grammatical elements. For purposes of reconstruction, I have selected consonant plus vowel segments that may constitute whole words or morphemes in some languages, but are found only as root segments in others. Especially valuable are syllables in particular languages that can be assessed as having once constituted morphemes because the segment occurs, usually initially, in more than one word with a similar meaning. These roots are submorphemic because unanalyzed segments cannot be counted as morphemes.

From this broad base I have extracted what seems to be the earliest system of meaningful oral sounds, the phememes, diagrammed in Table 11.2.[17] These sounds are systematically organized as stops, continuants, and semivowels, which like those in the hypothetical phonemic chart of Table 11.1, are distributed from front to back of the oral cavity. Originally there seem to have been no phememic vowels; only an epenthetic, or meaningless, central vowel, [a] or [ə] separating consonants and providing unobstructed sound. Later, semivowels became vocalic in certain positions, or fused with the epenthetic vowel to form new vocalic nucleii.

While each new phememe probably was added after a long period of time, and *p, *m, *w and *y were perhaps earliest because most visible, iconically derived sounds began to form systemat-

Table 11.2. Reconstructed Phememes

	Labial	Dental	Alveolar	Velar	Laryngeal
Stops	p	t	c	k	ʔ
Continuants	m	n	l	r	h
Semivowels	w		y		

ically distributed bases to which sounds with new points or manners of articulation could be added as the semantic need arose.[18] PIE maintained all of these phememes unchanged as phonemes except *ʔ and *h, but added others because of phonetic fusion when *ʔ and *h preceded stops with no intervening vowel. However, *h was conserved in Hittite, an early Indo-European dialect, unless it had earlier fused with a preceding *ʔ and was accordingly lost. Some of these phonemes changed either the point or the manner of articulation as languages separated through time. These provide isoglosses (points of divergence) of particular subgroupings. We have seen this in the Germanic shift of *p, *t, and *k to spirants at the same (or similar) point of articulation. Also, Primordial *c early became PIE *s (see earlier discussion of Table 11.1 for phonological discussion of symbols). This may well have served as the analogic model for the later Germanic stop to spirant shift. Analogic change is a common phenomenon in language history.

The meanings of the phememes were a function of their mimetic articulatory characteristics, as shown in Table 11.3. The reader is invited to follow the discussion of phememic meaning experientially by making the designated oral gesture and thus appreciating mimetic articulatory characteristics firsthand.

The phememic meaning of *p was "outwardness," "forwardness," "protrusion," or "thrust," in analogy to what was probably an exaggeratedly forward thrusting of the lips in pronunciation of *p. (It should be remembered that early hominids were also much more prognathous than modern humans.) Some examples of protrusion or outward extension in words with initial *p can be illustrated by English words with initial *f* (the regular Germanic reflex of *p): forth, first, flow, flee, fling, finger, feather, fang, fat. and so forth.

The phememic meaning of *t resulted from striking the tongue tip against the back of the teeth or the alveolar ridge. This received the iconically derived meaning of "contact," or "precise placement." Some examples of this meaning in English, with initial /θ/ (as the regular reflex of *t) are: through, throw, the, this, that, there.

Table 11.3. Phememic Meanings

Thrust	Contact	Dislocation	Descent	Onset
p	t	c	k	ʔ
Interrelation	*Centrality*	*Laxity*	*Mobility*	*Vector*
m	n	l	r	h
Bulk		*Lineality*		
w		y		

As against the contact, or precise placement meaning of *t, *c indicated "displacement," from contact plus slippage of the tongue against the alveolar ridge. Some English examples (with s as the regular reflex of *c) are: slip, strip, sink, spit, start, soon.

The descent of the tongue from the velum, or soft palate, prompted the meaning of the phememe *k, "downward." Again following the Germanic conversion of stops to spirants, some examples in English of this meaning found in words with initial *h are: hole, heavy, hard, hang, hut (the last from a PIE root *keu-, meaning "to shelter under") and home, (from a PIE root *kei-, meaning "to lie").

Contact between the two lip surfaces in production of *m resulted in a meaning of "interrelationship," or "between," often involving interrelationships between like entities. Some English examples are: mimic, middle, measure, much, more, many.

Meanings of *m and *n tend to be similar; both are frequently found in words for negation, and both are also found in locative particles or affixes. To give examples from just one language, in Egyptian we find m as an imperative mark of negation, and n and nn "no, not." We also find Egyptian m "in, into, from, on, at, with, out from, among, of, upon, as, like, according to, in the manner of, in the condition or capacity of," and n "for, to, on account of, in, while, because, since, in respect of, belonging to." Despite the seeming semantic overlap between the two nasals, *n, produced with inner articulatory contact, as well as closure of the velum to produce nasalization, was used to express more intimately inner meanings, such as the temporal "while," or the spatial "belonging to," that is, "inner-ness" rather than "between-ness" as in the case of *m. Examples similar to those in Egyptian are found in PIE.

*l expressed "looseness," lack, or "laxity." It is found initially in those English words as in many others, such as lazy, limp, lose, languish, or as the second phoneme in such words as slip, sloppy, slow, flap, flop, and flow. These meanings derive iconically from relative lack of tongue tension in its articulation.

In contrast with that of *l, the phememic meaning of *r was "mobility," perhaps originally "upward mobility." These meanings were derived from the upward flapping or trilling of the tongue against the upper surface of the mouth. In English we find these meanings in, for example, rise, run, race, rush, reach, rip, roll.

Laryngeals *ʔ and *h, expressed "beginning," "becoming," or "causing," for the former, and something like "trajectory," or "vector" for the latter. The glottal stop pushes the air forward from the glottis with a sudden plosion, miming the beginning or first source. *h, as the least obstructed continuant, with air passing the length of the vocal tract, mimed a trajectory of time or space. Because of loss of these consonants in English, I must illustrate with two languages in which they have persisted:[19] Egyptian and Yana (Hokan) of California. Both languages also have the advantage of possessing only one or two consonant root morphemes so that primordial meanings are not obscured by a great deal of early affixal modification.

Egyptian hieroglyths do not include vowels. These can sometimes be conjectured if a Coptic derivative from Egyptian is available. Some examples are: Eg. ʔ "to come" (from PL *ʔ "to begin"), ʔt "to bring forth" (*ʔ plus *t "placement" results in "beginning placement"), ʔrʔ "to embark in a boat" (PL *ʔrʔ from *ʔ "begin" plus *r "move" plus *ʔ "begin"). In Yana we find -ʔa "causative, to be, to become," -ʔu- "to be (there), "(PL *ʔ "beginning/being" plus *w "bulk": "to be there in bulk." The Yana term is equivalent to Spanish *estar* "to be (there)," as against *ser* "to be."

In both Egyptian and Yana *h has become /x/. Egyptian gives us x-t[20] "products of," x-t "learning, literature," x-t "object, subject, matter, affair, fact, cause, concern," and, with a following -r, xr "by, with, from, towards, before." The simplest forms reflecting initial *h in Yana are: -xa (with noun stems) "former," and -xa (with verb stems) "remote past tense." All of these meanings express temporal trajectory. When the sequence includes *r, "movement," the trajectory meaning is more obvious. In the other examples the trajectory is implied by indirect reference to a starting point and an end result.

Primordial semivowels mimed the lineal mouth contour in pronunciation of *y (vocalically [i]) as spatial or temporal "lineality." Initial *y is scantily reflected in English, but is found in *year*, and *yoke*. The rounded mouth contour in pronunciation of *w (vocalically [u]) resulted in a meaning of "roundness," "circularity," or "bulk." In English it occurs especially in words with meanings of turning or surrounding, such as wind, weave, wring, writhe, wear, womb. As suggested earlier, reflexes of *w are very frequently found in words expressing speech or other vocalization, such as English word, or vocal (a Latin borrowing). Thus, mouth opening and rounding also originally mimed speech.

PHEMEME CONCATENATION

The consonant and vowel (C and V) structure of most roots in Proto-Indo-European, as in many other languages, is C(V)C. Presence or absence of a vowel depended upon stress and affixal patterns. After what were probably many millenia of early experimentation with utterances consisting of a single phememe, or a phememe plus a meaningless vowel, CVC constructions became common. Both of these constructions were originally words, in the sense that they could both follow and precede a pause. They remain words or bound morphemes in some languages, as, for example in the Egyptian and Yana examples cited above. In others they became so fused with other sequences, which originally were also meaningful, that the original meanings were obscured or lost. Languages differ in the extent to which they are *analytic* or *synthetic*, that is, in the extent to which CV or CVC segments came to be bound to one another or remained free, as separate words. Vowels separated consonants wherever stress patterns required it. Both semivowels and the epenthetic vowel [a] assumed this role. Semivowels also tended to fuse with [a] to form new syllabic nuclei. Most languages exhibit this kind of fusion.

One of the most fascinating aspects of global reconstruction is the extent to which analogy linking articulatory gestures with meanings can be seen to have continued to govern phono-semantic choices and the particular metaphoric and metonymic extensions of the meanings that the early exercise of the analogic faculty had produced. Meanings in historic languages are largely of this analogic nature. Not only can the earliest phememes be demonstrated through mass comparative research, but similar evolutionary paths of early development from phememe to phoneme can be demonstrated. It seems improbable both that languages all over the world would have followed similar early developmental paths and that divergences from the original path would be shared by geographically widely separated languages and language families unless there had been a single, monogenetic, origin.

The theory of monogenesis rests not on phonological evidence alone, but on additional criteria, for example the fact that two-consonant roots with consistent analogic semantic associations can be established, and that longer sequences and a variety of frequently found symbolic extensions of meaning can be shown both to derive from these underlying roots and from very early prototypes. It is possible to trace many features of the primordial language, features which were retained until the earliest changes, representing geographical branching of the evolutionary tree, took place. It is also possible to determine shared isoglosses: changes which took place at various prehistoric periods and involved certain language families but not others. Proof of this requires the presentation of a great many reconstructions, using data from a great many language families. Much of this research has already been carried out (see note 12 for references).

CONCLUSIONS

It is the discovery of phememic meaning that forced me to look at language as an analogic system with its deepest roots in bodily mimicry, expressing deeply sensed bodily relationships between the individual and his or her observed world. Loss of the immediate analogical oral principle as it gave way to increasingly complex analogical classifications of language seems to have loosened the conscious ties that our ancestors once felt to the environment. With this bodily alienation one can conjecture that in the gradual development of philosophical thinking, during which time Aristotle separated form as logic from content as illogic, and Descartes separated mind as thinking substance from body as mere extension, an overvaluation of formal reasoning, whether deductive or inductive, has tended to promote a lineal, mechanistic world view that rejects analogical thinking. Yet analogical thinking is a crucially *human* activity, in contrast to the thinking of other mammals whose thought processes, rather than being analogically mediated, depend more directly on cause and effect.

Filtering experience through an analogical network fostered by the bodily analogical categorizations underlying language provides us a social flexibility permitting virtually limitless possibilities for structured change. Because of our lineal focus (probably promoted to a great extent by the lineality of the written word), we have largely lost conscious sight of the analogical operations that drive and shape us, that still attest to the unity of mind and body, and that can still be discovered if we look closely at our culturally constructed world.

NOTES

1. Gordon Hewes, "The Invention of Phonemically-based Language," in *Glossogenetics, The Origin and Evolution of Language,* ed. Eric de Grolier (Paris: Harwood Publishers, 1983), 143–162, 144.

2. Mary Foster, "Symbolic Origins and Transitions in the Paleolithic," in *The Emergence of Modern Humans: An Archaeological Perspective,* edited by Paul Mellars, Vol. 2 (Edinburgh: Edinburgh University Press, 1990).

3. Noam Chomsky, *Aspects of the Theory of Syntax* (Cambridge, MA: MIT Press, 1965).

4. While the charting of the phoneme inventory of any actual language shows, as does this chart, a symmetrical systematization, there will also be assymetries of lack or addition. The tendency to correct these in the direction of resystematization is one reason for phonemic change.

5. Holger Pederson, *The Discovery of Language: Linguistic Science in the Nineteenth Century* (Bloomington: Indiana University Press, 1938), 18.

6. The *th* of *three* is voiceless, while that of *father* is voiced (i.e. đ rather than θ). These sounds are contrastive in the same vocalic environment (consider the difference between the *th* of *this* and the *th* of *think*), but the spirantal voicing in *father* can be explained on other environmental grounds.

7. An asterisk before a linguistic form indicates that it is a reconstructed (hence hypothetical) ancestral form.

8. Ferdinand de Saussure, *Course in General Linguistics* (New York: Philosophical Library, 1959), 67–70.

9. Patricia Kuhl, "Speech Categories as Represented by Prototypes." Paper delivered at the 5th annual meeting of the Language Origins Society, Austin, Texas, August 12, 1989.

10. J. Desmond Clark, "Africa in Prehistory: Peripheral or Paramount. *Man* (N.S.) 10 (1975): 175–198.

11. Roman Jakobson, "Why 'Mama' and 'Papa.'" In Roman Jakobson, *Selected Writings* I ('S-Gravenhage: Mouton, 1962), 538–545.

12. For earlier accounts of the oral mimetic origin of language see, for example, Mary LeCron Foster, "The Symbolic Structure of Primordial Lan-

guage," in *Human Evolution: Biosocial Perspectives*, edited by S. L. Washburn and E. R. McCown, Menlo Park, CA: Benjamin/Cummings, 1979, 77–121; "Solving the Insoluble: Language Genetics Today," in *Glossogenetics*, 455–480; "Reconstruction of the Evolution of Language," in *Handbook of Symbolic Evolution*, ed. A. Lock and C. Peters (Oxford: Oxford University Press [in press]).

13. See note 12 for references.

14. Charles F. Hockett, "The Origin of Speech." *Scientific American* 203: 89–96.

15. There is growing evidence that writing systems were invented in the Neolithic. See, for example, Winn, Shann M. M., "A Neolithic Sign System in Southeastern Europe," in *The Life of Symbols*, edited by Mary LeCron Foster and Lucy Jayne Botscharow (Boulder, CO: Westview, 1990), 263–284.

16. Linguistically, morphemes are minimal segments to which meaning can be assigned because of privileges of syntactic distribution. Phememes are not morphemes because they do not manifest such privileges, nor are they phonemes, because the latter are never meaningful.

17. In earlier papers, for which references are provided in note 12, I have included a series of voiceless spirants. I have omitted these here because I am currently exploring the possibility that they resulted from later phonemic fusion.

18. While the visible aspects of phememes *p, *m, and *w are readily apparent in lip-thrusting, lip-touching or -closing, and lip-rounding respectively, the visual aspect of *y as mouth lineality can easily be missed short of actual experience—of sounding the word *yes*, for example.

19. Inherited identities such as these are not considered evidence of close genetic relationship unless coupled with shared changes from an earlier evolutionary stage. It is the latter that constitute the true isoglosses marking a shared history.

20. -*t* in Egyptian is a feminine noun suffix.

Contributors

Mary LeCron Foster, an anthropological linguist, is currently Research Associate in the Department of Anthropology, University of California, Berkeley. She is engaged in research on symbolic origins and evolution. Among her many publications are two (edited) books on symbolism: *Symbol as Sense: New Approaches to the Analysis of Meaning* (Academic Press, 1980); and *The Life of Symbols* (Westview Press, 1990).

Eugene Gendlin, clinical psychologist and philosopher of psychology, is internationally known as the founder of the psychotherapeutic technique of focusing and as the author of the book, *Focusing* (Bantam, 1982). He is currently completing a philosophical manuscript on the relation between language and the body. He teaches at the University of Chicago.

Mical Goldfarb is a psychotherapist and artist. She has a clinical practice in Seattle and is associated with a group of Seattle artists. She is co-author of the recent article (in *The Humanistic Psychologist*) "Grounding Truth in the Body: Therapy and Research Renewed."

Albert A. Johnstone is an independent scholar who teaches philosophy at Oregon State University and at Western Oregon State College. He has studied extensively in France, England, and Canada, and is the author of a number of articles as well as the recent book, *Rationalized Epistemology: Taking Solipsism Seriously* (SUNY Press, 1991). At present he is working on a book that explores the pan-cultural bodily nature of the self.

Peter Levine, a pioneer in the emerging field of Somatic Education, holds doctorates in Medical Biophysics and in Psychology. A former teacher in residence at Esalen Institute, he has also taught in universities in the United States and in training programs in Europe and

South America. He has written the chapter on stress in the major scientific and medical source book, *Handbook of Psychophysiology*, and is presently completing a manuscript, *The Body As Healer: Transforming Trauma*, in which he examines the genesis of various traumatic syndromes and develops the treatment approach known as "Somatic Experiencing."

Robert Kugelmann, Chair and Associate Professor of Psychology at the University of Dallas, has just completed a manuscript entitled *Stress: The History and Nature of Engineered Grief*. His publications concern historical and philosophical aspects of psychology, particularly issues of embodiment. In addition to publications in the field of medical anthropology, he is also the author of *The Windows of the Soul: Psychological Physiology of the Human Eye and Primary Glaucoma* (Associated University Presses, 1982).

Daniel Moerman is Professor of Anthropology at the University of Michigan at Dearborn. He has been working on an analysis of the medicinal flora of North America. The analysis will appear in the *Journal of Ethnopharmacology*. He is also currently working on a new project: an attempt to account for the existence of ethnocentrism.

Shigenori Nagatomo teaches in the Department of Religion at Temple University. His interest is in comparative philosophy. He has co-authored the book, *Science and Comparative Philosophy* (Brill, 1989), and co-translated Hiroshi Motoyama's *Toward A Superconsciousness* (Asian Humanities Press, 1990) and Yasuo Yuasa's *The Body: Toward An Eastern Mind-Body Theory* (SUNY Press, 1987). He is currently working on a book, *Attunement Through the Body*, and co-translating Yasuo Yuasa's *The Body, Self-Cultivation and Ki-Energy*, both of which will be published by SUNY Press.

Robert D. Romanyshyn, Professor of Psychology at the University of Dallas and a clinical psychologist in private practice, has lectured widely in the United States, Europe, and Africa. The author of two books, *Psychological Life: From Science to Metaphor* (1982) and *Technology as Symptom and Dream* (1989), and of numerous chapters in edited books and journal articles, he is currently at work on a book concerned with the cultural-psychological history of the American dream. He has recently joined the core faculty of Pacifica Graduate Institute in Santa Barbara.

Maxine Sheets-Johnstone was formerly a professor of dance, dance artist and scholar as well as a philosopher. She is currently an independent scholar who was most recently Visiting Associate Professor of Philosophy at the University of Oregon. Among her many publications is the recent book *The Roots of Thinking* (Temple University Press, 1990). She is currently working on *The Roots of Power: Animate Form and Gendered Bodies,* which will be published by SUNY Press (1992), and on *The Foundations and Rationality of Caring: Forging a Viable Evolutionary Ethics.*